Labor Migration Under Capitalism

History Task Force
Centro de Estudios Puertorriqueños

Labor Migration Under Capitalism:
The Puerto Rican Experience

Monthly Review Press New York and London

Library of Congress Cataloging in Publication Data
New York (City). City University of New York. Center
    for Puerto Rican Studies. History Task Force.
    Labor migration under capitalism.
    Bibliography: p. 265.
    Includes index.
    1. Labor mobility—Puerto Rico. 2. Puerto Rico—
Emigration and immigration. 3. Puerto Ricans in the
United States—Employment. I. Title.
HD5744.A6N48   1979   331.1'27'097295   78-13918
ISBN 0-85345-444-2
ISBN 0-85345-494-4 pbk.

Monthly Review Press
62 West 14th Street, New York, N.Y. 10011
47 Red Lion Street, London WC1R 4PF

Manufactured in the United States of America

10 9 8 7 6 5 4 3 2 1

Contents

5

Preface

Although the making of this book began with a three-day conference workshop on migration and it contains three essays that were key documents in those discussions, it is not a conference report or a collection of conference papers. The main body of the volume is rather the product of a subsequent four-year effort by a small group, varying in composition during that time, to follow through on a research mandate roughly formulated in sometimes emotionally charged and agitated exchanges over those three days among Puerto Ricans of many conditions—students, community activists, and individuals professionally engaged in migration research. The 1974 Conference on Puerto Rican Historiography, sponsored by The City University of New York's then fledgling Centro de Estudios Puertorriqueños, was specifically designed to elicit from such a diverse group an approximate sense of research priorities, felt needs for new knowledge, as well as commitments and capabilities to materially advance systematic inquiry on topics of strategic interest to Puerto Rican communities in the United States.

In this sense, the question of migration—that is, the need to understand, interpret, and project the significance of the massive presence of Puerto Ricans in the United States—emerged as among the most salient concerns. In a wide-ranging, at many points diffuse, but insistently probing discussion, few aspects of migration out of and back to Puerto Rico remained untouched. What emerged was, of course, neither a research agenda nor even the outlines of a new framework for migration research, but a set of broad directives substantially derived from a critical appreciation of the three workshop papers that are part of this book. The critical appreciation and the papers themselves demonstrate the multiple sources of a rising consciousness of the systematic forces that define and reproduce a people's disadvantaged and unsettled condition. How did Puerto Rico become a nation of perennial mi-

grants, apparently destined indefinitely to circulate rest-
lessly from the Island to ever more far-flung concentrations in the United States? What is the point of the
repeated pain and sacrifice of dismantling and recon-
stituting the networks of kinship and sociability that give
life meaning, if the collective conditions of inequality and
exclusion that set us in motion are nowhere to be rem-
edied? If we are unwanted wanderers in the United
States because we are too numerous for a small island,
how is it that thousands from other lands find the accommodation in Puerto Rico that eludes the native born? What
are we to make of the fact that in the course of time eager
homecomers to Puerto Rico, anxious to pick up the
threads of a cherished way of life, may find themselves
strangers and intruders in their own land?

The three papers used as a platform for reflection and
debate in the workshop showed that partial answers to
such questions may be gleaned from a thoughtful analysis
of the fragmentary data available to us on the state and
movement of Puerto Ricans. Vázquez Calzada, in "Demographic Aspects of Migration," shows how slender is the
store of facts and theory which have formed the basis for
demographers' appraisals of the magnitude and consequences of Puerto Rican migration, as well as for their
advice to policymakers. Given the results of the migrants'
experience, he asks, is it morally or politically defensible
to premise the future of a people on a continuing dismemberment of the society?

The failure to take into account basic changes in regional economies, such as the New York metropolitan
area, that remain major destinations of migration, per-
petuates an invidious search for explanations of the migrant's maladaptation, or mobility "lags" in values, attitudes, or social characteristics, rather than in structural
features of labor markets. Clara Rodríguez, in "Economic
Factors Affecting Puerto Ricans in New York," ably
documents a point that has found substantial support in
later studies. Felipe Rivera, in "The Puerto Rican Farmworker: From Exploitation to Unionization," writing from

direct experience as an organizer, shows how structural conditions in specialized or regional labor markets interlock with and are reinforced by federal and Commonwealth legal and administrative provisions ostensibly mounted to protect migrants.

These pieces themselves make clear some of the many reasons why most university- and government-sponsored research sheds little light on matters so close to the inner concerns of Puerto Ricans. Yet the partial critique of past work articulated in these early discussions was plainly inadequately focused, restricted in scope, and weakest of all in posing convincing alternatives. This became, in short, the mandate to the Centro task force on history and migration, which formed as a result of this conference. People were calling for a theoretical approach to migration that would be responsive to the totality of the complex and contradictory movements so fresh in their experience. People were anxious to restore their own sense of the historicity of the migration process and of the sustained interaction between Island and United States economic and political changes that were driving it forward. They wanted to compare the situation of Puerto Ricans in communities scattered around the country, and, above all, to have a role alongside the researchers in generating new knowledge and in connecting such knowledge to practical struggles.

In responding to these conference directives, the task force set out to build on the basic insights and theoretical guidelines provided by Marx, chiefly in *Capital*, concerning population and labor force movements as essential components in the organization of production. One thing that has been brought home with increasing forcefulness in the course of these reflections is the richness of the Puerto Rican case as a historical instance of a global movement that has been a part of world capitalist development for nearly two hundred years. Puerto Rican migration is perhaps unique in the duration and relative magnitude of the population displacement, the depth and scope of related changes in the Island's economy, class configuration, and political organization. With the intensification in recent decades of the legal and illegal flow of workers from formerly colonized and peripheral economies to metropolitan centers, the case takes on a special pertinence, not only for countries that may be at various stages in a similar process of associated development and population exchange with the United States, but also for migration from all labor-surplus industrializing regions to metropolitan centers.

This book is thus an outgrowth of a complicated collective enterprise. An early form of Parts 1 and 2 was published in late 1975 by the Centro under the title, *Taller de Migración: Conferencia de Historiografía, Abril 1974*. That work has been extensively debated in seminars, courses, public meetings, and internal study sessions in many places in the United States and abroad. Numerous conference papers and articles have been written on specific aspects of the migration process that were only generally treated in the first version (for instance, the analysis of class changes that appeared in *Latin American Perspectives*, Summer 1976). An extensive search for statistical materials and documents pertaining to different historical periods has been undertaken; some of this material is being independently published, while some is partially integrated in the present volume. Three task force members—Frank Bonilla, Ricardo Campos, and Carlos Sanabria—are most responsible for this volume and earlier versions. Juan Flores contributed substantially to the present formulation of chapters 2, 3, and 4. Other persons who have shared in this and related task force work include Américo Badillo, Sonia Bu, Hector Colón, José Angel Cruz, Gilbert de Jesus, Julio Luis Hernández, and Virginia Sanchez Korrol.

For more and more peoples migration is becoming a way of life rather than a momentous event in a lifetime. This way of life cannot be comprehended by studying only the social and cultural adjustments and conflicts it generates, however crucial these may be to the emerging web of relations by which the life of major cities around the world is continuously reconstituted. It is rather helping to un-cover the complex and contradictory economic and politi-cal forces propelling the massive displacement of workers and nationalities of which we are part that is, in our view, the most important contribution the study of the Puerto Rican experience can yield for us all.

PART I

Issues and Theories

LA FAMOSA
BODEGA HISPANA
GROCERY
7up
PEPSI
diga Pepsi por favor
PEPSI
say
Sparkling
PARTY
ICE
Welcome!
CIGARETTES SOLD HERE!

CHAPTER 1

Critical Comments on Migration Studies

The migration of Puerto Rican workers is a far-reaching historical event. Unless it is understood, no sense can be made of the present situation of Puerto Ricans as a people. The urgency of the need to reexamine that experience is not based simply on the magnitude of the human contingents most directly affected by the migration of recent decades, although this alone would justify a close examination of the problem by anyone engaged in a serious study of Puerto Rican reality. More important, however, this massive transfer, dispersal, and circulation of population constitutes a dismemberment of the Puerto Rican nation that has yet to run its course and which is being achieved by setting into motion a sizeable proportion of the country's working class. Such a large-scale displacement is an essential feature in the total process of colonialism, not only as it has operated in Puerto Rico, but as it manifests itself around the world today. At a time when ethnically defined struggles are sharpening everywhere and Puerto Ricans are emerging as a significant political force in the United States, it becomes all the more necessary to trace the origins and dimensions of the movement by Puerto Ricans to the home territory of the dominant power. Only on such a foundation will it be possible to mount the kind of sustained and rigorous investigation needed to clarify the present position, collective development, and real prospects of Puerto Ricans in the United States.

The next few pages provide a critical sketch of the numerous studies and interpretations of Puerto Rican migration that have been widely accepted as objective accounts. The following chapter outlines an alternative formulation that we believe is more comprehensive, more coherent, and more closely rooted in the direct experience of migration as lived by thousands of Puerto Ricans. The remaining chapters test that view against some one hundred years of historical evidence, beginning with the advent of capitalism in Puerto Rico in the 1870s. Clearly, it will take many years to fully flesh out and articulate an argument of this scope, but these chapters should at least establish the centrality of aspects of the migration process that in previous analyses have been relegated to a subordinate position or even omitted altogether.

We do not propose to summarize all the material on the migration of Puerto Ricans to the United States. We will differentiate three clusters of writings about this migration, each of which may be described adequately, without serious distortion or omission, in the light of the work of one or two authors, and show that the variables dealt with, and the dynamics attributed to them, reflect a willful interpretation that is given concrete expression in both U.S. and Puerto Rican official policy and in a distinctly North American vision of society that is expounded and upheld by academics of both countries.

The first group includes a series of studies and interpretative documents that have been issued by the Puerto Rico Planning Board and the Migration Division of the Department of Labor of Puerto Rico. The dominant figure in these early investigations, and in the effort to rationalize and convert migration itself into an instrument of policy in planning for economic development in Puerto Rico, was the late Dr. Clarence Senior. We owe to his dedication and determined effort a large part of the basic information about the scope and nature of the movement of people from the Island to the United States. From the first postwar proposals for emigration and the massive colonization projects around 1946, through 1966, when the Commission on the Status of Puerto Rico sought an overall assessment of the migration of Puerto Ricans, it was Dr. Senior who played the leading role.[1] In this twenty-year period he served as an influential official and advisor to the government of Puerto Rico, and was for several years director of the Office of Migration which Puerto Rico maintains in the United States.

A second group of writings is concerned mainly with the experience of Puerto Ricans in the United States, and tends to treat the appearance of Puerto Ricans as just another wave in a steady process of incorporating newly arrived minorities into North American society. We believe that the last volume by Father Joseph P. Fitzpatrick, who has for many years been closely concerned with the evolution of the Puerto Rican community in the United States, represents clearly this current of interpretation.[2]

The third cluster of writings comprises the recent critiques by Puerto Rican scholars who reject the official perspective but who we feel also fall short of the mark by failing to provide an alternative analytic approach capable of adequately accounting for the diversity of situations that imprint a particular character on migration in Puerto Rican history. It includes the work of Puerto Rican scholars, demographers, and others who, like Vázquez Calzada in his contribution to this volume, have been questioning the official version of events and documenting some of the destructive effects of migration on Puerto Rican society and on the persons displaced from their homeland.[3]

The first two groups of writings have the combined effect of formulating and propagating a very particular vision of the origins and dynamic of population movement. This is an obstinately optimistic vision which has the following essential components:

(1) Puerto Rico has a problem of overpopulation. Poverty, unemployment, and retarded economic development are the consequence of an adverse balance between resources and population. Migration is one of the necessary means to attain a renewed growth in production and thus to arrive at a new equilibrium at a level comparable at least to that of the poorest regions of the United States. At that point migration will cease. Initial projections pointed toward 1975 as a reasonable target for the completion of this phase.

(2) Migration is a rational process. It is the better qualified individuals, those with initiative and imagination,

who choose to transfer to places which offer better employment opportunities and material conditions. Because there is a correlation between the movement of migrants and an improvement in the economic situation in the United States, it is implied that migrants adapt themselves to cyclical and regional differences in U.S. employment opportunities, while an unfavorable situation on the Island is assumed to be constant.

(3) The policy of the government of Puerto Rico is not to promote migration directly, but rather to provide the migrant with the information, orientation, and legal protection that will ensure a successful change of residence (i.e., a rapid adaptation in the United States and permanent settlement away from Puerto Rico).

(4) North Americans should understand that immigration has been an essential element in the formation of their country. The United States benefits from, and in turn benefits, the impoverished people from underprivileged countries by successively incorporating them into the lower ranks of its productive apparatus. Since Puerto Ricans are technically already citizens, North Americans should rise above the prejudice and distrust with which they have always received incoming foreigners. Although North Americans tend to view Puerto Ricans not only as foreigners but also as blacks, or at least as nonwhites, over time prejudice against Puerto Ricans will diminish.

(5) Thus, despite some problems of adjustment, destructive experiences, and unexpected costs, migration has had generally favorable results, for the immigrants, for Puerto Rico, and for the areas in the United States that have been the main reception centers.

This view has recently had to face some stubborn realities, which manifest themselves in acute form in a prolonged economic crisis such as that which surfaced in 1973, and which point to deep structural dislocations in the United States economy and its extensions abroad. These include:

(1) The deadend nature of Puerto Rico's strategy for economic growth, in which migration is a central ele-

ment, has been thrown into relief by recent reversals. Even government sources have publicly declared the need for a redefinition of economic and political relations with the United States, expanding local autonomy, and freedom of action. At the same time, government economic and social policy in Puerto Rico is desperately tied to ameliorative devices such as the federal food stamp program.

(2) The high cost and nettlesome international and domestic issues raised by the anomalous economic and political status of Puerto Rico, as well as the growing presence of Puerto Ricans within the United States, project these questions to the highest levels in U.S. politics.

(3) The return to Puerto Rico of a significant number of migrants whose children have been born and in part acculturated in the United States has aroused a good deal of concern. How will it be possible to stimulate a more substantial and diversified migration and manage to root the migrant more firmly away from home? How avoid, above all, massive returns in the event of a deeper economic crisis in the United States? There is a disquieting feeling in Puerto Rico that migration may be changing from a "safety valve" into a boomerang or time bomb.

(4) On the basis of only fragmentary evidence of advances in the process of "assimilation" among Puerto Ricans outside of New York (as measured by small gains in education, job status or income, and rates of marriage with non-Puerto Ricans), a systematic dispersion of the migrants within the United States is being proposed as a solution to the problems the new arrivals bring to U.S. communities. At the same time, Commonwealth policymakers talk about taking steps to ensure that the needs of Puerto Rican migrants are adequately met in the U.S. communities in which they reside in order to stem the return flow. They propose, in effect, to obtain for Puerto Ricans in the United States the minimal life conditions that they have been unable to provide for them at home.

It will become clear how precarious the principles underlying the cited interpretations really are if we refer to the treatment of some of the key variables in the groups of studies already mentioned.[4]

Population

Among the first acts of the invading government in 1898 was to take a census of the population and to make various economic surveys intended to estimate the investment opportunities in the new territory. There is, therefore, a fairly solid foundation upon which to estimate the degree of population growth in the following decades and to establish that this was relatively high. Such was not the case, however, with respect to productive capacity, resources, or level of production. The best-informed experts admitted that they lacked a basis upon which to estimate the total of goods and productive services in the country for the year 1944.[5] Their most cautious calculations led them to estimate that this exceeded $350 million, a figure that was unacceptable to them since it would indicate an average income of $1,000 per family in circumstances of such general social misery as to render such a supposition totally untenable. Nevertheless, to these experts it was already clear that the Island could not sustain a population of a million, and that it was obviously necessary to export Puerto Ricans. Since the cost of migration and colonization projects were out of reach (between $3,000 and $4,000 per family), and anyway offered little guarantee of success, it was decided to undertake "well-supervised individual migration." In other words, it was considered more efficient for the migrants themselves to finance the transfer from one country to another.

From this moment on the talk of population growth as an inexorable and catastrophic process was unceasing. Comparative population density statistics were cited to evoke cataclysmic images. Puerto Rico had in this period a density of 618 persons per square mile, as compared with 47 persons per square mile in the United States.[6] It was noted that if the United States had a similar density it would hold more than three-quarters of the world's population, but it was rarely mentioned that the majority of Puerto Ricans, in their flight from this human avalanche, were destined to land in New York City, where the population density was around 90,000 persons per square mile.[7] No work on migration produced in the United States raised any serious question as to the validity of the basic premise that Puerto Ricans are in the United States because they do not fit on the Island.[8]

Thus statistics about population have been used in a simplistic manner, setting up equations between growth and economic factors in which only one side is clearly defined. And those observers who insist that this treatment is inadequate have generally gone no further than to recommend the incorporation of some additional dimensions on the side of economic resources.[9] There is still no appeal to a theoretical framework that will aid in explaining the relation between the state of the population and economic processes. Yet as we shall see in the chapter that follows, to propose that it is the population that exerts unbearable pressure on the productive apparatus has entirely different implications than to propose that it is the system of production that has an adverse impact on the population.

Migration

Since the beginning of the present century there has been a count of departures from and entrances into Puerto Rico.[10] It is on the basis of these statistics that the relation between the migratory flow and the ups and downs of the North American economy have been established and insistently referred to.[11] Apart from the precariousness of such estimates and the problems arising in their interpretation, this method presents us with two difficulties. First, it leads to the view that migration is a uniform process. This false sense of homogeneity is reinforced by the parallels typically drawn to earlier migrations to the United States. The data portray a current of human movement of varying intensity over the course of nearly eight decades. What becomes most important, and is the only thing possible to ascertain from the data, albeit with an uncertain margin of error, is the volume of this flow. From time to time the census or an occasional survey allows us to appraise the composition of the migrant grouping at a given moment. It is here that we meet with the second difficulty. In the absence of any analytical framework for studying migration, its causes and dynamic can only be sought in the characteristics of the human beings who are set in motion and in oversimplified notions as to the manner in which they move within the labor force in Puerto Rico and the United States. Since each cross-section in time is taken without reference to changes in the migration flow over time, there is no way of knowing whether one such cross-section is more revealing than another or whether it obscures rather than sheds light on the events we seek to understand.[12]

Characteristics of the Migrants

The first systematic study of the Puerto Rican population in New York was published in 1948. Reacting in part to the adverse publicity generated by the intensified migration to the city, the government of Puerto Rico contracted Columbia University to carry out this survey. Its results, which were then used by the government and other defenders of the Puerto Rican community, showed that the majority of the migrants were family people of working age from urban backgrounds who had experience of factory work on the Island. Only 2 percent of the men had been out of work when they left Puerto Rico, while more than 70 percent said they had worked for the full year prior to their departure. The average income on leaving the Island was higher than that of most of their fellow workers at home.[13] The superiority of the migrant and the selectivity of the migration process was thus established, with all of the comforting implications for the general public and the New York City bureaucracy. The assumption that the city would be able indefinitely to accommodate newcomers was never questioned. Subsequent comparisons between migrants and the Island population, based on census data as well as on the so-called ramp surveys of the late 1950s (which interviewed people as they were leaving the Island), generally confirmed these impressions, even though the reliability of some of the statistics came to be seriously questioned. By the time the Status Commission was reviewing information on migration in 1966, an effort was under way to show that the exodus was not continuing to draw such strong contingents of its most skilled workers from the Island.[14] Shortly thereafter, the thesis of the superiority of the migrant once again regained currency—but this time in terms of those returning to the Island—in a careful study by a demographer, José Hernández Alvarez.[15] Now again this optimistic view of the return migrant is being questioned. Recent studies by the Puerto Rico Planning Board suggest that the migrant who eventually returns to the Island shows no signs of superiority over the worker who has never left, and that a returning worker tends to contribute disproportionately to unemployment. They hypothesize that the worker returns from the United States with a negative attitude toward the job market which, when combined with the particular features of the labor market on the Island, produces a pathological "instability of labor." These characteristics are then generalized as being common to all workers outside the so-called primary market in the United States.[16]

These new concerns promise a massive expansion of data on migration and a higher technical level of treating these data, as is already evident in the most recent publications of the Planning Board. But none of this will take us very far. For, as has been the case from the start, the reasons for the failures and frustrations of Puerto Ricans unable to find a stable means of securing a livelihood, whether on the Island, in the United States, or in a frantic back-and-forth movement from one to the other, continue to be sought in the characteristics of the migrants themselves. The best idea that has occurred to the new North American technicians working for the Planning Board is that they duplicate the 1948 New York study, *Puerto Rican Journey*, a journey that today, as then, seems to have no end in sight.[17]

Adaptation

The idea of the superiority of the migrant within the Puerto Rican population carried two implications. First, as we have seen, it substantiated the premise that migration was a rational and voluntary process. Secondly, it allowed for a certain optimism with regard to the adaptability of the migrant. In *Puerto Rican Journey*, the meaning of the term adaptation is clearly defined: the Puerto Rican who adapts well to the new environment will be able to "function inconspicuously and free of psychological discontent."[18] The presence of a large number of women and many poor people "of color" was considered at that time to be the main obstacle to a more complete adaptation; and perhaps to be less offensive to Puerto Ricans and cause less alarm to the public, it was claimed that the best-adapted Puerto Ricans had probably eluded the interviewers, who had limited their activities to the poor neighborhoods of Manhattan and the South Bronx.[19]

It cannot be said that there has been much headway made in the investigation of the impact of the migration experience upon the people who have been living it out, upon Puerto Rico, or upon the communities in the United

States where Puerto Ricans have made their homes. Statistics and specialized studies have piled up to document the persistent situation of disadvantage that weighs down Puerto Ricans even when compared with other deprived sectors in the United States. By the mid-1970s, even federally executed studies had become forthright in their pessimistic appraisals.[20] Highs and lows around the country in this generally bleak panorama are being carefully quantified, as in Aspira of America's report on Puerto Rican educational attainment in major metropolitan areas.[21] The particular dynamics and patterns of exploitation currently institutionalized in administrative practice, labor market structures, community attitudes, and the diverse other pressures that operate on thousands of seasonal migrants both in Puerto Rico and in the United States have been usefully delineated in such case studies as Nieves Falcón's *El emigrante puertorriqueño*. Similar studies in Boston and New York have revealed the structural similarities in the agricultural and urban labor markets open to Puerto Ricans.[22] But more technical studies by economists, increasingly sophisticated in method and occasionally insightful with respect to the implications of changes in the basic dynamics and composition of the migration flow, still remain tied to simple correlational models and ideas taken from decision theory and cost-benefit analysis. As applied thus far in Puerto Rico, these approaches have reaffirmed that employment levels and wage differentials are the key factors impelling migration but have not clarified how these operate at any given time or vary for particular sectors of the population. The difficulties are admittedly formidable, but the questions raised have not gone beyond puzzling over how migration currents may be manipulated to increase economic expansion and productivity. This is as true of Puerto Rican economists as of their North American colleagues.[23] Efforts to fill this void by more frankly political voices have so far suffered from the limitations of data and prematurely hardened theoretical stances and interpretations. This is unfortunately true of the most ambitious, and in its way groundbreaking, challenge to established views, that by the Marxist political scientist Maldonado Denis.[24]

Thus we have, over and against the celebration of alleged advances toward adaptation, as minute as they may be (the second generation, we are told, completes more years of school, has higher employment rates and income levels, enjoys higher social status, marries non-Puerto Ricans, and has fewer children), inescapable proof of nonadaptation, that is, of Puerto Ricans who will neither function inconspicuously nor remain silent about their discontent.[25] It is finally beginning to be understood that the intense interaction and circulation of the working population between the Island and a growing number of communities in the United States cannot be treated as just one more migration in the annals of U.S. history.[26] Nevertheless, the same set of concepts and types of information continue to be juggled in a sterile quest to rationalize a relation of colonial exploitation that becomes increasingly unequal and destructive for Puerto Ricans.

In conclusion, both official and academic studies have systematically excluded a historical and structural understanding of the economic reality that gives impulse to the geographic and political dismemberment of nationalities like the Puerto Rican. Unfolding events have in themselves borne out the integral character of the exploitation that sustains migration. On the Island, the Puerto Rican worker is offered up as a prize to expanding multinational capitalism. As economist David Ross has noted, this capital does not respond to modest advantages in the costs of production but to the prospect of bonanza profits.[27] On the continent, the Puerto Rican worker is offered to declining small-scale industries and services, in New York or in whatever squalid backwater of the economy the planners of our progress can locate. We will never come to understand these contradictions with the analytical tools offered to us by the very architects of that situation.

Notes

1. Clarence Senior's foremost writings on this topic are: *Puerto Rican Emigration* (Río Piedras: Social Science Research Center, University of Puerto Rico, 1947); *Puerto Rican Journey* (with C. Wright Mills and Rose Goldsen) (New York: Harper, 1950); *The Puerto Ricans: Strangers Then Neighbors* (Chicago: Quadrangle Books, 1965); "Toward a Balance Sheet of Puerto Rican Migration" (with Donald Q. Watkins), United States–Puerto Rico Commission on the Status of Puerto Rico, in *Status of Puerto Rico: Selected Background Studies* (Washington, D.C.: U.S. Government Printing Office, 1966).

2. Joseph P. Fitzpatrick, *Puerto Rican Americans: The Meaning of Migration to the Mainland* (Englewood Cliffs, N.J.: Prentice Hall, 1971). Part of the material in this volume, as well as essays by Clarence Senior, José Hernández Alvarez, and others, appears in "The Puerto Rican Experience on the United States Mainland," a special issue of the *International Migration Review* 2, no. 2 (Spring 1968).

3. Apart from his contribution to the Historiography Conference, see, by the same author: "La emigración puertorriqueña: ¿Solución o problema?" mimeo. (San Juan: Universidad de Puerto Rico, Escuela de Medicina, 1963); "El desbalance entre recursos y población en Puerto Rico," mimeo. (San Juan: Universidad de Puerto Rico, Escuela de Medicina, 1966); and "Las causas y effectos de la emigración puertorriqueña," mimeo. (San Juan: Universidad de Puerto Rico, Escuela de Medicina, 1968). Vázquez Calzada has also written extensively on fertility, sterilization, and family planning in Puerto Rico. José Hernández Alvarez has been able to improve considerably the body of information concerning return migration, although he does not adequately question the premises for previous writings on the subject, in his study *Return Migration to Puerto Rico* (Berkeley: University of California Press, 1967).

4. This set of partial and disconnected premises, observations, and proposals for action has more political than scientific importance. In fact, although the names of prominent North American academics from a variety of disciplines appear in the bibliographies alongside the individuals already mentioned, this is a field characterized by little or no theoretical

pretensions and a relative indifference to questions of method. We are referring to Nathan Glazer, Daniel Moynihan, Christopher Rand, Oscar Handlin, Oscar Lewis, and C. Wright Mills, among others. To all of them, with the possible exception of Lewis, the interest in Puerto Rico has been peripheral in their intellectual production.

At the same time, a new wave of research in Puerto Rico promises to break ground in the study of related themes, such as historical changes in the labor force, workers' organization, and the development of classes, but has not yet made a mark on the study of migration. The reference is to the research done by the Center for the Study of the Puerto Rican Reality (CEREP), and in particular to the writings of Angel Quintero Rivera and Gervasio García. These facts tend to diminish the usefulness of entering into a detailed, author-by-author critique of migration studies.

5. *A Development Plan for Puerto Rico* (San Juan: Puerto Rico Planning, Urbanizing, and Zoning Board, 1944), p. 64. The discussion on population in the plan begins with the following remark (p. 63): "The objective of every society is to have its population and resources in equilibrium." A second technical report by the board in that same year begins with eight quotations from authoritative research, all affirming the priority of the population problem. The three component parts of the projected development plan for the Island were "the restitution of land, industrialization, and migration" (Frederic P. Bartlett and Brandon Howell, *The Population Problem in Puerto Rico* [San Juan: Puerto Rico Planning, Urbanizing, and Zoning Board, 1944]). This study notes (p. 11) that if the income estimates made by the board staff at the time were correct, it would mean that the poorer 80 percent of the Island's population was subsisting on 20 percent of the national income. Cited in this same report is a 1935 resolution of the Puerto Rican legislature addressed to the President and Congress of the United States in which emigration is vigorously rejected as a solution to the Island's problems: "The immigrant everywhere is material for exploitation, and neither the psychology of our people nor its civic environment incline it towards migration. It is our duty to see to it that everyone who was born in this land and prefers it to another may remain here and to offer him every opportunity at our disposal to live a decent life" (p. 73).

6. See Senior, *Puerto Rican Emigration.*
7. Senior, Mills, *et al., Puerto Rican Journey,* p. 100.
8. In a master's thesis entitled "The Measurement of Over-population: An Analysis of Puerto Rico," University of North Carolina, 1954, James Beshers characterized Puerto Rico as a moderate rather than extreme case of overpopulation for an agrarian country. He argued that migration has different meanings in different economies and that whoever raises the cry of overpopulation should be prepared to answer the question: too many people where and for what?
9. See for instance, Vázquez Calzada, "El desbalance . . . ."
10. There is data from fiscal year 1908-1909 on. According to Senior, the U.S. Immigration and Naturalization Service had provided this information from that year until he prepared his report to the Status Commission in 1966. A more up-to-date summary of the information sources on the migration, together with an estimate of their limitations, appears in *Puerto Rican Migrants: A Socio-Economic Study* (San Juan: Puerto Rico Planning Board, 1972).
11. See the graphic representations in Senior, *The Puerto Ricans,* p. 38. *Puerto Rican Journey* has a similar graphic representation on p. 44.
12. Brazilian economist Paulo Singer presents an important discussion on this subject in "Migrações internas: considerações teóricas sôbre o seu estudo," a chapter in his book, *Economia política da urbanização* (São Paulo: Ed. Brasiliense, 1973).
13. Senior, Mills, *et al., Puerto Rican Journey,* p. 35.
14. Senior and Watkins, "Toward a Balance Sheet of Puerto Rican Migration," p. 711.
15. Hernández Alvarez, *Return Migration.*
16. Planning Board, *A Comparative Study of the Labor Market Characteristics of Return Migrants and Non-Migrants in Puerto Rico* (San Juan, 1973), ch. 8. See also Celia Fernández de Cintron and Pedro A. Vales, *Social Dynamics of Return Migration to Puerto Rico* (Social Science Research Center, Universidad de Puerto Rico, 1975). This study attempts a classification of "motives" for migration and return, as well as a typology of migrants, ranging from those who settle permanently in the United States, and in effect "assimilate," to a generally "alienated" group that seeks to reproduce and maintain its Puerto Rican culture and iden-

tity, thereby encountering conflict and rejection both in the United States and in Puerto Rico as they lose touch with changing lifeways. In between is a group of "successful" and "unsuccessful" sojourners, whose main base remains Puerto Rico as they make successive forays to the United States.

17. *Puerto Ricans: A Socio-Economic Study*, p. 106.
18. Senior, Mills, *et al.*, *Puerto Rican Journey*, p. 141.
19. Ibid., p. 155.
20. U.S. Commission on Civil Rights, *Puerto Ricans in the Continental United States: An Uncertain Future* (Washington, D.C., 1976).
21. Aspira of America, "Social Factors in Educational Attainment among Puerto Ricans in U.S. Metropolitan Areas" (New York, 1976).
22. Luis Nieves Falcón, *El emigrante puertorriqueño* (Río Piedras: Editorial Edil, 1975). See also Michael J. Piore, "The Role of Immigration in Industrial Growth: A Case Study of the Origins and Character of Puerto Rican Migration to Boston," mimeo., 1973, as well as Ruth Fabricant Lowell, *The Labor Market in New York City: A Study of Jobs and Low-Income Area Workers in 1970* (New York: Department of Social Services, 1975).
23. The more useful of these studies are those by Lois Gray, especially her unpublished dissertation, "Economic Incentives to Labor Mobility: The Puerto Rican Case," Columbia University, 1966. See also her "The Jobs Puerto Ricans Hold in New York City," *Monthly Labor Review* 99, no. 10 (October 1976), and Stanley Friedlander, *Labor, Migration, and Economic Growth* (Cambridge, Mass.: MIT Press, 1965). A model predicting net flow between Puerto Rico and the United States has recently been constructed by Rita M. Maldonado, "Why Puerto Ricans Migrated to the United States in 1947-73," *Monthly Labor Review* 99, no. 9 (September 1976). However, as early as 1960 it had become clear that no such model could be of much use unless it made separate forecasts of in-migration and out-migration. See Robert O. Carleton, "New Aspects of Puerto Rican Migration," *Monthly Labor Review* 83, no. 2 (February 1960). In this connection see also John Vanderkamp, "Migration Flows, Their Determinants and the Effects of Return Migration," *Journal of Political Economy* (September-October 1971). For

a more general assessment of econometric migration models, see Michael Todaro, *Internal Migration in Developing Countries* (Geneva: International Labour Office, 1976).

24. Manuel Maldonado Denis, *Puerto Rico y Estados Unidos: Emigración y colonialismo* (Mexico: Siglo XXI, 1976).

25. John J. Mascisco, "Assimilation of the Puerto Ricans on the Mainland: A Sociodemographic Approach," *International Migration Review* 2 (Spring 1968), pp. 21-38.

26. Joseph P. Fitzpatrick, *Puerto Rican Americans: The Meaning of Migration to the Mainland* (Englewood Cliffs, N.J.: Prentice-Hall, 1971).

27. David F. Ross, *The Long Uphill Path* (San Juan: Editorial Edil, 1969).

CHAPTER 2

A Theoretical Approach to the Migration of Workers

"But with modern compulsory emigration, the case stands quite opposite. Here, it is not the want of productive power which creates a surplus population; it is the increase of productive power which demands a diminution of population and drives away the surplus by famine or emigration. It is not population that presses on productive power; it is productive power that presses on population."
—Karl Marx and Frederick Engels[1]

As has been shown, previous studies of Puerto Rican emigration began with the supposition that Puerto Rico suffers from an endemic "overpopulation problem" which impels the constant geographic displacement of the people. Emigration and overpopulation are thus linked in a mechanical causal nexus.

The logic of this argument is clear and simple—Puerto Ricans emigrate because they are too many to be feasibly maintained in their own country. It is therefore necessary to reduce the population on the Island to match the available "resources." One of the "natural" mechanisms for attaining such a balance is "free" emigration, not managed by government but facilitated by informational, educational, and legal support. Thus, by virtue of individual, rational, and deliberate decisions, wisely supported by public policy, a process is initiated that is beneficial to both the expelling and receiving countries, and of course to the emigrant population itself. The sustained ability to find receiving countries that can accommodate the entering excess population is assumed, as is an equalization of population and social integration resulting from timely, planned population transfers.

This manner of understanding working-class migration is neither recent nor restricted to studies of the Puerto

Rican experience. Rather, in treating population as a force abstracted from the total historical process, it represents an advanced form of a debate over historical facts and theoretical approaches that dates from the early years of institutionalized social science. With some important qualifications having to do with intervening advances in sociological method, approaches to Puerto Rican migration are generally in the tradition of what has come to be known as Malthusian thinking,[2] even though Malthus himself viewed migration as a temporary palliative to population pressure. As is known, Malthus' response to early criticism of his philosophical premises was to incorporate into his famous essay an extensive review of the "empirical" evidence to substantiate his fatalistic claims and draconian proposals. Similarly, current criticism of research on Puerto Rican and other population movements from within mainstream social science has merely led to intensified data gathering, more elaborate policy formulations, and more complex model building. No substantial change in theory or in method has resulted.

The most thoroughgoing refutation of Malthusian theory and a consistent alternative to positivist interpretations of population growth is provided by a Marxist framework of analysis. It is true that recent Marxist critiques of social science have often not focused directly on migration, but on the larger issues of the international division of labor, the prospects of economic development for presently industrializing nations, imperialism as the political order of world capitalism, and the current possibilities of socialist transformation. But it is precisely such considerations which underlie any satisfactory account of Puerto Rican migration in its full historical dimension. Furthermore, the numerous references to and discussions of population growth and migration in the works of Marx and Engels provide a base for the construction of a systematic explanation of these demographic changes. Such an explanation bridges the major gaps in the research reviewed above by bringing in a sense of the history and changing character of the economic base of the migrating population, and by turning attention to the continuous expansion and increasing complexity of the migration flows.

A fruitful reconceptualization can only derive from an application of these concepts to real historical events and configurations. Puerto Rican migration, for example, while illustrative of certain general tendencies, is defined by a composite of particularities, an interplay of concrete social forces which largely post-date the original Marxian formulations. While there has been no decisive break with the Malthusian paradigm within the body of research on Puerto Rican migration, new information and a pertinent dialogue has begun. Thus a Marxist alternative must not only expose basic theoretical fallacies, but address the substantial body of available findings, and still be prepared at every turn to meet the challenge of a changing historical reality.

Marxist analysis begins neither with migration nor with absolute population size. Demographic conditions—including, of course, "overpopulation"—are at all times seen as being relative to the level of productive development of the society, or societies, in question; demographic facts are always situated and can only be explained in relation to the prevailing organization of social production. In a well-known passage from the introduction to the *Grundrisse,* Marx clearly states the basis of this approach:

> It seems to be correct to begin with the real and the concrete, with the real precondition, thus to begin, in economics, with, e.g., the population, which is the foundation and the subject of the entire social act of production. However, on closer examination this proves false. The population is an abstraction if I leave out, for example, the classes of which it is composed. These classes in turn are an empty phrase if I am not familiar with the elements on which they rest. E.g., wage-labour, capital, etc. These latter in turn presuppose exchange, division of labour, prices, etc. For example, capital is nothing without wage-labour, without value, money, price, etc. Thus, if I were to begin with the population, this

would be a chaotic conception (*Vorstellung*) of the whole, and I would then, by means of further determination, move analytically towards ever more simple concepts (*Begriff*), from the imagined concrete towards ever thinner abstractions until I had arrived at the simplest determinations. From there the journey would have to be retraced until I had finally arrived at the population again, but this time not as the chaotic conception of a whole, but as a rich totality of many determinations and relations.[3]

Historical Laws:
Population and Mode of Production

> "In different modes of social production
> there are different laws of the increase of
> population and of overpopulation . . ."
> —Karl Marx[4]

The same theoretical premises that led Marx to reject and reformulate the abstract concept of population advanced by Malthus lead to a redefinition of the attendant notion of population law. For Marx, within the specificity of each concrete case the dynamic of population change proceeds according to historical laws. These "laws" are, however, not universal but defined by the inner logic of each mode of production.

To say that "laws" of population are historical in character indicates that they arise, are transformed, and become inoperative over the course of time. The effective lifespan of each law corresponds to the prevalence of a given mode of production or stage in the development of social production: within each stage of productive development there reigns an appropriate law; and with the supercession of that mode of production, the dominant law of population is likewise changed.

Historical laws of population are the *form* assumed by concrete social facts in their temporal succession. As such, they express the dynamic movement of social processes. Social facts considered individually or in composite arrangement comprise no more than reified moments, since they appear divorced from reality as an objective process of ongoing transformation. It is in this way, on the basis of circumscribed social facts in disassociation from a fully unfolding historical process, that most interpretations of the Puerto Rican migratory experience have been undertaken. The time-frames chosen and demographic phenomena observed appear as accomplished facts, frozen analytical units treated as self-sufficient and revealing some permanent reality.

The Marxist approach recognizes population changes as indicative of general and dominant tendencies within a particular social formation. A tendency, in this sense, entails the constant reproduction of a certain social effect such that it persists as long as the factors which occasioned it are maintained. The tendency to convert part of the working class into a surplus population is a demographic "law" of the capitalist mode of production. This tendency remains as long as the basic motor of capitalist society—the interchange of labor power and capital—remains intact.

More specifically, population growth cannot be understood as an autonomous process occurring independently of the existing organization of social production. Such change is rooted in the mechanism of social reproduction of human labor power as it bears on the different classes of society. The terms "adequate population" or "overpopulation" are explanatory only in relation to the prevailing arrangement of productive activity. It is not a matter of establishing simple quantitative balances between resources and the volume of population. Rather, the population "law" in effect at any time can only be derived from an analysis of the manner in which these resources are produced and transformed.

The prevalence of systemic tendencies does not obviate the *contradictory* nature of historical processes. On the contrary, the social law which prevails at any given conjuncture is also caught up in a temporal motion propelled by the very antagonism of countervailing tendencies. For example, the capitalist mode of production tends not only to generate a relative population excess, but also to absorb it by means of successive transfers of workers from one branch of production to another, as well as by expanding. But countertendencies are not dominant, and therefore do not exert a determining influence. Thus, no particular instance of the law—whether its tendency or countertendencies—can reveal the law in its actuality, that is, in all its complexity and dialectical interaction. At the level of immediate observation it may appear that the effectiveness of a law has been exhausted when it has in fact but changed its form of historical manifestation.

Further, the same law may be manifest in diverse forms according to differences in time and place. Even during the reign of a given mode of production the population law manifests itself in a variety of ways. This diversity is not, however, random or accidental; indeed, it attests to the law-governed quality of social development. For, as stated, the Marxist law of population is not an absolute, abstract deduction; it is a relative premise grounded in concrete historical experience.

Thus "overpopulation" refers not only to the impact of varied conditions within a given mode of production, but also to differences in demographic patterns under distinct modes of production. Certain precapitalist societies also experienced relative overpopulation, for overpopulation under these conditions must be distinguished sharply from parallel phenomena arising with capitalist development. This analytical differentiation between the laws of population operative before and after the emergence of capitalist relations is crucial to an understanding of changes in demographic conditions in the history of Puerto Rico.

The general principle formulated by Marx with respect to all precapitalist formations is that the growth of human population—the principal force of production—appears as a threat to the reigning forms of property and appropriation. This is so because these modes of production, and, therefore, the social relations appropriate to them, do not rest on the constant growth and perfection of the productive forces.

In all previous forms of production the development of the productive forces was not the basis of appropriation; rather, a specific relation to the conditions of production—forms of property—appeared as an inherent barrier to the forces of production, and merely had to be continually reproduced. It follows, therefore, that the development of population, in which the development of all productive forces is summarized, would even more strongly encounter an external barrier and thus itself appears as something to be restricted. Only a certain amount of population was commensurate with the conditions of the community.[5]

The ancient Greeks and the Germanic peoples, as Marx noted in the lines following the passage just cited, were forced to limit their population in order to remain as they were. Since each individual or family required a certain amount of land and a certain number of production instruments, population growth posed a definite limit to the society's ability to reproduce its own economic conditions. This "barrier" was the driving force behind the historic migrations and invasions of these peoples. Contemporary research has helped to describe the particular patterns of growth and change, and the diversity of social forms present, in precapitalist societies. Serious investigation from this perspective, which addresses the case of Puerto Rico, is only beginning.[6]

We do know, for example, that in the early sixteenth century three streams of population transfer coexisted. Arawak and other Indian tribes were engaged in a broad migratory passage between Central and South America and the Caribbean islands, as a result of changes and adjustments in the primitive communal organization of their societies. Second, European colonizers were settling in Puerto Rico, not only in search of riches but because of population pressure in certain regions of feudal Spain. Third, slaves were shipped from Africa in answer to the growing needs of European commercial capital.

As different as these migrations were, all were governed by laws of population preceding the decisive onset of capitalist relations on a world scale or within the nations involved. Slavery, as distinct from indigenous migrations and early Spanish colonization, was an integral part of the primitive accumulation generating the basis for capitalism. It did not necessarily reflect population pressures in Africa, but formed part of the unfolding of production in the New World. The other movements did not originate with the expansion of productive forces but precisely because of obstructions to their development.

The Law of Population
in the Capitalist Mode of Production

Under capitalism population becomes population for capital. The capitalist mode has as its fundamental premise the dispossession of the majority of the population of the instruments and means of production. This majority is transformed into a wage-labor force, that is, a human mass defined not by its need for subsistence but by its production of capital, which involves both the accumulation and increasing concentration of social wealth and the reproduction of capitalist relations as such. While continuously expropriating the population of the means of producing its own livelihood, capitalist relations also demand a steadily expanding population of available wage workers.

But systematic expropriation and the demand for laborers are not matched by a capacity to absorb ever larger numbers of workers into the productive apparatus. In augmenting its numbers, therefore, the working class reproduces itself as a dispossessed population; it also reproduces its own superfluity within the society. In contrast to other modes of production, it is the very mechanism of capitalist development in its explosive revolutionary expansion that generates an ever larger relative overpopulation. Thus, in these circumstances it may be said that the labor force reproduces its own excess.

As is known, Marxist economic analysis recognizes

that, under capitalism, the work process is composed of two parts, or aspects: necessary and surplus labor. Necessary labor represents that part of the work process during which living labor power (the working population) is reproduced; consequently, the other part of the work process (excess or surplus labor) is that which takes the form of surplus value subject to capital accumulation. Correspondingly, capital is also divided, according to its organic composition, into constant and variable capital. The basis of capitalist appropriation lies in the first instance on the growth of a proletarianized population to carry on labor increasingly productive of surplus value. In the early stages of capitalism that part of capital designated for the reproduction of the worker—variable capital—makes up a considerable portion of the total. The accumulation process, however, is oriented toward a maximum extraction of surplus labor, and is thus propelled by the application of technology to intensify productivity. Thus, while constant capital—that spent on the means of production—is inclined to rise over time, the general, long-term tendency is toward a relative decline in the volume of employment purchased by variable capital. Although there is a rise in total capital, variable capital—and rates of profit—grow in inverse proportion to accumulation. In other words, the expansion of the productive forces generated by the relatively higher productivity of the worker alters the organic composition and causes the demand for labor—or, more specifically, for laborers—to decline. The various stages of this process stand out clearly in Puerto Rican economic development over the past hundred years. It is this tendency to generate a relative surplus population, or an industrial reserve army, that Marx identified as the general law of capitalist accumulation:

> With the magnitude of social capital already functioning, and the degree of its increase, with the extension of the scale of production, and the mass of the labourers set in motion, with the development of the productiveness of their labour, with the greater breadth and fullness of all sources of wealth, there is also an extension of the scale on which

greater attraction of labourers by capital is accompanied by their greater repulsion; the rapidity of the change in the organic composition of capital, and its technical form increases, and an increasing number of spheres of production becomes involved in this change, now simultaneously, now alternately. The labouring population therefore produces, along with the accumulation of capital produced by it, the means by which it itself is made relatively superfluous, is turned into a relative surplus-population; and it does this to an always increasing extent. This is a law of population peculiar to the capitalist mode of production and in fact every special historic mode of production has its own special laws of population, historically valid within its limits alone. An abstract law of population exists for plants and animals only, and only in so far as man has not interfered with them.[7]

Along with the expropriation of the working population, the conversion of its labor power into its only commodity, the alienation of the activity and product of its labor, and the constant reduction of socially necessary labor time, the creation of a relative surplus population stands as another consequence of capitalist production. This population excess, or industrial reserve army, comprises an available mass of workers for use by capital as it sees fit. The existence and growth of this reserve has the practical effect of intensifying competition for employment and maintaining a steady downward pressure on wages.

At one and the same time, then, the labor reserve *accelerates and counteracts* the tendency already noted toward a decline in the relative share of capital going toward labor costs. Since rates of accumulation, as well as profits, hinge directly on the relative amounts of variable capital (insofar as these reflect the quantity and quality of labor power engaged productively), it is at this point that the state of the population and its movement enters into the nexus of forces that both generate and cushion contradictions in the process of accumulation. To this effect Marx states:

If accumulation is to be a steady, continuous process, then this absolute growth in population—although it may be decreasing in relation to the capital employed—is a necessary condition. An increasing population appears to be the basis of accumulation as a continuous process. But this presupposes an average wage which permits not only reproduction of the labouring population but also its constant growth. Capitalist production provides for unexpected contingencies by overworking one section of the labouring population and keeping the other as a ready reserve army consisting of partially or entirely pauperized people.[8]

For this reason it is no insurmountable contradiction that the overproduction of the means of production runs parallel to relative overpopulation. That is, the increase of wealth is accompanied by a relative overpopulation which fights to stay alive with scanty means of subsistence, since the tendency generated by capital to increase the surplus working population is part and parcel of the tendency to reduce the portion of this population necessary for production.

In this way, then, the constant generation of a relative surplus population is inherent in the mechanisms which lie at the base of the capitalist economic system. Greater worker productivity spells a change in the organic composition of capital because it reduces the need to incorporate living labor in the productive process. This relative decline in variable capital underlies, in turn, another basic systemic tendency: that the rate of profit will fall. For it is only living labor, human labor power, which constitutes value capable of realization as capital. The living labor which is thus pressed into the condition of relative overpopulation serves at the same time as the reserve force used to counteract this tendency. By consuming the "excess" of workers in conditions more advantageous to capital (depressed wages, longer workdays, etc.), the system is able to restore a temporary upward trend to the rate of surplus value, and, as a result, to the rate of profit as well. As will be shown, this oscillating pattern and constant adjustment in the organic composition of capital explains much of the dynamic of the geographic movement of the Puerto Rican working class over the past century.

Furthermore, the unproductive use of human labor power—as, for example, in the realization of commodities in the form of market value or money—both absorbs and generates further reserves of labor. In general, workers—and capital—employed in the circulation process are "unproductive" in the specific sense that they do not participate directly in the extraction of surplus value but in its redistribution and transformation into commercial capital. They subsist and are reproduced socially using part of the surplus value generated in production, and are thus derivative of and conditioned by the sphere of actual production. Labor power consumed as a use value in the circulation sphere is thus ultimately subject to the oscillating contraction or expansion in the productive capacity of workers employed directly in capitalist production. Whether "unproductive" workers are part of the active or reserve army of labor, therefore, depends on the existence of a constant and expanded output of commodities, while their wage scale is determined by the share of surplus value redistributed to the commercial capitalist.

In general, the demand for workers in the circulation sphere tends to increase with the advance of capitalism, and thereby to absorb part of the labor surplus generated by commodity production. However, the relative speed of the circulation of commodities is of vital importance to the capitalist class, since circulation time is in effect the negation of production time. For this reason, all manner of technical innovations are introduced which would accelerate the pace of capital conversion and realization on the market and, once again, replace a growing portion of the employed workforce. As we shall see, the case of the Puerto Rican economy, especially in recent decades, makes abundantly clear that the same tendency to substitute variable for constant capital is at work in the circulation sphere as was characteristic of capitalist production as such. Instead of absorbing relative overpopulation, the realm of unproductive labor becomes still another source of the expanding labor reserve.

State intervention in the capital-labor relation also

exerts an important pull on the relative population "excess." The large-scale and growing absorption of the Puerto Rican working class into state-controlled corporations and bureaucracies has been crucial to the sustained subordination of the colonial economy. Though some workers have found productive employment in firms protected—or directly owned—by the state, unproductive labor accounts for the largest volume and provides the expansive dynamic of this process. Wages paid to this section of the working class are drawn from surplus value further transformed after its conversion into money capital. In this case, therefore, surplus value tends to be destroyed, since it is neither realized as capital nor does it participate directly in the production and circulation process. Nevertheless, the need to reproduce the conditions of capital accumulation and to both nurture and absorb a growing number of "excess" laborers makes this continual intervention by the state indispensable to the survival of the system as a whole.

Here again, the magnitude of the labor force drawn into this sphere of activity depends ultimately on the productive level and capacity of the society. The higher the rate of surplus value, the larger the share available to the state for this purpose. The scale of employment in the state sector varies not so much according to the relative need for labor, but according to the availability of funds and the growth of unemployment at critical historical moments. Thus as clearly as in the circulation sphere, labor use by the state depends on the accelerated production of surplus value.

As in commodity production proper, an increasingly efficient division of labor brings about the simplification of work in the spheres of circulation and state employment, and a progressive reduction in the importance of requisite skills, increasing the population "excess" expelled from these sectors. The history of the modern Puerto Rican economy, with its rapid transformations in agriculture, manufacturing, and early industrialization, illustrate well this impact of technological innovations. Some of the expelled workers enter the industrial reserve army and compete for whatever employment is available; for many of them, this means migration.

Thus, in spite of the appearance of new branches of production, and of the continuing growth of the labor force in the circulation and state sectors, there is a permanent regeneration and expansion of relative overpopulation. This population surplus, according to Marx, assumes a variety of historical forms, designated as *latent, floating,* and *stagnant.* It is important to keep in mind that the several types of relative overpopulation defined by Marx are not independent forms following each other in some ordered sequence, but tend to appear simultaneously in different areas of production, and to interact in different configurations over time.

Latent surplus population stems from the structural contradiction in capitalism that makes the entire working population a potential human surplus in terms of its employability. It is this root condition that leads Marx to assert that "it is already contained in the concept of the free labourer that he is a pauper, a virtual pauper."[9] At the same time, the expansion of capital involves a progressive dissolution of other relations of production, making those workers not as yet incorporated into the wage-labor force a part of the latent surplus population.

Marx considered the peasantry the most representative example of this process. As capitalist relations penetrate into agriculture, part of the peasant population is made superfluous by the exigencies of the new wage system, but the economy is unable to absorb them productively into the new relations of production. In the face of the eventual capitalist organization of agriculture, this human contingent is destined to become unemployed and is pressured to move in search of work. It is not a scarcity of "resources"—of land in particular—but the newly imposed dialectic of necessary and surplus labor that forces an ever larger portion of the peasantry to become part of a latent surplus population.

In the monopoly stage of capitalism the inflated demand

for bureaucratic and "emergency" labor on the part of the state and government also transforms the workforce in these sectors into part of the latent surplus population. The use of a large number of these workers is determined not by any direct labor need but by social and political considerations, making this latent population surplus severely affected by slight movements of the economy. This condition is endemic to the modern-day Puerto Rican working class on the Island.

Latent relative overpopulation, therefore, is basic and structurally inherent to capitalism. Every area of the economy—agriculture, industry, services, etc.—contains a mass of workers who are likely to be forced out of work by the continued concentration and centralization of capital. This tendency to expel workers, accompanied by a countervailing tendency to attract and absorb them, gives rise to what Marx called a *floating* surplus population. This labor surplus, commonly designated by bourgeois economics as the technologically, seasonally, or functionally unemployed, includes those most disposed to seek a reconnection to capital through migration.

Within this floating population, however, the dominant tendency is toward expulsion, creating a reserve whose prospect of being absorbed by any future expansion of capital becomes increasingly remote. As this situation has become acute with the advance of monopoly capital, some writers have called this surplus a growing "marginal" mass of unemployed auguring a deep crisis. But, in fact, a substantial portion of the surpluses that cannot realistically be regarded as "reserves" at the level of the social formation in which they occur become a reserve for capitalism at the international level. Migration is thus one of the mechanisms that makes it possible for these surpluses to recover their status as reserves, or to reenter the active workforce. The accelerated circulation of workers that is reflected in migration flows, however contradictory and costly in human terms, is evidence of the sustained capacity of monopoly capital to absorb parts of locally marginal reserves.

The *stagnant* (*stockende*) surplus population includes all variants of the sub- and semi-employed workers, those sectors of the working class that endure the worst labor conditions. While many of these workers work an overextended or incomplete day, wages in this category are always depressed below the minimum standard of subsistence. This is the poorest stratum of the active workforce in whatever sphere of the productive process. As a point having special pertinence in the Puerto Rican case, it is worth mentioning here that the petty bourgeoisie as a class may be regarded as *latent* surplus population. The contradictory workings of the subordination of the labor force by capital (that is, the attraction and repulsion of workers) permits the persistence of independent producers and workers in precapitalist relations of production. In the long run, however, and in very observable ways, members of this class are increasingly subjected to wage labor or drawn into the reserve army for capitalist production. At the same time, the prevailing conditions of work (minimal earnings, unstable employment) make a large part of this group part of the stagnant surplus population.

This stagnant surplus population is also *latent,* because the low organic composition of capital in these sectors coexists with technologically advanced methods for drawing *relative* surplus value from the workers. The extraction of relative surplus value depends on the capitalist's ability to reduce the proportion of socially necessary to surplus labor within a given work period. This may be accomplished by numerous means, such as improved technology, organization, or speedups. Whether the sectors with a low organic composition of capital are declining (as, for example, with many forms of light manufacturing) or just developing (as with some services), they are destined either to disappear or to move on to higher levels of technical organization. A principal mechanism of their survival at this stage is migration: both the movement of capital directly to reserves of low-cost labor and the attraction of such reserves to present concentrations of capital. At the same time, the frequent withdrawal or recombination of this capital throws workers from this sector into the floating reserve.

Taken together, all of these varieties of surplus population comprise what is called the "industrial reserve army," which today constitutes a majority of the working class in Puerto Rico and of Puerto Rican workers in the United States. The magnitude of this reserve and the structural features characterizing its components have generated a reexamination of the concept.[10] The most glaring contradiction of contemporary capitalism is that reproducing this reserve involves tremendous social costs. Together with the consumption of surplus value necessary to maintain various forms of "unproductive" labor, especially in the state sector, the channeling of social wealth to maintain these "reserves" represents a large expenditure, as capitalists are well aware. Thus by virtue of the very process of profit maximization and expansion, capitalist society creates a mass of "excessive" lives dependent for their survival on "public charity," and is forced to commit another significant share of accrued surplus value to alleviate its chronic "social problems."

State intervention to absorb the surplus population and diminish its explosive potential emerged as a prominent and necessary feature of capitalist society in the monopoly stage. The effective and timely transfer of surplus value to sustain growing branches of "unproductive" labor is carried out through the intervention of the state. The fact that the state's ability to exercise this function rests wholly on the extraction of maximum surplus value indicates that the very maintenance of the reserve army is dependent on the intensified productivity and exploitation of the active labor force.

The economic history of Puerto Rico in this century is an extended example of continually magnified state involvement and control, and there can be no doubt but that the colonial economy is at present thoroughly dependent on the designs, agencies, and devices of the U.S. federal government. It is equally clear, however, that state intervention will never provide a possible solution to the contradiction, and that whatever adjustments are made, the course of capitalist development and the particularities of the imperialist subjugation of Puerto Rico will continue to engender an ever expanding relative overpopulation among the working class.

The Marxist critique of Malthus and of neo-Malthusian population theory centers on the tendency to take as natural and universal what is in fact a historical law, one appropriate to the capitalist mode of production. Marx and Engels did not deny that population grows absolutely; on the contrary, they affirmed it. But overpopulation in capitalist society is the result of contradictions in the conditions of accumulation, contradictions that exert constant pressure on the increasing population. Not only do these contradictions generate a population "excess," but the excess is itself an outcome of the absolute growth of the population, which in turn responds to increases in the productivity of labor. Population growth and rising labor productivity are dialectically interconnected in specific ways, no less problematic than those envisioned by Malthus. As Engels comments: "The pressure of population is not upon the means of subsistence, but upon the means of employment; mankind is capable of increasing more rapidly than modern bourgeois society can stand. To us a further reason for declaring this bourgeois society a barrier to development which must fall."[11] Engels clearly recognized that population growth can go beyond the powers of absorption of capitalist production, because of the particular mechanisms through which this mode of production renews its workforce. He pointed out, from this perspective, that should population growth reach excessive proportions, only a society organized on the basis of socialism will be able rationally to confront this problem: "There is, of course, the abstract possibility that the number of people will become so great that limits will have to be sét to their increase. But if at some stage communist society finds itself obliged to regulate the production of human beings, just as it has already come to regulate the production of things, it will be precisely this society, and this society alone, which can carry this out without difficulty."[12]

International Capital and Migration

As we have seen, overpopulation relative to the available means of employment in capitalist societies is an inherent condition of capitalist production in general. Continued and expanding reproduction of this excess population and its varied historical manifestations are based, in turn, on another systemic reality: the permanent geographic mobility of the labor force. In other words, labor power, the workers' only commodity, enters into circulation in search of employment (or variable capital) as a field of exchange. The movement of the workforce may thus be perceived as the exercise of that "freedom" operative within free market conditions.

However, it is clear that the amount of available employment, or the demand for labor, does not depend on the desire of workers to exchange their commodity. Thus "free will" is conditioned and limited by the ongoing reduction of the living labor required by capitalist production. The resulting fluctuations in the labor market occur independently of the "liberty" of the working class to produce or not. Thus to ensure the maximum use of the commodity labor power it is necessary to assure the mobility of workers, even between nations. In fact, all major changes in the capitalist division of labor have been accompanied by the large-scale transformation of the latent surplus population in the rural areas into floating and stagnant surpluses in the urban centers. It is capital that geographically distributes the labor force in accordance with its need to constantly optimize the exploitation of the working class. The migration of workers, therefore, runs parallel to the incessant production and circulation of capital; it is the necessary counterpart to the process of capital accumulation.

When labor power becomes a commodity, it is transformed from being a use value—the capacity to produce useful goods—into an exchange value. It enters into the labor market opened up by variable capital, a circulation process that presupposes the spatial mobility of the workforce. Migration, then, is a displacement set in motion by the same economic relations that engender relative population surplus. Worker migration is one crucial way for capital to consume labor power most effectively. Like the productive process as a whole, and conditioned by it, migratory currents undergo a continual change of composition and direction.

In whatever concrete social context, early capitalist development witnesses massive movement from the countryside to the towns. This internal migration actually involves the conversion of small proprietors into wage workers; it is a migratory flow resulting from the expropriation and proletarianization of small cultivators, including those who may also be engaged in servile labor relations. In these cases labor power is already functioning as a commodity, and recurrent adjustments in the social division of labor demand an ever increasing velocity of labor circulation. Even such early population movements, therefore, cannot be understood as simple geographic transfers, but as the circulation of labor power according to the exigencies of capital accumulation. The relative territorial permanency of the producers become elastic, while innovations in the means of transport and communication serve as a forceful lever in this accelerated process of commodity circulation.

At no point, however, have these consequences of capitalist development been limited to a single national formation. Since its mercantilist beginnings, capital has assumed an international dimension, and the intensification of international commerce gave the necessary impetus to primitive accumulation in different countries. Thus, at the same time that the social relations of capital laid the base for the evolution of national economies and the hostile contention among competing nations, there arose a need for international cooperation to carry through the full-scale realization of surplus value. Corresponding to the growing network of commodity exchange was an international division of labor according to which certain nations came to specialize in the production of specific commodities. International trade thereby supports the diversity of nationally produced goods. The nationally placed working populations are likewise conjoined in this system of international commodity exchange. Simply put, each localized productive process is increasingly subordinated to the overriding demands of non-local forces. Commodity production may begin in one national setting and extend to others at different stages of production and distribution, with several national labor forces participating in the same overall process. The international division of labor that emerges from capital investment by one country in the economy of another thus occurs within the process of commodity production, and may involve the successive and multiple participation of nationally different working classes.

The determining movement in these cases is the investment of capital outside of its original national context, consuming a different labor force in the new area. But this capital outlay also involves the reproduction of capitalist relations of production. These interchanges of capital and labor power give rise to a constantly magnifying relative overpopulation among each national working class engaged in the entire sequence of capital expansion and realization. With the full unfolding of capitalist relations, the elaboration of world trade, and the rapid advance in the productive forces, this structural impact of capital investment as the exportation of social relations themselves becomes increasingly prominent.

For centuries, the slave traffic constituted not only a circular exchange of commodities, but the socialization of slaves as workers also generated profit in the form of surplus labor incorporated into the commodities. Thus, although the exploitation of slave labor did not occur under capitalist productive relations, it clearly formed the basis for primitive accumulation and subsequently came to coexist as a crucial subordinate aspect of the capitalist mode of production. In this sense, slave migrations were integrally tied to the origins of capitalism.

With the industrialization of capitalist production in Europe, labor circulation became a constant social phenomenon, exhibiting differences according to the phase of capitalist development and its uneven manifestations within distinct national formations. These diverse stages of capital expansion determine the points of origin and destination as well as the social composition of the migratory currents. The volume of the working population set in motion grows in proportion to the organic composition of capital and the velocity of its circulation. Until recent times, both in the competitive and the monopoly stages of capitalism, permanent transfers were the main tendency of geographic labor mobility. Over time, however, the movement has tended to become a circulation of the labor force, and the permanent component of population transfer has been reduced. The accelerated circulation of capital and its extended reproduction on a world scale give rise to larger movements of an increasingly diversified stream of workers from different countries.

From an international point of view, then, labor transfers do indeed reinforce an amplified capital accumulation process, but at the same time they require a growing surplus population that defies social absorption into the new international division of labor. It is no surprise, therefore, that the process results in large-scale return migrations to traditional labor-exporting countries, often accompanied by immigration from several other countries. With this network of simultaneous integrations, turnovers, and dispersals of national labor forces throughout the world, the composition of working classes in the entire imperial chain undergoes basic alterations. At the same time, the contradictions of relative overpopulation are intensified in both expelling and receiving countries.

For the imperialist bourgeoisie, all labor power in the international chain represents potential surplus value.

The exploitation of the working classes in subordinate social formations is intended to supplement the profits extracted from the workers—active or inactive—in the home country. This configuration of capital investment in "underdeveloped" societies and the resultant expulsion of workers toward the dominant imperialist centers is sometimes proposed as a "model" for national development. It is important to understand, however, that the imperialist bourgeoisie can only develop this process in alliance with local ruling classes. Imperialism, in fact, is not simply a relation among nations, but a pattern of subordination and exploitation among social classes on an international level. The national form in which this class contradiction is manifested must not obscure the motor that propels the entire system—the extraction and realization of surplus value.

All capital investment serves to deepen the subordination of the local working class, both to the imperialist bourgeoisie and to its domestic counterpart. Though the colonial bourgeoisies may grow increasingly dependent on imperialist financing, this system of dependency unquestionably serves to bolster its local class position in the long run. Would-be "models" of progressive national development based on the exchange of invested capital and colonial work forces actually reflect designs for more efficient control and exploitation of the reserve army. When implemented, they serve only to highlight the class character of imperialist oppression. For not only are local bourgeoisies forced to reformulate their alliances along strictly class lines, but the various working classes more and more frequently stand up to combinations of capitalists from different nations. As the existence of Puerto Ricans and workers of other nationalities in the United States—as well as the multinational composition of the proletariat in the advanced capitalist countries of West Germany, France, and England—shows, the objective conditions for an internationalization of the class struggle are being laid.[13]

The wide variety of migratory flows, the pattern of continued displacement and dispersal, and the periodic waves of migratory return point to the complexity of the social development of labor in its international dimension. The mobility of the worker allows for his or her transfer to positions of more optimal benefit to capital, which can only assist in counteracting the declining rate of profit. The availability of workers accustomed to less favorable working and living conditions means that for a time the cost of reproducing labor power can be reduced and the extraction of surplus value augmented. For the expelling country, emigration involves a decline in the supply of workers, and may raise the possibility of a rise in the overall wage scale within that national economy. Migrations thus tend to reduce wage differences among national economies, just as the circulation of commodities has the general effect of leveling national prices to an international average.[14] The tendency to equalize wages internationally is accompanied by more severe and effective exploitation of the migrant labor force, wherever it is active. The mobility of the worker only improves his or her potential service to capital.

It is not to be assumed that this transfer of workers under the control of monopoly capital proceeds free of contradictions. On the contrary, the international circulation of labor presents serious economic and political dangers to the system as a whole. Once the labor force becomes mobile, it stands to a significant extent outside the control of capital and of the capitalist class. However "legal" any given migratory current, migrant populations invariably seem to aggravate social "problems" for both expelling and receiving countries. One reason for this negative outcome is what might be termed the "overflow" factor, the fact that impelled migration sets more workers into motion than are specifically needed by capital, including workers drawn out of precapitalist relations of production who would otherwise be to a certain extent self-supporting.

This unanticipated upset in the desired balance may also be felt in the expelling society, which often loses that

sector of the workforce most needed within its own development plans. The noted cases of "brain drain" (e.g.,
India, Jamaica) and the migration of industrial workers
from Puerto Rico in the 1940s and 1950s are examples of
this phenomenon, the other side of which is that the receiving country often fails to use these workers productively.
Very often, the migrants carry with them their status as a
"reserve" to the place of destination, where they remain a
dead weight on capitalist production and an essentially
unproductive expense.

In general, then, the multiplicity of migratory alternatives escapes the designs of capitalist planners. Even the
highly programmed movement of "guest workers" into
European countries has entered into a vicious circle. Like
masses of Puerto Ricans in New York City, the "guest
workers" in France, Switzerland, and West Germany, imported to fill acute labor shortages, are fast becoming a
labor "excess" in their own right. No program to return
the immigrants to their homelands can conceal the underlying structural quality of relative overpopulation under
conditions of advanced capitalism.

The practical impact of migration on the production
process also eludes the precise expectations of imperialist
planning, since capitalists are at a perennial loss to pre-
dict with any accuracy whether any given migration will
result in the transfer of workers from the reserve to the
active workforce, or the contrary, or whether the expanded supply of workers will be available primarily for
productive or unproductive labor. Such considerations are
of course crucial, since they go to determine directly the
relative cost of socially reproducing the additional labor
force, and thereby of the working class as a whole. This
perpetuation of costly "reserves" in certain branches of
production makes subsequent planning measures all the
more arbitrary, and at times blatantly defensive of the
political and economic system as a whole. Further, the
costs not only of these reserves and of unproductive labor,
but of the very conversion of labor power from a use value
into an exchange value, are all drawn from the labor of the

employed working class. As mentioned earlier, the intro-duction of additional workers into the labor market itself presupposes increased productivity of wage labor, which means intensified exploitation of the active producers.

Capitalist Development and Migration in Puerto Rico

As allusions to the Puerto Rican case in the foregoing pages make clear, the effort to recapitulate Marx's essen-tial insights with respect to worker migration and to situate these within a contemporary context was under-taken with the knowledge of that particular experience in mind. The principal directive flowing from this formula-tion is, of course, for a global historical analysis of that experience, clearly differentiating transformations in the mode of production and phases within them. The histori-cal periodization set forth in the three chapters that follow seeks to define and explain the variety of relations be-tween capital and labor, and the movement of each of these in Puerto Rico over the course of the last hundred years. Each chapter covers a major phase in the develop-ment of capitalism in the Island, from its beginnings in the last century to the present. In general, each proceeds from a mapping of basic economic structures and trends to the delineation of class configurations and related polit-ical and ideological practices, going on to an account of attendant changes in population, and especially in worker migration. Throughout, this requires a close interweaving of national and international forces and events, chiefly with regard to relationships with the United States, but also with Spain in the initial period and with other points in the shifting network of imperialism along the way.

The period from 1870 to 1898 constitutes a transition toward the establishment of capitalist relations within ag-riculture which was nevertheless uncompleted by the end of the period; the concentration of land and the introduction of machinery into sugar cultivation, along with a steady growth in population, generated diverse migratory movements, both internal and directed abroad, all on a modest scale but symptomatic of changes in the economic order.

The U.S. occupation in 1898 accelerated the ongoing transition and quickly consolidated the establishment of agrarian capitalism. The plantation economy, along with its manufacturing complement (first tobacco and subsequently the needle trades), became a part of the international system at the service of the new metropolis. This second period, which lasted until about 1940, saw the formation of a growing relative overpopulation, and the generation of numerous migratory currents, as well as a substantial internal redistribution of population paralleling the investment of U.S. capital. There were two phases of outward flow. The first was a dispersion of population along related links in the imperialist network. Then, after World War I, there was a concentration of movement toward the commanding center of this network. Emigration, though still small in volume, put to a test the capacity of the Puerto Rican labor force to move into new settings. The accumulation of relative overpopulation during these years was still cushioned by the persistence of precapitalist relations in rural areas, but with the collapse of the plantation system and related manufacturing activity toward the end of the period, the accumulated human surpluses began to constitute an acute social problem.

With the early 1940s and the beginnings of industrialization, the human mass that could not be absorbed into the new scheme of production intensified the move to the United States. The period opened with a first phase of investment in light industry (i.e., that with a low organic composition of capital), and passed in the early 1960s into a second phase in which finance capital with a much higher technological component (a high organic composition) became dominant. By the time of this second phase the mobility of the Puerto Rican labor force had reached unprecedented proportions. The progressive absorption of the colonial economy within the productive system of the metropolis has intensified the circulation of Puerto Rican workers within what is in effect a single labor market controlled by the U.S. bourgeoisie. Since this "redundant" population reproduces its condition as a surplus within the metropolis, as in Puerto Rico, it continues to disperse throughout the United States and to return to Puerto Rico in a restive search for a reconnection to capital. At present this circulating workforce is made up in large part of such "reserves" who find no stable source of employment within the ever widening circuits they now traverse. Clearly, Puerto Rico's problem of "overpopulation" is today more acute and more difficult to solve than it was in 1940. Only the action of the state, dependent almost entirely on local disbursements by U.S. federal agencies, allows for the maintenance of this human mass (now a majority of the population) and prevents it from occasioning more serious social and political conflicts.

This rough sketch gives only the general contours of the analysis presented in the following chapters. The periodization is no more than a complex set of hypotheses intermingling insights and guidelines from the theoretical approach with broad knowledge of the recent history of Puerto Rico. The text to follow begins the work of successively confronting concepts and data so as to refine and deepen our understanding of the contradictions faced by the working class in Puerto Rico, and by Puerto Ricans living and working in the United States. Hopefully, this analysis will help illuminate the position of the millions of other workers around the world set into motion by the same historical forces.

Notes

1. Karl Marx and Frederick Engels, "Forced Emigration," in *Ireland and the Irish Question* (Moscow: Progress Publishers, 1971), p. 57.
2. Thomas Robert Malthus, *An Essay on the Principle of*

Population (New York: Augustus Kelley, 1971), book III, ch. IV.

3. Karl Marx, *Grundrisse* (New York: Vintage, 1973), p. 100.
4. Ibid., p. 604. Our discussion of historical "laws" of population is an attempt to draw together ideas on the dialectics of social change and tendencies found in a wide range of Marxist texts, from *The German Ideology* and *The Critique of Political Economy* to *The Dialectics of Nature, Anti-Dühring*, and Engel's letters on historical materialism.
5. This is a slightly freer translation of Marx's text than Nicolaus' version in *Grundrisse* (p. 605), which is more literal but awkward and potentially confusing.
6. See, for example, Maurice Bloch, ed., *Marxist Analyses and Social Anthropology* (London: Malary Press, 1975). For a Marxist approach to pre-Columbian Puerto Rican economy, see Francisco Moscoso, "The Theory of Tribal Consciousness and the Taino," mimeo. (Binghamton: State University of New York, 1975).
7. Karl Marx, *Capital,* vol. 1 (New York: International Publishers, 1967), pp. 631-32.
8. Karl Marx, *Theories of Surplus-Value,* vol. II (Moscow: Progress Publishers, 1968), p. 447.
9. Marx, *Grundrisse*, p. 614.
10. According to José Nun, for example, the industrial reserve army is a function of competitive capitalism and is transformed in the monopoly phase into a "marginal mass" made obsolete by advancing productive techniques and the incapacity of monopoly capitalism to create employment equal to the growth of the labor force. For Cardoso, on the other hand, the industrial reserve army springs from contradictions in capitalist development as such, and continues to emanate from the many new sources of employment engendered by monopoly capital. While Cardoso is certainly justified in arguing for the persistence of the reserve army as a symptom of capitalism in all stages, and cites ample evidence of the continued generation of productive activity under monopoly conditions, he appears to underestimate the impact of sustained population growth. More important, perhaps, is to keep clearly in sight that these new fields of production give rise not only to more employment but also to magnified unemployment. As Harry Braverman's analysis of monopoly capital has shown, new employment categories inevitably produce new labor surpluses. Needless to say,

this process manifests itself differently in different parts of the world, but the contradiction remains the same and the category of "industrial reserve army" remains in force. The tendency of capitalism to employ workers and to deprive them of employment is constant; its further internationalization as a system has given birth to an international industrial reserve army of great mobility. The matter to be investigated is the forms these contradictions take in this new context.

See José Nun: "Sobrepoblación relative, ejército industrial de reserva y masa marginal," *Revista Latinoamericana de Sociología* 2 (1969); Fernando Henrique Cardoso, "Comentarios sobre los conceptos de sobrepoblación relativa y marginalidad," *Revista Latinoamericana de Sociología* 1/2 (1971); Harry Braverman, *Labor and Monopoly Capital: The Degradation of Work in the Twentieth Century* (New York: Monthly Review Press, 1974); Paulo Singer, *Economia política da urbanização* (São Paulo: Ed. Brasiliense, 1973).

11. Engels to Lange, March 29, 1865, in Ronald L. Meek, ed., *Marx and Engels on the Population Bomb* (Berkeley: Ramparts Press, 1971), p. 86. By 1844 Engels had pointed out how the capitalist means of production, upon reaching a certain degree of development, would become a contradictory barrier to population growth. "The Malthusian Theory, however, was an absolutely necessary transitional stage, which has taken us infinitely further forward. Thanks to this theory, as also thanks to economics in general, our attention has been drawn to the productive power of the soil and of humanity, so that now, having triumphed over this economic despair, we are forever secure from the fear of overpopulation. From this theory we derive the most powerful economic arguments in favor of a social reorganization; for even if Malthus were altogether right, it would still be necessary to carry out this reorganization immediately, since only this reorganization, only the enlightenment of the masses which it can bring with it, can make possible that moral restraint upon the instinct for reproduction which Malthus himself puts forward as the easiest and most effective countermeasure against overpopulation."—"Outline of a Critique of Political Economy," in ibid., p. 62.

12. Engels to Kautsky, February 1, 1881, in ibid., p. 120. From this vantage point the Marxist position with regard to the

practice of birth control can be understood as part of a conscious process of controlling and determining all of the forces of nature, including humans. In this sense it is possible to disassociate the practice of birth control from the theory that attempts to justify it under capitalism. As Lenin indicated, "Birth control as the democratic right of workers is one thing, while neo-Malthusian theory in bourgeois society is quite another."—V.I. Lenin, "The Working Class and Neo-Malthusianism," *Collected Works*, vol. 19 (Moscow: Progress Publishers, 1973), pp. 235-37.

13. V. I. Lenin, "Capitalism and Workers' Immigration," in ibid., pp. 454-57.
14. Nicolai I. Bukarin, *Imperialism and World Economy* (New York: Monthly Review Press, 1973), p. 45.

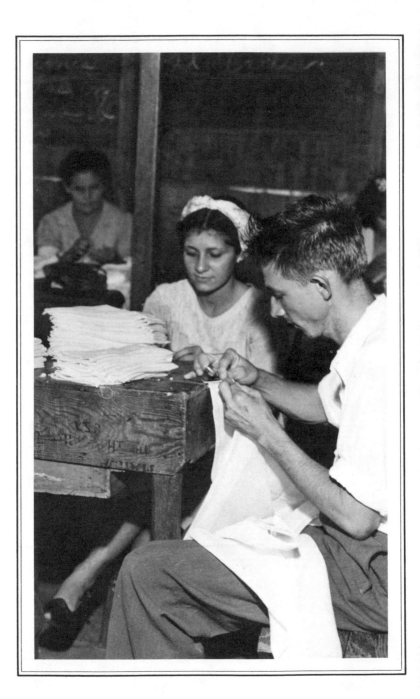

PART II

Capitalist Development and Migration

CHAPTER 3

The Colonial Contradiction, 1873–1898

The colonial contradiction that is the subject of this chapter can be stated in deceptively simple terms: Spain, as a waning colonial power in the latter part of the nineteenth century, was unable to fulfill its role as a metropolis for its colony, Puerto Rico. It is important to understand that the simple enunciation of such a contradiction, of a relationship set against itself, is but a point of departure. It is the complex trajectory of this relationship, the conflict-ridden process of its unfolding, that requires analysis. The contradiction appears in the first instance as a juxtaposition of structural conditions and contrary historical forces and agents. The contradiction reflects, generates, and renews these forces; they in turn act *within* the contradiction, transforming themselves, investing the contradiction with new content and bringing new actors into play. This is, of course, a difficult form of exposition, especially since these processes are neither smooth nor linear, but are marked by forward spurts, reversals, and periods of stagnation. We believe that the entry of Puerto Rico into the orbit of capitalist relations in the closing decades of the last century cannot be well understood until this analysis is accomplished.

Puerto Rico as a Spanish Colony

During the last third of the nineteenth century, then, the hold of the Spanish metropolis on Puerto Rico became increasingly tenuous. Throughout most of Europe, the system of capitalist production was consolidating, as evidenced in changes in the means of transport and communication, population growth, technological innovations, the opening of new markets, the continuing institutionalization of "free" labor, and enormous increases in industrial production. The Spanish metropolis was unable to adjust its relations of production so as to enter fully into this process, and the result was an obstruction to the emergence of capitalism in one of its colonies, Puerto Rico, and the channeling of Puerto Rico's external commerce to other expanding nations. Spain had since much earlier lacked an adequate economic base for extracting agricultural products and primary resources from Puerto Rico, and for providing the colony with manufactured goods in return. Spain was a predominantly agricultural country, and so competed in agriculture and industry with its own colonies; it therefore was maintaining an order of political domination without the economic structure to sustain it.[1] In short, the Spanish bourgeoisie, still struggling to consolidate its position as a class at home by bringing a greater part of the peninsular labor force under its control, was unprepared to move effectively to exploit the colonial labor force in Puerto Rico, still largely engaged in precapitalist forms of production.

The original interest of the Spanish monarchy in Puerto Rico was in its search for precious metals. But once mining production had been exhausted around 1535, Spain abandoned the colony's external commerce, which fell largely into contraband with other nations. The colony's agricultural production continued to stagnate at a subsistence level. Not until 1756, when the Barcelona Company was established in order to revive colonial agriculture, was there an attempt to develop agriculture by creating commercial conditions that would guarantee a market for crops. But the result was only more contraband. In 1765 the Aguirre-Aristegui Company attempted to supply the colony with slaves in exchange for Island products, but this project also ended in failure.

The major commercial experiment of the eighteenth century was the establishment, in 1765, of La Factoría, a mercantile institution whose main purpose was to organize the export of tobacco and other products to Holland.[2] La Factoría only served to confirm once again Spain's inability to exploit the colony. At best, it could only seek to obtain some benefit by legalizing part of the illegal trade with other nations over which it had no effective control.

A new mercantile policy, embodied in the Cédula de Gracias of 1815, opened the way for colonial commerce with other nations, giving impetus to agricultural production. Previously undeveloped land was divided up, and immigrants were attracted in an attempt to break the independent producers who were disposing of their agricultural surplus as contraband. St. Thomas, then a Danish possession, became a major source of imports, occasioning such comments as Tapia y Rivera's: "Well, what a novelty, the arrival of a boat from St. Thomas loaded with merchandise! What movement, what vitality!"[3]

The Puerto Rican colonial market became divided among various nations which supplied the colony with manufactured products and consumer goods, and extracted the major share of the Island's agricultural output. While Spain could do nothing to harness either the boom in commercial cultivation or the new economic needs that resulted from it, its high customs barrier had the effect of diverting currency to Spain, creating further obstacles to trade with other nations and to the expansion of the money supply in Puerto Rico.

The figures on Puerto Rico's foreign trade in Table 3.1 indicate the extent to which Spain was not fulfilling its function as a metropolis and had, by the 1870s, become a costly intermediary between the colony and other nations. As can be seen, the major part of Puerto Rico's external commerce depended on trade with other nations, while the metropolis played a minor role.

Meanwhile, the United States increasingly was becoming the market for Puerto Rican sugar and molasses, the colony's major products during this period. The level of cane cultivation thus came to be determined by the buying capacity of the U.S. market. The political implications of this contradiction were clear to Spanish observers, who from the middle of the century had been troubled by the significant United States participation in the colony's

Table 3.1
Trade Between Puerto Rico and Spain, 1870–1897
(as percent of total)

	Imports to Puerto Rico	*Exports to Spain*
1870	14.4	5.3
1873	24.0	6.5
1878	24.7	5.5
1879	19.3	7.7
1881	29.2	9.4
1882	22.3	11.7
1883	20.4	12.5
1884	29.6	12.1
1885	22.8	15.1
1886	28.0	12.3
1887	23.3	16.7
1890	30.8	26.1
1893	20.0	25.0
1896	32.6	29.0
1897	40.0	27.2

Source: Estadística general del comercio exterior de la provincia de Puerto Rico, 1870–1897.

commercial export trade.[4] North Americans were competing strongly with the Spanish metropolis, to such an extent that the volume of purchases made by the United States in the colony surpassed that made by Spain. The attraction of the United States market was its ability to absorb a large share of the colony's production. Only at the end of the century, in the 1890s, did Spain increase its purchases from the colony, and even then it received less than 28 percent of Puerto Rico's total exports.

Table 3.2 illustrates the share of Puerto Rico's exports absorbed by the Spanish market. What is interesting is that sugar and coffee, the most important colonial products, were far less important both in volume and value

Table 3.2
**Percent of Exports of Major Products
to the United States and Spain, 1870–1897**

| | *Molasses* | *Sugar* | | *Coffee* | *Tobacco* |
	U.S.	*U.S.*	*Spain*	*Spain*	*Spain*
1870	92.0	68.6	0.8	26.0	16.3
1873	90.0	59.6	1.2	24.3	0.1
1879	—	54.0	1.4	10.7	30.0
1881	89.3	57.0	2.0	12.3	56.4
1882	89.0	56.3	2.2	15.7	43.4
1883	68.1	66.5	5.3	20.0	72.0
1886	73.6	69.2	9.2	9.4	57.0
1887	95.0	70.3	11.2	21.1	42.1
1890	88.0	51.4	36.0	17.0	70.2
1893	96.6	68.2	26.0	24.1	67.5
1896	67.3	62.2	35.4	28.0	56.0
1897	74.4	60.6	32.0	29.0	12.0

Source: *Estadística general del comercio exterior de la provincia de Puerto Rico,
1870–1897.*

than tobacco, and this was not exported to the metropolis
in significant quantities until the last third of the century
(until 1869 Spain did not consume any Puerto Rican tobacco *at all*).

Modes of Production in the Colony

The essential characteristic of Puerto Rico's colonial
contradiction was thus Spain's inability to fulfill its role as
a metropolis; the uneven and fragmentary development of
Spanish capitalism impeded the optimal exploitation of
the colony. The second half of the nineteenth century is
the period in Puerto Rican history when this colonial contradiction reached its highest expression, as a conse-

quence of the development of commercial export agriculture (coffee, sugar, and tobacco) and the formation of a class of *hacendados* intent on expanding and modernizing the means of production. Modernization here meant the establishment of capitalist relations and the dissolution or subordination of coexisting relations of production, a struggle that took place over several decades among the diverse class sectors linked to the several systems of production.

Table 3.3
Distribution of Farms by Size, 1899

Size in acres	No. of farms	Percent	Acres under cultivation	Percent
0–4	22,327	57.2	50,274	10.4
5–9	7,417	19.0	48,815	10.1
10–19	4,503	11.5	58,760	12.2
20–49	2,929	7.5	83,783	17.3
50–99	994	2.6	69,940	14.5
Over 100	851	2.2	171,398	35.5
Total	39,021	100.0	482,272	100.0

Source: Report on the Census of Puerto Rico, 1899.

Spain's failure to encourage production in the colony led to the formation of a network of independent subsistence producers and to a fragmentation of rural property. Slaves, day laborers (*jornaleros*), tenant farmers (*agregados*), and small farm owners coexisted. The increase in trade in the early 1800s sparked a process of change in the mode of production, leading slowly to a transformation from subsistence to commercial cultivation. The productive apparatus, formerly divided into independent family units, began to move toward the creation of a system of *haciendas*. In Puerto Rico the sugar *hacienda* best represented the form of agricultural cultivation propelling the transition to a capitalist mode of production. Major changes began to be felt around 1870, with the establishment of the first sugar refineries (beginning the process of proletarianizing agricultural workers), the legal abolition of slavery and various forms of servile labor, the appearance of political parties and of agricultural, mercantile, and craft associations, the creation of savings banks, the growth of public transportation, the growth of the press, and so on. A social and economic movement began toward the modernization of the colonial structure and the establishment of capitalist relations of production.

Nevertheless, great obstacles stood in the way of the unfolding of this process. The main obstacle to the development of commercial agriculture, principally sugarcane, was Spain's policy of neither protecting nor taking any interest in such activity, primarily because Caribbean sugar meant competition for Andalusian producers, who put strong pressure on the central government to raise duties on sugar entering the Spanish peninsula.[5] The same pressures led the Spanish government in 1865 to withdraw the grants of credit to indebted Puerto Rican sugar producers, which up to then had prevented seizure of their lands. Producers found it impossible to acquire sufficient credit to finance their production, and interest on loans sometimes reached the astounding level of 36 percent a year. Sugar producers faced the double risk of usury and expropriation, since the absence of banks meant that the financial operations necessary for agricultural development could not be regulated. A chaotic and arbitrary tax system added to these financial difficulties.

Failure to aid production on the part of the metropolis represented heavy burdens on the Puerto Rican sugar producers. They were further obstructed by competition from the cultivation of beet sugar, technological innovations in other sugar-producing countries, and a tariff policy that prevented technologically advanced machinery from entering the colony—a tariff policy similarly affecting all industrial activity.[6] Spain feared any development that would increase agricultural competition or create an industrial competitor, and recognized that a strengthening of economic ties between Puerto Rico and other nations would inevitably lead to the eventual loss of the colony.

The Dynamics of Class Struggle:
Hacendados *vs.* Comerciantes

Only a partial view of the class dynamics in the transition to agrarian capitalism can be provided here. Two essential aspects of the backdrop to class contention in late nineteenth-century Puerto Rico have already been sketched. The first is the "colonial contradiction," the constraints on the Spanish state, domestic and foreign, that blocked it from adequately performing a metropolitan role for Puerto Rico. The second is the actual combination of precapitalist modes of production present as the movement toward agrarian capitalism began. We now turn to the key social forces and lines of movement in class struggles of the period. Much of the detail necessary for a full treatment can only be mentioned in passing—for instance, the role of the merchants and landowners, and of nationals of countries other than Spain or Puerto Rico; differences within the landowning class according to their chief crop; the political projection of institutions and social groups such as the military, the clergy, and the bureaucracy. Important as these may be to a rounded understanding of the period, for present purposes it will be enough to focus on those in active contention for class ascendancy in Puerto Rico itself, and on the working class in formation, whose coming into being was the most important outcome of the whole process.

Small farms based on familial or servile relations of production were predominant in the Puerto Rican economy until the end of the nineteenth century, despite the beginnings of agrarian capitalism. A comparison of statistics pertaining to tenure in Cuba and Puerto Rico makes this situation clear. According to the census of 1899, 43.5 percent of the area under cultivation in Cuba but 91 percent in Puerto Rico was owned by its occupants; 28 percent of farms in Cuba but 93 percent in Puerto Rico were owned by occupant farmers. In Puerto Rico, in striking contrast to Cuba, no class of *hacendados* emerged with the strength and solvency to finance large-scale projects that would lead to major social change. The fragmentation of rural property was an index of the structural weakness of Puerto Rican *hacendados* as a class.

At the same time, and as a pure manifestation of the colonial contradiction, the bourgeoisie in Spain did not function as the dominant class on the Island; it controlled neither the means of production nor the means of exchange. The two social forces in contention for this role were Puerto Rican *hacendados* and Spanish merchants, or *peninsulares* in Puerto Rico. To the extent that land remained in the hands of Puerto Ricans while commerce was controlled by *peninsulares,* two social forces, one of which had appropriated the means of production and the other of which controlled the means of exchange, stood against one another; each fought to establish itself as the commanding nucleus of a new bourgeoisie.

But it was the *peninsulares* who had the support of the Spanish state, whose primary interest was to assist those who had come to the Island solely to enrich themselves through mercantile activity. At the same time, the *peninsulares* did not want to face the many risks that agricultural operations entailed, since their aim was not the development of agriculture but immediate financial benefit.

In time, the *hacendados* found themselves increasingly in debt to the Spanish merchants, which led them to seek control of the circulation of money and commodities in an effort to win command of the socioeconomic structure of the colony. The merchants, who at first had no intention of appropriating the means of production, could nonetheless not allow the unification of production and exchange under the control of class rivals. This conflict came to a head in 1887 with a broad-based movement among *criollos*, small merchants and farmers as well as professionals, to boycott Spanish goods and businessmen. The repres-

sion unleashed against all those suspected of being conspirators in the boycott—including mass arrests and
tortures—indicates the determination of Spanish merchants to preserve their monopoly over commerce.

Capital accumulation does not, however, originate in
usury, or in the simple hoarding of money, the characteristic activities of the *comerciantes*. It needs the development of production through increased productivity and
technological advances. Only the *hacendados* were in a
position to initiate the changes necessary to move the
colonial economy toward capitalist development; but a
substantial investment, far beyond their means, would
have been essential. The merchants could not initiate the
process because their power on an economic level depended on the metropolis, which, as we have seen, sought
to block the development of agriculture. To initiate the
unification of production and exchange would have engaged the merchants in a struggle on two fronts: with the
hacendados and with the metropolis.

As long as the merchants could continue enriching
themselves without serious risk to their social and economic position, they drew back from this double confrontation. If the merchants could have been sure of controlling the progressive institutions proposed by *hacendado*
spokesmen, they would have offered no resistance, but
since they enjoyed no such assurance, they preferred to
oppose liberalizing change of any kind, from education to
urban services.

As agriculture moved through the transition from subsistence to commercial farming, however, the merchants
were the only ones with enough liquid money to finance
the harvests. Many *hacendados* came to depend on this
financing, which made them more dependent and indebted to the merchants. With much of the land and even
the harvests themselves mortgaged at usurious rates,
merchants moved into a more commanding but also more
conflictual position. As a sector of the merchants became
involved in agricultural production, they too came into

conflict with metropolitan policy and formed unstable alliances with *hacendados* in moments of economic crisis.[7] By the end of the century, when the situation was increasingly difficult for all classes in the colony,[8] some *peninsulares* were openly engaged in a partial boycott of Spanish products and in organizations supporting autonomy.

The merchants' dilemma was that agricultural progress tended in the long run to undermine their dominant role. They were forced, therefore, to do everything in their power to detain the unfolding of the forces of production. The class contention underlying the colonial contradiction was thus manifest on the national level as the antagonism between *criollos* and *peninsulares,* and in the political realm as a polemic between liberals and conservatives. The merchants played a reactionary role, which by no means derived simply from their ideological loyalty to the metropolis but was a function of their position in the economic structure of the colony. They represented mercantile and usurers' capital that, not realized by its application to social production, could not operate as capital in the strict sense of the word.

The *hacendados*, on the other hand, were the progressive force and aspired to revolutionize the colonial relations of production. It was this class, and those who spoke for it (the elite *criollo* professionals), who made up the nucleus of a potential national bourgeoisie. Their petitions to Spain for the establishment of banks, universities, schools, means of transport and communication, political rights and liberties, colonial representation, free trade, and so on, constituted a set of revolutionary class claims that signaled a historic advance for Puerto Rican society. Their interests clashed with those of a backward metropolitan state. In giving in to *hacendado* petitions the metropolis was strengthening the *hacendados,* allowing them to stand up to the colonial power, and eventually to claim sovereignty for the Island; it was thus undermining its own political control. Not to give in, on the other hand, was to invite the attack of this class. But these attacks were few because of the financial and structural weakness of the *hacendados,* who, although they may have presented a broad front, were never strong enough to produce open and effective opposition to Spain.

It was not until the end of the century, and to a great extent as a consequence of the international situation faced by the metropolis, that the party of the *hacendados* was able to achieve partial political and economic victory. The events of 1898 arrested this process abruptly and threw the *hacendados* into a new struggle.

The Dynamics of Class Struggle: The Persistence of Servile Labor

The *hacienda* system necessitated a continual concentration of land, an extension of commercial cultivation, and the employment of large numbers of agricultural workers. Once established on this base, the Puerto Rican economy was geared toward production for export, and therefore toward integration into a world capitalist market.

At first the *haciendas* used both slave and servile labor, although servile labor predominated. Even before abolition (in 1873), slavery had been widely felt to be a negative factor in economic progress, and its juridical abolition was clearly foreshadowed.[9] What little resistance to abolition that there was among the *hacendados* was directed at being guaranteed indemnity and assured a sufficient labor force.

It is significant that by 1872 slaves made up only 5.12 percent of the population, and only one-third of these were employed in agriculture. In addition, the slave population was aging and was not reproducing itself, due to a low birth rate and high infant mortality, and to the increase in the number of freed men, to the suspension of the slave traffic in 1845, and to a cholera epidemic which took some thirty thousand lives, mainly among slaves and *jor-*

naleros, in 1855. Thus, by the middle of the century slaves constituted an ever diminishing component of the labor force, and a range of measures was proposed that would guarantee a sufficient agrarian workforce, particularly for the cane *haciendas*. Two early measures, the Bando de Policía y Buen Gobierno (1838) and the Reglamento de Jornaleros (1849), legalized the system of servile labor at a time when the number of independent producers and *agregados* (tenants) made impossible a ready supply of free labor. These measures were intended to end the system of *agregados* and establish a system of *libretas* (work passes).[10] The *libreta* system did not end *agregado* labor, however, and it continued to predominate. Thus these legal alterations in the system of work, which were aimed at creating a class of unpropertied rural workers, did not succeed. Although land became increasingly concentrated and *jornaleros* and independent producers were expropriated, there was not sufficient money, even on those *haciendas* most developed in the direction of the plantation system,[11] to pay the workers in cash alone. The *libretas*[12] were not abolished until 1874, but this did not end the system of servile work, since even then the *haciendas* could not pay cash. Payment in *vales* (scrip), legally abolished in 1863, was maintained until well into the twentieth century.[13]

In 1874, during a brief period of liberal ascendancy in Spain, it was ordered that "free" work be unregulated so as not to tamper with the "interest of capital and worker" and the "laws of supply and demand."[14] But while a political party in the metropolis was facilitating the creation of a labor force available to work for wages, existing fiscal and tariff policies served to impede the process of proletarianization in the colony. These policies therefore expressed clearly the underlying contradiction: the metropolitan legal order, reflecting the relations between metropolis and colony, and the colonial social structure, corresponding to internal relations of production, were altering at different tempos.

The first large-scale sugar refineries (*centrales*) were

established in the early 1870s, but the owners' inability to keep pace in modernizing production put them at a competitive disadvantage on the world market. In 1878-1879 the first sugar refinery (Central San Vincente), which had been established in Vega Baja, declared bankruptcy. In the last two decades of the century, Puerto Rican sugar production declined drastically, falling a full 40 percent between the early 1870s and the 1890s.[15] The value of exports to the United States declined similarly. By the end of the century those *centrales* in operation lacked the technical and financial base to compete with new corporate investment from the United States. At the same time, however, coffee was securing an increasingly prominent place in the European market. Coffee production required less labor and capital investment while enjoying a more favorable price, and by 1888 it had replaced sugar as the chief export product and source of revenue in the colonial economy. At the time of the takeover by the United States, the amount of land dedicated to coffee far surpassed that in cane, while the average farm in coffee cultivation was substantially smaller.

The ascendancy of coffee provides further evidence of the failure to establish a capitalist plantation system under Spanish rule and to break with the predominantly servile relations of production. Pay in *vales*, the indebted *agregado*, seasonal labor, access to small landholdings by the *jornaleros*—in a word, all of those characteristics which tended to delay the onset of capitalist agricultural development—found renewed life as the Puerto Rican economy turned to coffee.

All aspects of life in the colonial economy were thus influenced by the demands of the world market, and especially by conflicting Spanish and U.S. policies and commercial needs. Lacking any effective internal market, the economy was locked into commercial dependence. Early capitalist development, which would have favored the consolidation of an anticolonial movement and the securing of national sovereignty, was blocked by the persistence of precapitalist relations of production.

Population:
Growth and Migration

Over the course of the second half of the nineteenth century the population of Puerto Rico doubled in size (see Table 3.4). Although there was generalized growth throughout the entire Island, the increase was disproportionately high in the central and western areas, while such large towns as Aguadilla, Mayagüez, Caguas, and Bayamón-San Juan also grew rapidly.[16]

Although along the coastal rim there was some cultivation of fruits, tobacco, and cane, the central and western area was the traditional coffee belt. In the post-1870 period, the region became the center of Puerto Rican commercial agriculture. Due to the dictates of world commerce, human labor power, the most productive force, was drawn away from that sector of production to which it was best suited—sugar—and which was inclined toward initial capitalist accumulation, and into the coffee farms. From the regions surrounding the large cane *haciendas*, the growing "excess" *jornaleros* gravitated westward and inland to take up work in coffee, many of them returning only seasonally to the coastal canefields. But coffee cultivation was characterized by precisely those features of economic organization that tended to fetter the onset of capitalist development: a fragmentation of landholdings, servile labor, and continued access to small holdings for subsistence production. Thus the population surplus was absorbed, but at the same time it contributed to the persistence of precapitalist relations of production.

Gradually, however, population increase came to constitute a burden on the continued reign of precapitalist production, because the small holders and tenant farmers were unable to produce enough for their use and to meet the growing needs of a larger population on the small and middle-sized *haciendas*. It comes as no surprise, therefore, that in the last three decades of the nineteenth century large numbers of small landholding and peasant families emigrated from the Island. The Puerto Rican colo-

Table 3.4
Slave Population for Selected Years

	Population	Slaves	Slaves as a percent of total
1802	158,050	13,333	8.43
1812	183,014	17,536	9.58
1820	230,622	21,730	9.42
1827	287,673	31,878	11.08
1830	323,838	34,240	10.57
1834	357,082	41,818	11.71
1846	443,090	51,216	11.51
1860	583,208	41,738	7.15
1872	617,328	31,635	5.12
1877	731,648	—	—
1887	998,565	—	—
1899	953,243	—	—

Source: Report on the Census of Puerto Rico, 1899.

nial society, which had for centuries attracted a continual and considerable flow of immigrants, began on the
path toward becoming a land of perennial emigrants.

At the same time that there began to be "overpopulation" in the coffee area, the cane growers were constantly
lamenting an acute labor shortage. But the cane *hacendados* not only failed to attract workers; they were also
unable to raise the capital to buy land or the necessary
machinery. They also could not understand that there was
no real labor shortage, but rather that what was lacking
was a mass of agricultural workers who were available for
contract wage relations. What was needed was a working
class, but what existed was a labor force, dispersed and
fragmented according to the diverse forms of servitude to
which the laborers were then subjected. *Hacendados* thus
considered the labor shortage to be the problem in and of
itself, and so devised a variety of schemes to remedy the
situation, including the import of Asians, which was authorized in 1854, and a plea for the introduction of con-
victs. The main immigration flow, however, was made up

of Spaniards, who either were or became soldiers, merchants, clerks, and public employees. French and Italian immigrants became merchants and landholders, and to a lesser extent artisans in the urban areas. The steady flow of Europeans was thus of limited value in the search for rural day laborers, and in addition had no substantial effect on overall population growth and movement.[17]

Despite all obstacles, there was a steady extension of land under commercial cultivation, an expropriation of small farmers, and an ample growth in population. The dispossessed subsistence farmers moved in three directions: toward the coast, toward the inland and coastal towns, and abroad. Neither the agrarian capitalist enterprises nor the poorly developed craft and industrial enterprises[18] were able to absorb significant numbers of these groups, while those who did have jobs were facing sharp increases in the price of basic goods, stagnating wages, and levies of labor for public works. Both the breakup of precapitalist farms and the incipient distribution of capitalist relations displaced people, and for some of these emigration became an attractive or inescapable alternative.

There was also, beginning in the 1860s, another type of emigration taking place, the voluntary or imposed exile of the *criollo* professional elite. Born in Puerto Rico but educated in Europe and imbued with the liberal ideas of the epoch, many of these young professionals, who represented the interests of the class of *hacendados*, were in favor of social and economic progress, and were at the forefront of the anticolonial movements of the period. After the failure of Puerto Rican and Cuban representatives to negotiate liberalizing reforms with the Spanish parliament through the Junta Informativa y de Reformas of 1865-1867, and after the suppression of the Lares insurrection of 1868, part of this elite left the Island and established itself in New York. Men who had been deported, such as José Julio Henna, and survivors of the Lares revolt who went into exile, such as Juan de Mata Terreforte and Antonio Vélez Alvarado, began to consolidate contingents of Puerto Ricans in New York dedicated to the struggle for the Island's independence. In 1892 the Club Borinquen was founded, with Sotero Figueroa as president. Joining forces with Cuban exiles, they issued such newspapers as *La Revolución* and *El Porvenir,* and promoted the struggle for the liberation of all the Antilles. Political repression during Governor Laureano Sanz's incumbencies in 1868-1870 and 1874-1875 increased the number of exiles, as did the harsh crackdown in 1887, Spain's frantic response to the formation of secret societies whose aim was to boycott Spanish commerce.

The period of the most intense political activity began in 1895, the year of the outbreak of the second Spanish-Cuban War and of the second armed uprising against the Spanish in Puerto Rico, the insurrection of Yauco (1897). Militants came to New York and joined in the founding of the Puerto Rican section of the exiled Cuban Revolutionary Party, and a number of Puerto Rican conspirators in New York went to Cuba to participate in the war of independence.[19] Despite the obvious difference in conditions and motivations, the emergence of the exiled political opposition was but another dimension of the colonial contradiction that gave rise to and sustained the larger volume of worker migration.

The workers, as opposed to the elite, migrated to a variety of places. In the early 1870s Santo Domingo became a point of attraction for laborers from the cane areas in the south of the Island,[20] a movement that some authors attribute to the despotic rule of General Sanz, then governor of Puerto Rico.[21] By the end of the decade, the situation was considered alarming, and attempts were made by the metropolitan government to dissuade the workers from emigrating. In 1879, for instance, the Spanish government declared: "Without depriving the emigrant of his liberty, the government should deter the emigration, insisting on the instruction that your excellency has communicated to those functionaries authorized to issue passports, calling their attention and that of the town mayors to this important matter, with the aim of making clear to those who propose to emigrate the risk they run of being deceived in their hopes."[22] In spite of these admonitions, Puerto Rican laborers continued to emigrate, not only to Santo Domingo but to Cuba, Venezuela, Guatemala, and New York.

During the next decade Spanish government policy changed, seeking to direct emigrants to other of its colonies in a more organized way. Governors of the period took an active hand in the matter. In 1882 General Portilla issued a circular that allowed the exit of emigrants, mainly to Santo Domingo. In 1887 General Palacio encouraged the emigration of Puerto Rican *jornaleros* to Cuba, following upon negotiations with an agent dispatched to San Juan for that purpose by an association of Cuban *hacendados*. In 1889 General Ruiz Dana continued the policy of promoting emigration to Cuba.[23]

These policies rekindled the debate over the consequences of emigration for the development of the colonial economy. Liberal journalists saw a very serious social problem. In 1888 Manuel Fernández Juncos wrote in *El Buscapié:* "It's been two or three years since an emigration movement was initiated in Puerto Rico. The young laborers, having no family obligations and driven by necessity—or, perhaps, by hunger, which is felt for the first time in Puerto Rico—accept offers for work in Santo Domingo or in the Panama Canal and ship out to those countries."[24] This view of the migration as a drain of human resources was echoed by José Ramón Abad: "It is worth noting that because of an upheaval characteristic of all social malaise, the emigrants do not tend to be those least capable of holding up under hard labor but, on the contrary, they are often men of great energy and strong disposition. Thus the damage is all the greater since it diminishes the useful forces available to work without lessening the cause of the upheaval."[25]

Interestingly, Abad also called for the establishment of manufacturing industries, which would "constitute a remedy for misery and a corrective to the emigration of laborers not usable in agriculture." Fifty years later, of course, this formula was reversed. Only substantial migration, it was then affirmed, could open the way to a successful industrialization. But such remedies were impossible: the metropolis continued to obstruct the entrance of machinery and primary resources into the colony until the end of the century. The lament over the loss of "useful forces" was the lament of a member of the liberal *criollo* class, which was imbued with a vision of a Puerto Rican society based on modernization and progress. To fulfill this dream they believed it was necessary to have an "enlightened" labor force, skilled and ready to submit to "intelligent" exploitation.

Despite this protest, measures to encourage the emigration of Puerto Rican workers were even more organized in the 1890s. In 1893 boats came from Venezuela to transport workers to that country. Shiploads of *jornaleros* contracted by the Dominican agricultural syndicate of San Pedro de Macoris embarked from Santo Domingo. In the same year, the head of the *Diario de Puerto Rico* observed that "now that the emigration is taking other courses, it becomes more tempting and attractive. Not too long ago boats arrived chartered especially by Venezuelan enterprises or from other neighboring republics to take strong and healthy laborers from this country . . . and we have seen that the representative of a rich syndicate from Brazil has established agencies and information to prepare for and promote a major emigration current in that direction."[26]

The emigrations of the 1890s occurred in the context of a severe economic crisis in Puerto Rico itself and were evidence of the expansion of the relative overpopulation in the rural areas. They anticipated the first emigration movement organized under U.S. auspices: the expeditions to Hawaii in 1900-1901.

Notes

1. For a more complete account, see Tulio Halperin Donghi, *Historia contemporánea de América Latina* (Madrid: Alianza Editorial, 1969), ch. 1, "El legado colonial."

2. See Bibiano Torres Ramírez, *La Isla de Puerto Rico, 1765-1800* (San Juan: Instituto de Cultura Puertorriqueña, 1968), p. 86, and Juana Gil-Bermejo García, *Panorama histórico de la agricultura en Puerto Rico* (Seville: Instituto de Cultura Puertorriqueña—Escuela de Estudios Hispano-Americanos, 1970), pp. 173-76.

3. Alejandro Tapia y Rivera, *Mis memorias* (Río Piedras: Editorial Edil, 1971), p. 17. See also Andrés Viña, *Estudios sobre la Isla de Puerto Rico* (Madrid: Imprenta de Don Antonio Pérez Dubrull, 1856).

4. Andrés Viña, *Relaciones mercantiles entre España y Puerto Rico* (Madrid: Imprenta de Don Antonio Pérez Dubrull, 1855). In this report, written by the ex-secretary of the Board of Commerce and Economic Development and directed to the Ministry of State, Viña declares: "At the same time, there appears another matter of supreme importance, the political question, which more than once has occasioned uncertainty, and caused considerable losses to colonial commerce. No one doubts that the agricultural and industrial interests will carry with them the sympathies and the most adverse dispositions. The *Balanza mercantil,* published by me in 1851, which relates to the previous year, indicates that United States interests exported from Puerto Rico 47 percent—almost half—of Puerto Rico's production. This fact alone provides evidence that none of the flags that compete in that market offers more benefit to Puerto Rico than the American: it is the only one in which exports exceed imports by a large amount; it is the only commerce which does not pay cash for the merchandise it sells to that island, and which offers reciprocal and direct exchange. You have in your hands today the means to neutralize this preponderance which every day is more threatening . . . ."

5. Isidoro Araujo, *Derechos de importación en la península sobre los azúcares de Cuba y Puerto Rico* (Madrid: Imprenta de Antonio Andrés Babi, 1855). See also "Exposición de los hacendados de caña, por conducto del Gobernador, pidiendo franquicia para el azúcar que se envía a la Península 1876," in *Boletín Histórico de Puerto Rico*, vol. XI, compiled by Cayetano Coll y Toste, 14 vols. (San Juan: Tipografía Cantero y Fernández, 1914-1926), henceforth referred to as *BHPR. La Prensa* (September 24, 1876) also indicates the collapse of the cultivation of sugarcane at the cost of enriching peninsular regions.

6. Asamblea de Aibonito, *Informes presentados por las comisiones departamentales. Acta de las sesiones—Exposición al Excsmo. Sr. Ministro de Ultramar. Documentos varios* (Mayagüez: Tipografía Comercial, 1886). Also, *Memoria Unión Mercantil e Industrial de Ponce* (Ponce: Establecimiento Tipográfico "El Vapor," 1886), and Federico Asenjo y Arteaga, *El catastro de Puerto Rico* (Puerto Rico: Editorial Don Carlos B. Meltz, 1890).

7. Even in 1872 a partial conciliation between liberals and conservatives had taken place in some electoral districts (see *Boletín mercantil*, April 13, 1872). In 1879 there was a temporary general conciliation (see Sotero Figueroa, *Ensayo biográfico* [Ponce: Establecimiento Tipográfico "El Vapor," 1888], p. 221).

8. In 1895 the merchants who supported Spain's policies unconditionally ("los incondicionales") petitioned the people to boycott Andalusian sugar producers, as well as the wheat producers of Santander, Barcelona, Bilbao, and Baleares. See Lidio Cruz Monclova, *Historia de Puerto Rico. Siglo XIX* (Río Piedras: Editorial Universidad de Puerto Rico, 1970), vol. III, pt. II, p. 278.

9. Segundo Ruiz Belvis, *et al., Proyecto para la abolición de la esclavitud en Puerto Rico, April 10, 1867* (San Juan: Instituto de Cultura Puertorriqueña, 1969); Rafael María de Labra, *La abolición de la esclavitud en las Antillas Españolas* (Madrid: Imprenta a Cargo de J.E. Morete, 1869); *La abolición de la esclavitud en el orden económico* (Madrid: Imprenta de J. Noguera, 1873).

10. See the excellent unpublished monograph by Gervasio García, "La economía natural colonial de Puerto Rico en el siglo XIX," mimeo. (Río Piedras: CEREP, 1974). Also Angel Quintero Rivera, "Background to the Emergence of the Capitalist Economy," mimeo. (Río Piedras: CEREP, 1973). These constitute two conscientious works on the precapitalist society of the nineteenth century.

11. Andrés Ramos Mattei, "Apuntes sobre la transición hacia el sistema de centrales en la industria azucarera. Contabilidad de la hacienda Mercedita, 1861-1900," *Cuadernos* (San Juan) 4 (1975).

12. For more information on the system of *libretas,* see Labor Gómez Acevedo, *Organización y reglamentación del trabajo en el Puerto Rico del siglo XIX* (San Juan: Instituto de Cultura Puertorriqueña, 1970).

13. Angel Quintero Rivera, "Conflictos de clase en la política colonial. Puerto Rico bajo España y bajo los Estados Unidos, 1870-1924," *Cuadernos* 2 (1974).

14. "Circular Gobernador Primo de Rivera," July 13, 1873, in *BHPR*, vol. XI, p. 177.

15. José Antonio Herrero, "En torno a la mitología del azúcar: Un ensayo en historia económica de Puerto Rico. 1900-1970" (Río Piedras: CEREP, 1971).

16. *Anuarios estadísticos de España, 1854-1860; Censos de población de España, 1877 y 1887; Memoria estadística referente a la Isla de Puerto Rico, 1860.*

17. Estela Cifré de Loubriel, *La inmigración a Puerto Rico durante el siglo XIX* (San Juan: Instituto de Cultura Puertorriqueña, 1964), and *Catálogo de extranjeros residentes en Puerto Rico en el siglo XIX* (Río Piedras: Editorial Universidad de Puerto Rico, 1962). For information on the immigrations at the beginning of the century, see Rosa Marazzi, "El impacto de la inmigración a Puerto Rico 1800-1830: Análisis estadístico," in *Revista Ciencias Sociales* 18, nos. 1-2 (1974), and George S. Ulibarri, *Nineteenth-Century Puerto Rican Immigration and Slave Data* (Conference on the National Archives and Statistical Research, May 1968).

18. Compare *Memoria descriptiva de la Cuarta Feria y Exposición Pública de la Agricultura, la Industria y Bellas Artes de la Isla de Puerto Rico* (Puerto Rico: Imprenta de Acosta, 1865) and George W. Davis, *Report on Industrial and Economic Conditions of Puerto Rico: 1899* (Washington, D.C.: U.S. Government Printing Office, 1900). See also *El Buscapié* (September 29, 1878), where expropriation of small proprietors by means of tax pressure and the reduction of these former proprietors to *jornaleros* are denounced. (Here, too, there is serious concern over worker emigration.)

19. See César Andreu Iglesias, ed., *Memorias de Bernardo Vega* (Río Piedras: Editorial Huracán, 1977), pt. II.

20. *Boletín mercantil*, January 10, 1874. See also, Lidio Cruz Monclova, *Historia de Puerto Rico*, vol. II, pt. II, pp. 919-21.

21. For example, Eugenio M. de Hostos, "Diario," in *Obras Completas* (San Juan: Editorial Coquí, 1969), vol. II, p. 134.

22. "Real Orden" (September 3, 1879) in *BHPR*, vol. X, p. 61.

23. Lidio Cruz Monclova, *Historia de Puerto Rico*, vol. II, pp. 360-65. In 1889 General Ruiz Dana sponsored an emigration to Cuba in accordance with an authorization granted by the

Supreme Government to the governor of that island for the establishment of colonies with families from the peninsula, the Canaries, and Puerto Rico. These families were provided with free transportation, six months' support, a house, and twenty-six *fanegas* of land.

24. Cited in ibid., vol. III, pt. III, p. 359.
25. José Ramón Abad, *Puerto Rico en la Feria–Exposición de Ponce en 1882* (Ponce: Establecimiento Tipográfico "El Comercio," 1885), p. 174.
26. Cited in Lidio Cruz Monclova, *Historia de Puerto Rico,* vol. III, pt. III, p. 361.

CHAPTER 4

Imperialism and Agrarian Capitalism, 1898–1930

U.S. Intervention in Puerto Rico: The New Metropolis

The U.S. military invasion of Puerto Rico in 1898 was the political culmination of a slow expansive process through which U.S. capitalist interests penetrated the Puerto Rican colonial economy and directed the lines of its development. During the entire nineteenth century Puerto Rican sugar production depended on the U.S. market. Those Puerto Rican *hacendados* who were producing for the northern market found in the United States a commercial tie that provided a material complement to their ideals of modernization and class control of the colony. As Angel Quintero Rivera has pointed out, "The golden dream of Puerto Rican land owners bent on commercial expansion was access to the extensive U.S. market."[1]

The change of colonial master not only accelerated the consolidation of capitalist relations in the Island; it also altered the colonial relationship because the colonizing nation was able to impel an abrupt overhaul of the Puerto Rican social and economic structure.

Changes in the patterns and proportions of trade show the ability of the new metropolis immediately to appropriate the productive process in the colony and adjust it to U.S. internal needs. Between October 1898 and April 1900 imports from the United States to Puerto Rico totaled $6.6 million and exports to the United States totaled $4.1 million, while imports from and exports to other countries totaled $9.4 and $9.8 million respectively. But between April 1900 and February 1901, while the Puerto Rico–United States trade remained roughly the same—$6.4 million in imports and $3.4 million in exports—trade with other countries dropped to $1.6 million in imports and $2.4 million in exports.[2] Between 1893 and 1896 the Spanish metropolis received only about 28 percent of Puerto Rico's exports per year, but ten years later, in 1905-1906, the United States received an average of 84.7 percent; this had increased to 92 percent in 1930 and to 94 percent in 1935.[3]

Table 4.1
Value of Exports for Principal Commodities

	1895	1906
Coffee	$5,640,055	$ 3,481,102
Sugar	$2,404,872	$14,184,667
Tobacco	$ 414,869	$ 3,554,833

Source: Commercial Porto Rico in 1906.

To a great extent the substantial increase in exports absorbed by the United States was made up of sugar. In 1897 sugar amounted to 21 percent of total exports; by 1901 this had climbed to 54.9 percent and, with some variation, it was maintained at about 50 percent until 1935, when it increased to 60 percent.[4] The relative importance of sugar had been evident since the beginning of the century, when marked changes in production affected the export value of the three principal crops. Sugar remained the principal export, but tobacco continued to expand into the 1920s. Coffee, on the other hand, although it grew in value, continued to decrease in proportion to tobacco and sugar. With the Depression, both coffee and tobacco suffered a sharp and fatal downturn.

Once the United States had occupied Puerto Rico, U.S. companies established control over all aspects of the Island's economy, including transport, communications, finance, agriculture, and small-scale manufacturing. Sugar was unquestionably the most attractive investment, since it was needed in the United States and offered the most favorable terms of trade. According to the report of the governor (1900-1901), the cost of sugar production per ton in Puerto Rico was $10 less than in Java, $4 less than in Hawaii, $12 less than in Cuba, $17 less than in Egypt, $19 less than in the British Antilles, and $47 less than in Louisiana or Texas. Three of the four U.S. sugar companies that came to dominate Puerto Rican sugar production were established in those years: the Aguirre Central in 1901, the South Porto Rico Sugar Company in 1902, and the L. Fajardo Sugar Company in 1905. Eastern Sugar Associates, the fourth of these giants, arrived in 1926.[5] It was through this rapid control of sugar production that the United States consolidated its economic hegemony over the Island.

The legal underpinnings for this swift economic takeover were dictated by decrees of the military government (1898-1900), which were subsequently incorporated into the legislation establishing a civil government, the First Organic Act of 1900 (known as the Foraker Act).[6] Measures that facilitated the quick appropriation of production (especially land) included the fixing of an exchange rate of $.60 (U.S.) per Puerto Rican dollar (*pesos provinciales*) and tight restrictions on local credit operations, which served to further weaken the position of the already heavily indebted Puerto Rican landowners.[7] All local production was brought under U.S. tariff, thus reducing access to European markets for local production, coffee in particular. Coffee was also singled out for exclusion from the U.S. market. At the same time, shipping to Puerto Rico was brought under the legislation governing all coastal traffic in the United States.

The Foraker Act extended the administration of insular affairs by the War Department, with ultimate power clearly retained by the federal executive, legislative, and judicial authorities. A local political apparatus dominated by U.S. presidential appointees was to exercise limited local functions.

Agrarian Capitalism:
The New Mode of Production

The main impact of the U.S. economic invasion is commonly believed to have been a break with the old agrarian capitalism. In fact, the measures taken by the new metropolis were directed toward fostering the growth of agrarian capitalism, a process that had begun much earlier. The new metropolis proceeded to revolutionize the relations of production in agriculture, particularly through the rapid concentration of lands, the extension of areas devoted to export production, and the proletarianization of the working population.

Table 4.2
Farms by Size Groups, 1899 and 1910

Acres	Percent of farms		Percent of area under cultivation	
	1899	*1910*	*1899*	*1910*
Under 5	57.2	35.4	10.4	3.0
5–9	19.0	19.4	10.1	4.1
10–19	11.5	17.2	12.2	7.0
20–49	7.5	15.2	17.3	13.4
50–99	2.6	6.3	14.5	12.2
100 or more	2.2	6.5	35.5	60.3
Totals	39,021	58,371	482,272	1,570,304

Sources: Census of Porto Rico, 1899 and 1910.

As Table 4.2 shows, by 1910 this land concentration was well advanced. Farms of over one hundred acres accounted for only 6.6 percent of all farms but 60.3 percent of all cultivated land; a decade earlier farms this size had controlled only 35 percent of cultivated lands. By contrast, holdings of fewer than twenty acres amounted to 72 percent of all farms but made up only 14 percent of cultivated land. The change is even more dramatic when it is

Table 4.3
Average Size in Acres of Farms for Puerto Rico and for
Principal Sugar Municipalities

	1910	*1920*	*1930*	*1940*
Puerto Rico	35.7	49.2	37.4	34.0
Salinas	129.2	450.3	736.3	353.0
Santa Isabel	162.8	444.0	594.6	1405.1
Fajardo	56.7	176.1	108.8	72.9
Vieques	276.9	335.4	196.4	116.4
Guánica	—	651.6	667.1	323.0
Arroyo	71.9	141.8	130.9	100.8
Ponce	69.4	112.9	84.5	87.7
Guayama	106.7	106.5	86.3	95.3

Source: Puerto Rico Census of Agriculture, 1910, 1920, 1930, and 1940.

realized that at the same time the area under cultivation almost quadrupled, reaching 1.5 million acres. The concentration process was most intense in the coastal sugar areas, as is evident when one compares the average size of all farms with that of farms in the sugar-producing municipalities (Table 4.3).

Not only were landholdings expanded and concentrated, but cultivation was increasingly aimed at the production of export crops, as the Table 4.4 shows. But while sugar production continued to expand until 1935, coffee and tobacco declined in the late 1920s. Thus while sugar production increased from 3.2 to 8.3 million tons between 1910 and 1935, coffee declined from 52.7 to 25.8 million pounds in the same period.

The extension of commercial cultivation and the process of the concentration of land, principally in the coastal areas, meant that structural changes of major importance were taking place. Thousands of small proprietors were forced to sell their land, entering a rural proletariat along with peasants who had relied on ready access to land without enjoying legal ownership. Land dedicated to sub-

Table 4.4

Acres in Cultivation of Major Export Products

	1899	1909	1919	1929	1935	1939
Sugarcane	72,000	145,433	227,815	237,758	245,154	229,750
Tobacco	6,000	22,142	39,068	52,947	45,720	28,584
Coffee	197,000	186,875	193,561	191,712	182,316	181,106

Source: Puerto Rico Census of Agriculture, 1940.

sistence was reduced and the economic position of the *jornalero* was fully transformed into that of the agricultural wage laborer. Even farmers with small and medium holdings soon fell under the sway of the large foreign-owned corporations.

The process of converting the Puerto Rican labor force into a rural proletariat was neither automatic nor immediate.[8] Earlier relations of production persisted in the shadow of the large corporations. In 1916, and again in 1919, rural strikers demanded an end to such signs of promissory relationships as the *cantinas* or company consumer goods, and the *vales,* which had been outlawed in 1908.[9] Such practices were most common among the small and middle-sized landowners in the interior. A decade after occupation, nonwage employment survived, a sign of the economic limitations of the old *hacendado* class in the new setting.

At the same time, there was a growth of manufacturing in the tobacco and needlework trades, although neither engaged a substantial part of the population. While the tobacco "boom" occurred during the first two decades of the twentieth century, needlework did not take off until the 1920s and flourished in the wake of the Depression. Cigar production, which went from being an artisan trade to a manufacturing process, began to generate a new vanguard within the urban proletariat-in-formation. Needlework, on the other hand, was a rural "cottage industry," the means by which women and children were introduced into the labor force. Both of these manufactures, stimulated principally by U.S. investment, were natural complements to agrarian production.

Tobacco and needlework both represented capitalist manufacture in a classical sense, using a low level of technology. Both quickly became "outmoded" by changing demands of the market—cigars were replaced by cigarettes in the 1920s when U.S. cigarette production boomed, and "cottage industry" textiles were superseded with the imposition of new economic priorities in the 1940s. But their rapid supercession does not negate their historical importance as the industries in which the modern class struggle between capital and wage labor was initiated in Puerto Rico. The *tabaqueros* made clear for the first time in Puerto Rican history that Puerto Rican workers stood against a collective class enemy, made up of both foreigners and Puerto Ricans.

Class Struggle in Puerto Rico: New Stage, New Actors

Imperialist occupation transformed the dynamic of the class struggle in the colony and lent it a new content. The peninsular merchant class left the political and economic panorama and was soon replaced by a new metropolitan mercantile bourgeoisie, and by "native intermediaries," many of whom were actually Dutch, English, French, or remnants of the former Spanish commercial elite.

For the class of Puerto Rican *hacendados*, North American domination meant eventual disappearance. Through the Autonomous Charter of 1897, Spain granted local political power to the *hacendado* class, many of whom at first greeted the invading troops with enthusiasm, believing that the United States would provide them with a secure market for their agricultural produce, as well as the necessary "democratic" reforms to buttress their position in society. But the U.S. offer of a secure market extended only to tobacco and sugar, which the United States needed, and the coffee growers quickly fell in wealth and prestige. As for the larger surviving sugar or tobacco *hacendados,* whatever design they had as a national bourgeoisie was blocked from the outset by the plans and interests of U.S. investors. The establishment of the civil government in 1900 was but the political expression of this fundamental subordination. It represented nothing short of a retraction of the liberties, guarantees, and relative power conferred three years earlier in the Autonomous Charter.

The *hacendado* class did not depart from the scene without a clamor. Rallying around such men as Luis Muñoz Rivera, sectors of this class founded the Partido Unionista in 1904, helping to direct part of Puerto Rican politics against U.S. imperialism. [10] But this was the call to battle of a class unable to retain its social and economic hold, a call that was quickly reduced to a nostalgic plea for the reconstruction of a way of life, undisturbed by the intrusive presence of monopoly capital. Despite major changes in the economic order and in the political system—such as the curbing of local legislative powers in 1909 and the imposition of U.S. citizenship over the protest of the Resident Commissioner and the opposition of the house of delegates—the Partido Unionista failed to launch a decisive national struggle. [11] When there was a call for a plebiscite on the political status of Puerto Rico in 1917, Unionista delegate José de Diego brought the project to a halt by rallying support for the efforts of the United States in the world war. "We are citizens of the United States," he declared; "we live and twenty thousands of our soldiers will fight and die under its glorious flag. . . . We should wait until Puerto Rican blood brightens the splendor of the flag of the United States, so that our spilled blood enriches our right and speaks for us to the American people in those jubilant and triumphant days of world peace." [12]

The inability of the *hacendados* to unite as a class was in part due to internal divisions within the class and among its representatives in the *criollo* professional elite. As early as 1896 this elite had divided over the matter of alliances, with parties in Spain willing to support Puerto Rican autonomist claims.[13] Among these class spokesmen there were also advocates for the new metropolis, which represented for them the ideal of progress and the promise of social ascent. This pro-American elite thus spoke for those *hacendados* who were able to modernize production, secure financial backing and markets, and coexist within the new order. They comprised what Quintero Rivera has called an "anti-national bourgeoisie."[14] Their policy of collaboration and support of the "Americanization" process weakened the struggle of *hacendados* as a class and their potential allies.

Whether anti-American or pro-American, the political action of the *hacendados* was blocked by the metropolitan bourgeoisie. At the same time, and as a result of the same process, the divided *hacendados* also faced a growing threat "from below," as the emergent working class took up a conscious struggle for its own interests.

Beginning in the last third of the nineteenth century, town-based Puerto Rican artisans began to voice and practice new forms of solidarity as workers. In resistance and mutual-aid organizations, a small vanguard among wage-working typesetters (*tipógrafos*) emphasized the need for ideological and organizational unity among craftsmen. At this stage, however, workers' organizations remained largely disconnected from the rural world. In the first decades of the new century, the center of organizational gravity moved to the more numerous and more radical cigar makers, and the workers' movement widened to involve the struggles of all those exploited by the *hacendados*. During the agricultural strike of 1905 the class abyss that separated them from the *hacendados* became clear to many workers. This workers' movement assumed organizational form first in the Federación Libre de Trabajadores (1899) and then in the founding of the Partido Socialista in 1915.[15] After 1901 the Federación was an affiliate of the American Federation of Labor.

But the *tabaqueros*, as part of a preindustrial, manufacturing workforce, could play only a limited role as a class vanguard. The absence of any significant industrialization of cigar-making, or any other production, meant a very slow growth for the urban proletariat. The Puerto Rican working class was still overwhelmingly made up of a rural labor force undergoing the transition to wage-labor relations. Up to the time of the 1905 rural strike, it was agricultural workers who stood in open contradiction to the *hacendados*, while the artisans tended to arrange unstable tactical alliances with the party of the landowners. From that time until 1920, workers' organizations established independent political positions, frequently at odds with the *hacendados*. While the workers' organizations tended to oppose the *hacendados*, they at the same time recognized some advantages in the judicial and political structure introduced by the United States. In contrast to the rigid restrictions on labor organizing made by the prior colonial regime, the new political order contained minimal guarantees for workers, including the right to organize as workers, to strike, and to form political organizations. Workers' organizations made a clear distinction between the need to oppose imperialism and U.S. corporate power and the use of constitutional and legal features of the colonial superstructure in defense of class interests. In the words of the labor leader Eduardo Conde in 1915, "It is not necessary to argue whether the Americans in power are worse or better than the Puerto Ricans, for at least with them we are free to protest their errors, which we cannot do with the Puerto Ricans, because in so attempting they will beat in our ribs [*moler las costillas*] and we will lose our liberty."[16]

This dual vision of the class struggle and resistance to imperialism in the colony brought a majority of labor leaders to concentrate on economic issues and increasingly to oppose class alliances oriented toward national liberation. At the fourth convention of the Partido Socialista in 1919, this tendency was defined and reaffirmed. Worker delegates rejected resolutions declaring independence to be a necessary objective for the working class. During the 1920s, demands for increased autonomy successively formulated by *hacendados,* professionals, and others grouped in the Partido Unionista were expressly rejected by labor leaders. They chose instead periodic unstable alliances with *criollo* capitalists (as in the elections of 1920 and 1924), who, from within the Republican Party, opposed independence. These alliances culminated in a formal Socialist–Republican coalition in 1928, which in 1932 proved the winning combination at the polls.

This bizarre combination of class forces, by then thoroughly torn by the Depression and the accentuation of the inner contradictions that came with the economic crisis, managed to wrest a last electoral victory in 1936. A workers' revolt against the operative pact between capitalists and labor leaders was signaled by the 1934 strike of sugar workers, who rejected the collective contract for the industry accepted by their labor representatives. This spontaneous workers' action, among the most extensive in Puerto Rico, failed, however, to produce a lasting new alternative organization. Despite efforts by communists, nationalists, and dissident socialists (Afirmación Socialista) to direct and build on this movement by seeking to link the working class and the independence struggles, a new central labor organization was not to take shape until 1940. By then, as we shall see in the next chapter, a markedly new combination of social forces had taken shape, with the endorsement and active participation of New Deal planners from the United States.

Relative Overpopulation and Migration

The U.S. military invasion and the subsequent large-scale investment in Puerto Rican agriculture inserted the Puerto Rican worker into the larger network of colonial and semicolonial populations who were to serve as the reserve workforce for the imperialist chain emanating from the United States. Workers from Hawaii, Mexico, Central America, Panama, and even from the colonies still under British rule were effectively subjected to the changing demands of U.S. capital expansion, and their diverse migratory movements were shaped accordingly. In all of these countries, regardless of their specific and altering political status, the impact of monopoly capital resulted in the breakup of precapitalist relations of production and the conversion of their workforces into highly mobile labor reserves of the metropolitan economy.

In each area, this transformation was experienced differently. The relative proportion of active and inactive producers—or "adequate" and "excess" population—was different in Puerto Rico than it was, for example, in Hawaii, which at the end of the nineteenth century still found itself largely at a much earlier, semifeudal stage of social and economic organization. In addition, population density in Hawaii remained low, so that it became a center of attraction for migrant workers from a host of other countries, including Japan and Portugal. Yet all of these migratory currents—whether emigration from an "overpopulated" colony, such as Puerto Rico, or immigration to a labor-deficit dependency, or the ongoing internal population movements—were governed by the same historical processes.

Between 1898 and 1940 the growth, employment, and patterns of movement of the Puerto Rican population were conditioned by the establishment and decline of the capitalist plantation system on the Island. The degree of relative overpopulation varied in the major branches of production—cane cultivation, sugar manufacture, tobacco, and needlework—and this engendered both the movement within the colony and the emigration out.

The changes in the different branches of production create basic changes in the social division of labor. Figure 4.1 shows that there was a steady increase in the number of males outside the labor force during these decades, only a small number of whom were drawn into the schools.

Figure 4.1

Activity of Males Ten Years and Older, 1899 to 1935

(in percent)

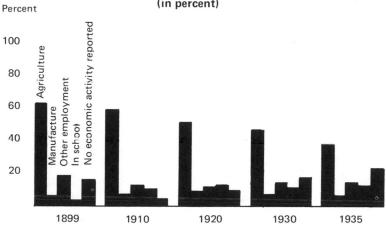

Figure 4.2
Females

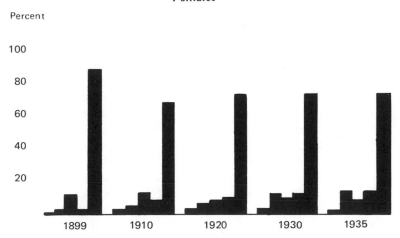

Sources: U.S. War Department, *Report on the Census of Puerto Rico, 1899*; U.S. Bureau of the Census, reports for 1910, 1920, 1930. The 1935 data are from the Puerto Rico Reconstruction Administration census of that year.

Unemployment among men was high even at the beginning of the century, and reached alarming proportions after 1920. At the same time women, as Table 4.5 shows, were increasingly becoming incorporated into the labor force. This was especially the case in manufacturing: women were dominant in the needle trades from their inception, and had become a majority of the tobacco workers by the 1920s; by the 1930s they had become the majority of those engaged in all manufacture.

After 1920 there was a continued reduction in the number employed in agricultural labor and "personal services" (domestic work, the traditional female domain), while manufacturing increased steadily after 1910. This shift was a result of the changing uses of U.S. capital on the Island. The expropriated labor force, forced to go to the site of invested capital, began to move from the mountainous inland areas to the coastal canefields and urban tobacco factories, a sharp reversal of the pattern of movement of the previous fifty years, when the inland coffee-producing municipalities were magnets that attracted migrants. But tariff regulations imposed on Puerto Rican coffee coming into the United States steered U.S. investment into sugar. Between 1899 and 1940 there was a relative depopulation of the central-western mountain region—extending from Morovis to Mayagüez—but the non-coffee-producing mountain zone in the northeast actually increased in population. The coastal cane-growing municipalities and the San Juan–Río Piedras area also grew, and the latter emerged as the main urban concentration on the Island. Of the fifteen major destinations of internal migration between 1899 and 1940, ten were centers of cane cultivation and sugar production, and three were part of the urban San Juan–Río Piedras area, which grew by a dramatic 448.9 percent. By 1940 the population of these fifteen areas was six times what it had been in 1899.[17]

As an example, Quintero Rivera's analysis of Guánica, the site of the largest sugar *central*, shows that between 1899 and 1910 the population of this municipality rose by

Table 4.5

Population Gainfully Employed by Sex, 1899–1935

	Total population	Ten years and older	As percent	Gainfully employed	As percent	In school	As percent	No economic activity reported	As percent
1899									
Male	472,261	322,567	68.3	268,664	83.0	9,630	2.9	45,173	14.1
Female	480,982	336,727	70.0	47,701	14.1	6,119	1.9	283,677	84.2
1910									
Male	557,301	386,516	69.3	317,256	82.0	48,495	12.4	20,765	5.6
Female	560,711	395,084	70.5	76,892	19.5	38,916	9.8	279,276	70.7
1920									
Male	647,825	447,777	69.1	322,466	72.0	72,968	16.3	52,343	11.7
Female	651,984	456,646	70.0	86,462	19.0	40,789	8.9	329,395	72.1
1930									
Male	771,761	544,184	70.5	378,033	69.5	68,690	12.6	97,461	17.9
Female	772,152	549,239	71.1	125,777	22.9	61,405	11.2	362,057	65.9
1935									
Male	861,635	615,983	71.5	384,118	62.3	82,859	13.5	149,006	24.2
Female	861,899	621,966	72.2	138,707	22.3	74,741	12.0	408,518	65.7

Source: See Fig. 4.1.

121.4 percent, compared to an increase for the entire country of only 17.3 percent. More generally, the seventeen major sugarcane areas grew by an average of 45.4 percent, compared to a 4.2 percent drop in the main centers of coffee cultivation.[18]

Emigration during these years was less significant and was as yet irregular in direction and volume. As can be seen from Table 4.6, although the total demographic impact of these movements is slight because the net figures are small, this obscures the magnitude of the human movement involved, for this is a circulation of people. There are two periods of net gain, one at the end of the first decade of the century and the other during the early depression years (1931-1934)—and three periods of sustained out-migration, the first at the end of World War I, the second during the 1920s, and the third toward the end of the 1930s.

An analysis of the complex and diverse currents underlying these trends must situate them in both national and international contexts, and relate them to the different types of relative overpopulation. On a world scale, the entire Puerto Rican labor force served as a reserve army of labor for the metropolitan countries; within the regional economy of Puerto Rico, there was primarily floating overpopulation, as rural subsistence and coffee-growing farmers drifted toward sugar and urban areas. At the same time, there was stagnant overpopulation, seen in the unstable employment, long working days, and low wages characteristic of nonseasonal activity in the urban zones.

The earliest and most important out-migration after the U.S. takeover was the shipment of eleven expeditions of 450 contract workers to Hawaii between December 1900 and October 1901. Organized by representatives of the Hawaiian Sugar Producers Association, these expeditions were intended to provide badly needed labor for the Hawaiian sugar plantations and to partially remedy the unemployment situation in Puerto Rico. This early experiment was a failure, however. Many workers perished on the long trip, which involved travel by rail across the

Table 4.6
Movement of People Entering and Leaving Puerto Rico, 1909 to 1940

Year ending June 30	Incoming	Outgoing	Balance Gain	Balance Loss
1909	5,085	1,974	3,111	—
1910	5,693	2,193	3,500	—
1911	5,953	4,478	1,475	—.
1912	5,028	4,833	195	—
1913	3,895	3,873	22	—
1914	6,806	7,394	—	588
1915	6,221	6,560	—	339
1916	7,293	7,260	33	—
1917	8,458	10,812	—	2,354
1918	11,122	15,334	—	4,212
1919	22,472	25,784	—	3,312
1920	15,003	19,142	—	4,139
1921	17,749	17,137	612	—
1922	14,154	13,521	633	—
1923	13,194	14,950	—	1,756
1924	14,057	17,777	—	3,720
1925	15,356	17,493	—	2,137
1926	16,389	22,010	—	5,621
1927	18,626	27,355	—	8,729
1928	21,772	27,916	—	6,144
1929	20,791	25,428	—	4,637
1930	20,434	26,010	—	5,576
1931	20,462	18,524	1,938	—
1932	18,932	16,224	2,708	—
1933	16,215	15,133	1,082	—
1934	16,687	13,721	2,966	—
1935	18,927	19,944	—	1,017
1936	20,697	24,145	—	3,448
1937	22,793	27,311	—	4,518
1938	23,522	25,884	—	2,362
1939	21,165	25,653	—	4,488
1940	30,002	31,906	—	1,904

Source: Harvey Perloff, *Puerto Rico's Economic Future* (Chicago: University of Chicago Press, 1950).

United States and an extended sea voyage from the West Coast; physical conditions on the plantations took a further toll. Yet the Hawaiian sugar producers complained of the emigrants' poor quality and lack of discipline, the usual response of employers to worker protest over brutal mistreatment and the denial of their rights.[19]

Nevertheless, the following years saw thousands of emigrants move to Cuba and Santo Domingo to work in agriculture and mining.[20] This migration continued into the second decade of the century; the construction of a railroad from Guayaquil to Quito attracted further workers to Ecuador, and in the same years the first tobacco workers, carpenters, masons, and other artisans began to settle in New York City. Beginning in 1899, workers from islands under British rule also began to move into Puerto Rico.

By the middle of the second decade of the century, there were large public protests and strikes in agriculture and tobacco, organized by the unions and led by the newly founded Partido Socialista. The colonial government responded that the "problem" of overpopulation was the source of all evil affecting workers. On October 22, 1915, Governor Yager said that "the only effective remedy" to this problem was "the transfer of large numbers of Puerto Ricans to some other region."[21] In a memorandum of April 17, 1917, to the secretary of war, General McIntyre, chief of the Bureau of Insular Affairs, wrote: "Overpopulation in Puerto Rico. Permanent remedy: Emigration to Santo Domingo. Possibility of temporary use of men and agricultural workers and laborers in general for the railroads in the United States." His message continued: "Pending the establishment of a government in Santo Domingo with which it will be possible to make some arrangements to colonize with Puerto Ricans that Republic and protect them afterwards, between 50,000 and 100,000 could be transported to the United States to be used in agricultural jobs for which they are perfectly prepared, or to be employed in the railroads or in similar work that requires manual help."[22] This plan was accepted enthusiastically by Governor Yager, but was never put into effect. In 1918 another plan proposed regulated migration to the sugar plantations in Cuba. Meanwhile, the Guánica Central was transferring large contingents of workers to "La Romana," its huge partner plantation in Santo Domingo.[23]

There seems to be no way of establishing the numbers of workers involved in these movements, but the most important scheme of the 1917-1920 years was the plan to transport Puerto Rican workers to meet acute and war-related labor shortages in the United States. It was at this time that the direction of the migratory movement began to shift away from other colonies toward the metropolis itself.

The Department of War and the Bureau of Insular Affairs brought between 12,000 and 13,000 Puerto Ricans to work in the United States. Like the earlier migration to Hawaii, this experiment also ended in failure as hundreds died en route and in military work camps.[24] There followed a series of legislative gestures by the colonial authorities to control the process and offer some protection to the emigrants. There was no intention of halting the flow, however, since the official thinking was still that the overpopulation "problem" could be solved by shipping people out. In 1919 hundreds of workers went to Cuba, Venezuela, and the United States, and in 1921 there was a further "expedition" to Hawaii.[25]

In the 1920s there were crises in coffee and tobacco cultivation, as well as the accumulated overpopulation in the canefields, and large numbers of workers began to make their way from the countryside to the cities. The population of Río Piedras increased by 180 percent, and that of San Juan by 61 percent.[26] The social impact of the movement, including health and housing problems, brought forth proposals to use military transport to "decongest" the Island by moving the excess to the United States. There followed the second major spurt of emigration to the United States, which overshadowed simultaneous movements to Santo Domingo and the Virgin Islands. Between 1923 and 1930 there was a net overflow of 38,000 persons. This increased emigration occurred despite the growth of needlework manufacturing in these years. The values of exports in this branch of production rose from $107,000 in 1920 to $15 million in 1929,[27] and by 1930, 42,222 women and children were employed in this rural "cottage industry."[28]

During the Depression, unemployment rose to 37 percent of the labor force, as every branch of production but needlework faced drastic cutbacks.[29] In the late 1930s, employment in the agricultural phase of sugar production rose by 33 percent, and this, together with a significant reduction in the workday, resulted in a cut in the real wages of the workforce.[30] As in the United States, the crisis necessitated decisive state intervention to counteract its most severe consequences. Agencies like the Puerto Rican Emergency Relief Administration organized public works programs, financial aid, and donations of food and clothing, and helped alleviate the misery of thousands of working-class families.

The crisis led to a net return of over 8,000 Puerto Ricans from the United States between 1930 and 1934, but once the federal "economic reconstruction" programs had been set in motion there was renewed emigration. After 1935, sugar production declined, and the needlework trades began to face the same fate as had coffee, tobacco, and cigar production in previous periods. By 1940, the collapse of all sectors of the economy made the relative overpopulation problem more acute than ever. The unrelenting accumulation of people in the towns was compounded by growing floating overpopulation in the plantation areas. The necessity for a massive emigration became a basic premise of all new development schemes. The conditions were set for the migratory explosion of the 1940s.

Notes

1. Angel Quintero Rivera, "Conflictos de clase en la política colonial. Puerto Rico bajo España y bajo los Estados Unidos, 1870-1924," *Cuadernos* 2 (1974).

2. Governor of Porto Rico, *Annual Report 1900-1901*.
3. Governor of Porto Rico, *Annual Report 1930*.
4. Arthur D. Gayer, *et al.*, *The Sugar Economy of Puerto Rico* (New York: Columbia University Press, 1938).
5. Ibid.
6. Lyman J. Gould, *La Ley Foraker: Raíces de la política colonial de los Estados Unidos* (Río Piedras: Editorial Universidad de Puerto Rico, 1975). See also Carmen Ramos de Santiago, *El desarrollo constituciónal de Puerto Rico: Documentos y casos* (Río Piedras: Editorial Universidad de Puerto Rico, 1973).
7. For the effects of this change on prices and salaries, see U.S. War Department, *Report of the U.S. Insular Commission to the Secretary of War Upon Investigations into the Civil Affairs of the Island of Porto Rico* (Washington, D.C.: U.S. Government Printing Office, 1899); and Henry K. Carroll, *Report on the Island of Porto Rico* (Washington, D.C.: U.S. Government Printing Office, 1899).
8. *Special Report of the Bureau of Labor to the Legislature of Porto Rico* (San Juan), no. 1, 1912.
9. Bureau of Labor, *Fourth Annual Report*, February 1916.
10. Luis Díaz Soler, *Rosendo Matienzo Cintrón: Orientador y guardián de una cultura*, vol. I (San Juan: Ediciones del Instituto de Literatura Puertorriqueña, 1960). See also Bolívar Pagán, *Historia de los partidos políticos puertorriqueños*, vol. I (San Juan: Libería Campos, 1959).
11. Néstor Rigual, *Incidencias parlamentarias en Puerto Rico* (San Juan: Instituto de Cultura Puertorriqueña, 1972). The conflict of 1909 centered around the refusal by the House of Delegates to approve the budget for the coming year as a reprisal against the Executive Council (appointed by the U.S. president) for not having ratified certain legislative projects proposed by the House. The intervention of President Taft and his recommendation to Congress permitted a modification of the Foraker Act aimed at extending the previous budget. In this way the only bargaining power the House of Delegates had under the terms of the Foraker Act was brought to an end. See Luis Muñoz Rivera, *Campañas políticas 1901-1916* (Madrid: Editorial Puerto Rico, 1925), speech before Congress, p. 342; José de Diego, *Nuevas campañas* (San Juan: Editorial Cordillera, 1966).
12. José de Diego, *El plebicito* (San Juan: Editorial Cordillera, 1960), p. 59.
13. Pilar Barbosa de Rosario, *La Comisión Autonomista de*

1896 (San Juan, 1957). The pact with Sagasta signified the culmination of the "opportunist" politics of the Partido Autonomista, signifying as it did an agreement with any party in the metropolis that would support colonial autonomy. The international situation in Spain permitted Sagasta, leader of the Partido Liberal Fusionista Español, to endorse the autonomy plan, and yet until that time Sagasta had been a strong opponent of colonial autonomy. In response, a sector of the Partido Autonomista bolted the party and found a new party (Partido Autonomista Histórico y Ortodoxo) around the figure of José Celso Barbosa.

14. See Quintero Rivera, "Conflictos de clase."
15. For these first years, see Gervasio García, "La primera década de la Federación Libre de Trabajadores de Puerto Rico" (San Juan: CEREP, 1974).
16. *Justicia,* June 5, 1915.
17. The History Task Force acknowledges the valuable contributions to this chapter made by Americo Badillo Veiga, who provided us with two extended notes on internal migration in Puerto Rico, the first on the period from 1899 to 1910 and the second on the period from 1898 to 1940. These notes are on file at the Centro library and may be consulted there.
18. Angel Quintero Rivera, "De campesino y agregado a proletario. La economía de plantación," mimeo. (Río Piedras: CEREP, 1974).
19. For these first emigrations, see *Report of the Commissioner of Labor on Hawaii,* Bulletin of the Department of Labor 47 (Washington, D.C.: July 1903); Igualdad Iglesias, *El obrerismo en Puerto Rico. Epoca de Santiago Iglesias, 1896-1905* (Palencia de Castilla: Editorial Juan Ponce de León, 1973); Azel Ames, "Labor Conditions in Porto Rico," *Bulletin of the Bureau of Labor* 34 (May 1901); and Walter Weyl, "Labor Conditions in Porto Rico," *Bulletin of the Bureau of Labor* 61 (November 1905).
20. Bureau of Labor, *Second Annual Report,* February 1914.
21. Arthur Yager, "Fundamental Social and Political Problems of Porto Rico," Lake Mohonk Conference, October 22, 1915.
22. Santiago Iglesias, *Luchas emancipadoras, 1910-1917* (San Juan, 1962), vol. 2, p. 284, and Manuel F. Rojas, *Estudios sociales o frutos del sistema* (San Juan: Federación Libre Press, 1918).
23. Joseph Marcus, *Labor Conditions in Porto Rico,* report for the U.S. Department of Labor (Washington, D.C.: U.S. Government Printing Office, 1919).

24. See *Official U.S. Bulletin*, October 3, 1918.
25. See *Octavo informe anual del negociado del trabajo* (May 1921) and *Noveno informe anual del negociado del trabajo* (February 1923).
26. Angel Quintero Rivera, "La clase obrera y el proceso político en Puerto Rico," *Revista de Ciencias Sociales* 3, no. 19 (1975).
27. Victor Clark, *et al.*, *Porto Rico and Its Problems* (Washington, D.C.: The Brookings Institution, 1930).
28. Harvey S. Perloff, *Puerto Rico's Economic Future* (Chicago: University of Chicago Press, 1950), p. 401.
29. "Unemployment in Porto Rico, 1929," U.S. Department of Labor, *Monthly Labor Review* 31, no. 3 (September 1930). Workers under eighteen years of age are not counted; nor are the underemployed in agriculture due to the seasonal nature of the crops. See also "Labor Conditions in Porto Rico, 1930," *Monthly Labor Review* 31, no. 35 (December 1930), and "Unemployment in Puerto Rico, 1928-29," *Monthly Labor Review* 31, no. 5 (May 1930). This article points out the high percentage of unemployment among tobacco workers. Of the 40,000 workers regularly employed in coffee, not even 20 percent of them were employed in 1928-1929. On the other hand, a number of farms had to pay the worker in food. Part of the crisis was due to the hurricane of 1928.
30. Angel Quintero Rivera, "La clase obrera."

CHAPTER 5

Migration and Industrialization, 1930 to the Present

The New Deal Design: Industrial Production, Agrarian Reform, and Migration, 1930-1947

The contradictions being so profoundly experienced in Puerto Rico during the 1930s between the development of the productive forces and the deteriorating situation of the working population were shaking capitalism everywhere at that time. In Puerto Rico the crisis was compounded by the character of the colonial controls that had followed on annexation: direct appropriation of the principal means of production (land) by elements of the metropolitan bourgeoisie and the direct lodging of the reins of state power and administration in the U.S. Congress and federal bureaucracy. In 1934 federal supervision was transferred from the War Department to the Department of the Interior, a shift that signaled recognition in Washington that something new was required if Puerto Rico was to move into a new stage of growth.

The situation in Puerto Rico appealed to New Deal theorists and cadre, already seasoned in struggles to bring emergency relief, fiscal intervention, and state management and planning to bear against the opposition of conservative agricultural and business interests. "Almost without its being noticed by the taxpayers in the states," writes one of these men, "sufficient economic assistance could be extended now to bring the insular economy into a wholly new stage, a self-sustaining one with a promise of indefinite expansion."[1] In this enterprise New Dealers were counting on the collaboration of U.S.-trained Puerto Ricans (chiefly Luís Muñoz Marin and the *Liberales* in his camp), even though these people were calling for fundamental economic reconstruction rather than relief measures, and even though they remained committed to the ideal of independence for the Island under appropriate conditions.

But the missionary zeal of the New Deal reformists foundered against the intransigence of sugar interests, the Republican-Socialist coalition, which still wielded considerable influence in local politics, and their political allies in the United States. An increasing number of strikes and other disturbances, along with a rising tide of nationalist violence and threats of armed insurgency, were equally chilling. This resistance was met with harsh repression on the Island and ominous rumblings from Washington: "Put aside radical notions about separation from the United States or be cut adrift to certain economic doom."[2] The laboriously constructed Puerto Rican Reconstruction Administration (PRRA), which was to undertake a major agrarian reform, lay the base for public ownership of essential utilities, and embark on the first industrialization projects, was abandoned in 1938 rather than leave any independence-minded Puerto Ricans in positions of importance.[3]

Although there is considerable detail on this stormy and tragic period, from varied class and political perspectives, in the sources thus far cited, much remains obscure about the constitution and role of the diverse class fractions, and the political groups that gave them voice, that were attempting to link up with sympathetic political forces in the United States in order to launch a new economic era in Puerto Rico. It is clear, however, that nothing less was at stake than the historical chance that industrialization might be accomplished in a way that would consolidate rather than undermine national aspirations.

The depth of the economic crisis, the level of misery and despair, as well as the pitiful inadequacy and heavy handedness of the emergency relief machinery added to the harshness of the strife. But at the root of the matter was a wrenching turnover of internal class forces and an attempt to impose newly fashioned forms of colonial control. A similar reshuffling of forces and casting about for effective class alliances was in process on a world scale. Puerto Rico became a political testing ground for the exportability of New Deal recovery strategies, for experiments in which more daring ventures in the socialization of farm production and light industry than could be entertained in the United States seemed urgently necessary and even possible. But the changes in perspective and practice within the colonial administration and its complementary political apparatus in Puerto Rico proved more than could be managed by the new breed of technicians and planners and their political counterparts in Puerto Rico, who were still piecing together the coalition of forces that would later give them undisputed local control for nearly thirty years.

The 1930s attempt to assemble a program and a combination of political forces capable of moving Puerto Rico into a new productive stage was thus aborted. It took the war to bring about a regrouping of Island and U.S. class forces and personalities behind a new project for change and accommodation, by then under the banner of "Operation Bootstrap." This project built on the political experience and extensive research of the New Deal years. It provided the ideological foundation for a design for economic development and political adjustment under external domination that continues to find multiple expression around the world. Both celebrators and critics of that design have focused on the movement of capital rather than migration as the factor sustaining capitalist expansion in its contemporary manifestations. Yet the Puerto Rican case is but one outstanding instance of an ongoing massive deployment and circulation of both workers and capital across national boundaries and between metropolitan centers and their colonized extensions. The ideological support for this population dispersal was being fashioned at that time.

The premise that Puerto Rico's economic ills were a consequence of population pressures was by then established doctrine. One of the earliest technical papers on this theme cited to that effect eight major studies, mostly carried out in the 1930s, by Puerto Ricans and others.[4] The first development plan from the agency that was to become the Puerto Rico Planning Board stated forthrightly that "the pressure of population on resources, which is already great, will become intolerably greater."[5] The Island, it was declared, could provide abundantly for one million persons and in a limited way for two million, but on reaching three million Puerto Ricans would find themselves face to face with disaster. These projections were offered in spite of the fact that the authors of the document also stated candidly, "We do not know what the total production of goods and services is." At the same time that massive migration was seen as the immediate solution, there was considerable skepticism that the necessary volume of outward movement could be achieved, and so education and birth control were looked to as important additional measures.

Thus, although planners talked about population and production, their proposals and projections were only tenuously grounded in any theory or data that linked the two. The compelling and persuasive facts were the sizeable and growing population, the miserable wage scales of those fortunate enough to have any employment, however intermittent or precarious, and the substantial mass of people outside the labor force. How this situation had come about and continued to deteriorate was taken as self-evident: an unfortunate ratio of people to resources, inefficient agriculture, and the absence of industry. The solution to "population pressure" was a new and different pressure, the pressure on people to leave or to curb their numbers.

Between 1899 and 1940 the Island population did in fact nearly double, but the annual rate of increase only rose slightly. Death rates declined very slowly until 1940, migration played only a small role in keeping numbers down, although, as has been seen, basic patterns of movement and key enclaves in the United States and elsewhere were established.[6] Since the proportion of gainfully occupied individuals remained roughly the same during these years (see Tables 5.1 and 5.2), the workforce approximately doubled in size. There was no really impressive surge in natural increase until well into the

Table 5.1
Population of Puerto Rico and the Annual Rate of Population
Increase for the Census Years 1899–1960

Year	Population	Annual rate of increase (percent)
1899	953,243	
1910	1,118,012	1.5
1920	1,299,809	1.6
1930	1,543,013	1.7
1940	1,869,255	1.9
1950	2,210,703	1.7
1960	2,349,544	0.6

Source: Stanley Friedlander, *Labor, Migration, and Economic Growth* (Cambridge, Mass.: MIT Press, 1965), p. 48.

1940s, and it was not until then that a significant extension of sanitary and health services into rural areas began, despite easy assertions about great strides in this connection during the early decades of U.S. occupation. As late as 1947 life expectancy at birth stood at forty-six years.

Production and income figures are more difficult to obtain and less reliable, but there is no doubt that production far out-paced population growth in this period. Sugar production increased from 70,000 to one million tons between 1897 and 1934; yields per acre tripled and the value of sugar production rose by a factor of twenty (from about $2.5 million to over $54 million).[7] The industry earned a steady profit of about 25 percent throughout the depression years (when 12 percent was considered a fair return by government analysts). Despite restrictions on landholdings above 500 acres established in a resolution of the U.S. Congress in 1900, aggregations of 20,000–60,000 acres were assembled.[8] Benefits from tariff protection, estimated at about $35 million in 1935, were going almost entirely to absentee producers, with Puerto Rican con-

Table 5.2

Employment by Industry, Selected Years, 1899–1948
(in thousands)

Industry group	1899	1910	1920	1930	1940	1948
Agriculture	198	240	245	263	229	242
Sugarcane	n.a.	84	85	n.a.	124	126
Tobacco	n.a.	7	30	n.a.	18	24
Coffee	n.a.	38	48	n.a.	26	12
Other farms	n.a.	111	81	n.a.	61	80
Manufacturing and handicrafts	23	45	62	98	101	116
Trade and transport	24	35	35	57	74	105
Construction	n.a.	8	9	13	16	33
Services (including government)	67	61	49	67	85	119
All other	4	4	7	5	7	12
Total	316	393	407	503	512	627
As percent	(33.2)	(35.2)	(31.3)	(32.5)	(27.2)	(28.6)

Source: Harvey Perloff, *Puerto Rico's Economic Future* (Chicago: University of Chicago Press, 1950), p. 64. The percentages for employed labor force against total population have been added. The figures are for April of each year except in 1899 and 1920. The data for 1899 are for December (and are calculated on the basis of the War Department Census), while the data for 1920 were collected as of January 1. The figures for 1899–1930 are for "gainful workers"; those for 1940 and 1948 are for "employed labor force."

sumers bearing about 90 percent of the cost in higher prices. By contrast, wage scales remained at or below subsistence.[9] Sugar workers, who comprised about 20 percent of the workforce, were by no means the most disadvantaged. As spokesmen for the major sugar corporations were quick to observe, "The most serious resistance to higher wage standards does not come from the stronger producers but rather occurs at the level of marginal employers."[10]

Such fragmentary data are no substitute for a careful

economic analysis of this important transition point in Puerto Rican development. But they are sufficient to advance the argument that it was the form of the demand for labor in the first decades of the century that created the pressure on population rather than the reverse. As even the Bureau of Insular Affairs observed, sugar "falls short of sustaining its due proportion of the population of the Island."[11] The steady proliferation of low-skilled jobs with broadly fluctuating demand, both in and out of agriculture, exerted a strong downward pressure on earnings but stimulated rather than restrained reproduction. As long as the outcome of failure to raise two or three children to maturity is destitution, fertility is not likely to drop.[12]

On the eve of war, then, the Island plantation economy was sputtering and viable alternatives remained hazy. The tenor of the preamble to the 1941 Land Reform Act conveyed the generalized revulsion against the pattern of the sugar corporations and operations on the Island. New Deal experiments had gone as far as the sponsorship of major cooperatives in sugar production, though these, along with other agrarian reform measures and goals of diversification, soon took a backseat to more exciting schemes for industrialization.[13] The Island thus remained essentially rural, with close to 45 percent of the workforce in agriculture, more than half of these in sugar cultivation. Manufacturing employment was, for men, restricted almost entirely to food processing, including the refining of sugar, and for women to needlework and related tasks performed as piecework in the home. Census employment data show that about half the women over fourteen years of age were in the labor force, and only one in ten of these was out of work and seeking employment.[14]

Women substantially outnumbered men as operatives, both in cities and in rural areas, and as professionals, where they were mostly schoolteachers; the other major category of employment was domestic service. A 1941 survey of two thousand families in industry and farming gave a glimpse of the economic reality facing these wage earners. The average family had 5.53 persons and 1.58

wage earners, and eked out an income of less than $10 a week.[15] When debate arose over the application of the U.S. minimum wage ($.25 per hour) to the Island with the passage of the Fair Labor Standards Act in 1938, Puerto Rican women doing handkerchief piecework were earning less than a nickel an hour.[16]

It was in these circumstances that Puerto Ricans were called upon to tighten their belts and make patriotic sacrifices on behalf of the war effort.[17] Some 76,000 men and a few women did military service in the early 1940s, while those who remained in civilian employment faced other hardships. The war dramatized the total dependence of the Island on the United States for food and the most basic of material needs, and the menace of economic strangulation was added to the threat of armed attack as supplies were diverted to the military. Governor Tugwell's (1941-1946) memoirs chronicle the indifference and cynicism with which the material and civil defense needs of the population were dealt with at every level of government.[18] Between 1941 and 1942 inflation rose to 53 percent and the number of unemployed increased from 99,100 to 237,000.[19]

What is interesting in this connection is that although nearly 400,000 foreign contract workers entered the United States between the fall of 1942 and the end of the war, few Puerto Ricans were included in this stream. In mid-1944 the War Manpower Commission suspended the carefully selected trickle that had begun in 1942 because it said it was unable to enforce the return of the migrants to the Island. Those who did come established new enclaves in southern New Jersey and Pennsylvania and dispersed through twenty of the forty-eight states.[20] Here they met with a similar movement among workers from the black South who also gravitated to the northern cities with the breakup of the southern plantation system, which paralleled developments on the Island in many ways.[21] In the early months of 1940 unemployment in those U.S. cities matched or exceeded the official rates in Puerto Rico; but the war drew nearly eight million more people into the labor force in the United States than would have been there—including women, youth, older people, minorities, and the handicapped. At the end of the war, with demobilization and the departure from the labor force of many war workers, especially women, with the drive to repatriate imported contract workers and expel any workers remaining illegally, and with the expectation of accumulated demands on civilian production, government economists projected a shortage of nearly two million workers for private industry by 1950.[22] Puerto Rican planners moved energetically to claim for Island workers a share in this expanding job market in the United States, particularly in farm work, domestic employment, and unskilled and semiskilled factory work.

As noted earlier, the political, technical, and ideological base for the changes in Puerto Rico between 1945 and 1965 was laid in the late 1930s and consolidated during the years Tugwell was governor. This required not only a major reorganization of government and the mounting of a technically oriented bureaucratic complex (some forty-one new agencies were created in the space of a few years), but also juridical and constitutional adjustments to permit the minimal decentralization of power required to engage the energies of Island political leaders and the coterie of technocrats gathered around them.[23] Overall command and the definition of the limits within which reform and development policy were to unfold were clearly retained by the U.S. component of this power bloc. The political instrument to effectuate the program, however, had to be local and to cover a broad range of class sectors and supporting groups with a direct interest in the projected transformations. This instrument, absent in the New Deal years, had been molded in the interim under the leadership of Muñoz Marin. The Popular Democratic Party was to become a prototype for populist, democratic, and reformist parties building on appeals to rural and newly urban workers and holding out the attractions of integrity in leadership and political practice, a tempered nationalism, and concrete economic and social goals.

These goals included extensive land redistribution and resettlement, as well as state administration of basic agriculture and of new light industry. This was a moving combination that carried the party quickly beyond the early catchwords of "bread, land, and freedom" into an ambitious program of industrial development.

But the limits of the fledgling colonial bureaucracy in the financing and administration of basic services and industry soon became apparent. With the end of the war, the impetus behind this first stage of industrialization soon began to evaporate, as imperialist controls were reasserted. The telling signal of total surrender on this front was the sale of state-owned industries and the passage of the 1947 Industrial Incentives Act. With these steps the government abandoned its role as entrepreneur and became instead the assiduous promoter of private investment, which meant providing U.S. companies guaranteed conditions for accumulation at several times U.S. rates. This latter version of the New Deal and Popular Party design was merchandised abroad by international capital under many guises, including a short-lived rebirth as the Alliance for Progress.

Industrialization and Absorption into the U.S. Economy, 1947-1965

Considerable thought has been given to the question of just when an alteration of national development goals as articulated by the *Populares* in the 1930s occurred.[24] The idea of independence as a goal to be gradually approached and negotiated peaceably was not new, but it was clear that the economic course charted by the *Populares* at war's end implied as the price for U.S. collaboration not only the abjuration of any radical policy of separation from the United States but moderation in demands for autonomy.[25] The "miracle" of industrialization about to be achieved had three interlocking components: industrialization, migration, and the consolidation of juridical and constitutional ties to the United States that would be more appropriate to the new nature of economic relationships.

There is no question that the mounting of an industrial apparatus in Puerto Rico during the late 1940s and through the following decade constitutes a signal achievement for a country starting from material conditions such as have been described. There is also no question that without emigration, the effects of that accomplishment on living standards would have been negligible. Between 1948 and 1965 Puerto Rico saw the "unusual spectacle of a booming economy with a shrinking labor force and . . . shrinking employment."[26] This seemingly paradoxical situation was made possible because migration reduced the labor force, while productivity gains were sought through an increased capital–labor ratio. On the one hand, there was a substantial rise in real wage rates; on the other, a declining or stationary labor force and permanent, double digit (13-16 percent) unemployment (see Table 11 in the appendix to this chapter). Between 1950 and 1960 average hourly earnings in manufacturing rose from 29 to 41 percent of the U.S. average and continued to mount after that point (Table 12, appendix); the national product quadrupled, yet the number of workers remained practically unchanged.

Wages rose, but not because of pressure from Commonwealth officials, who generally strove to keep wages low as an attraction to investors. It was the U.S. unions and other business interests, concerned about "unfair competition" in Puerto Rico, who pressured for higher minimum wage rates. Further, this pressure was strongest on the minimum scales for semiskilled and unskilled workers. Despite this, the net effect between 1952 and 1962 was to *increase* the difference between the median weekly earnings of laborers and managers from $32 to $48 and between laborers and professionals from $30 to $40 weekly; the differences between farm and nonfarm labor as well as within skill levels increased or remained substantially the same despite relative wage gains. But the pressure on minimum pay scales and the quality of the labor force cannot be blamed for business failures or decreases in profitability; the biggest factor in these closings, according to a Yale study of the period, was deficient management. Local firms readily achieved the productivity of U.S. units when workers were provided the same training, equipment, and management as their U.S. counterparts.[27]

The increased capital–labor ratio required to sustain productivity as wage levels crept upward transformed the Fomento sector into an extension of the mainland economy. By 1960 only about 10 percent of Fomento firms represented local investment.[28] This meant *the price of labor and other commodities, as well as profit ratios,* were being determined by market relationships and economic policies in the United States rather than by relationships among local firms and their workers. By the 1960s it was unclear in what sense one could continue to talk about a Puerto Rican "economy."

Industrialization proceeded with an almost limitless supply of labor despite the massive export of workers. Estimates of the population siphoned off between 1950 and 1965 run from 900,000 to one million, including the children born abroad to migrants. This was substantially the migration of a single class. Friedlander proposed that such an outflow could produce real benefits only if it was large and the outgoers were "redundant" (i.e., unskilled and uneducated),[29] and he concluded that Puerto Rican migration in this period was a success in these terms; he in fact urged it on other Caribbean nations as a solution to their similar problems.[30] Friedlander explained the flow and composition of the migrant stream in terms of wage differentials for unskilled workers in the Island and the United States. Although unemployment in the United States was higher, occupation by occupation, than in Puerto Rico (especially in New York) in 1950 and 1960, the migrants kept coming. "The Puerto Rican migrants," he tells us, "seem to be moving not in response to greater employment opportunities . . . in fact, they are moving to worse employment opportunities . . . but in response to significantly greater absolute and relative earning differentials from prospective jobs."[31]

By the early 1960s, then, it was clearly established that the Commonwealth mode of industrialization had considerable dynamism and was capable of producing impressive rates of economic growth. Economists tended to attribute this success to migration and to the low cost, skill, resilience, responsiveness, and general docility of the Puerto Rican worker under Popular leadership. The politicians, planners, and jurists who created the design for industrialization and fashioned the Commonwealth framework under which it was brought to fruition credited the newly proclaimed political status: "Economic growth under Commonwealth results from a successful blend of economic integration (e.g., common market, common currency) and economic autonomy (e.g., partial exemption from Federal wage and tax legislation)."[32] Commonwealth status, it must be made clear, took the economy into a set of relations that could no longer be described or dealt with in terms of ideas about a foreign presence, penetration, control, or dependence. The result was closer to an effective fusion of economic systems. When the Status Commission reviewed the question in 1966, it was forthright in stating that the elements of "integration" far outweighed the elements of autonomy.[33] The kind of autonomy enjoyed by the Island in terms of wage minimums, for example, was made only too plain in the Commission's own description of the applicable legislation:

> Under special provisions introduced in the Fair Labor Standards Act in 1940, minimum wage rates for employees engaged in interstate commerce in Puerto Rico can be set at or below the U.S. minimum. Minimum wages must, however, be raised as "rapidly as economically possible" to the mainland level without substantially curtailing employment. On the other hand, *rates are not to be set so low that a Puerto Rican industry enjoys a "competitive advantage" over its mainland counterpart* (italics added).[34]

These kinds of controls on competition from the Island were to be maintained even though, again in the Commission's own appraisal,

> The shares of total U.S. investment and the overall mainland market necessary to sustain a satisfactorily high rate of development in Puerto Rico are so insignificant that, even if the results of all individual statistical studies proved adverse, it would still be impossible for an objective program of economic studies to demonstrate conclusively that a future state could not attract sufficient investment funds or obtain adequate markets.[35]

The point, of course, is not that command over decisions was placed abroad; that was the reality before Commonwealth. What Commonwealth did was to reaffirm and consolidate, within a framework of apparent increased autonomy, an obliteration of economic boundaries without the effective, institutionalized provision for the minimal defense of local interests that federated states or independent nations are sometimes able to articulate.

Commonwealth officials and their economic advisers were mainly concerned with the continued profitability of already established enterprises and with the viability of development programs to attract new investors. Nevertheless, a number of effects were beginning to become obvious. Some of these contradictions were part and parcel of the forced draft industrialization; others were made more acute by the effort to represent this as a successful instance of national development, realized in association with a stronger power, but essentially managed from within and intended to enlarge local command of the economy and *ensure the benefits of expansion to Puerto Ricans*. In brief:

First, productivity gains to offset the upward pressure on wages were sought chiefly through increasing the ratio of capital to labor. This in turn had several effects:

(1) It necessitated a shift to capital-intensive, heavy industry, which had to be almost entirely financed from

abroad. This meant a further erosion of the already precarious economic base on which aspirations to enhanced
autonomy or independence had traditionally rested.

(2) The demand for massive inputs of capital brought
new actors into the picture. International conglomerates
and multinational corporations with complex and far-
flung operations and a new order of economic and political
power began to replace smaller producers and move into
positions of dominance in the Island economy.[36]

(3) As this happened, profitability began to be judged
with reference to other low-labor-cost locations around the
world.[37]

(4) At the same time, prospects for multiplying jobs by
introducing labor-intensive techniques in the industrial
sector became even more remote.

A second contradiction was that migration had become
a way of life rather than a temporary or one-time solution,
with complex economic, social, and political repercus-
sions. Although these were by no means fully understood,
it was plain that problems were arising on this front:

(1) In the early 1960s net migration fell off sharply, and
return migrants began to increase the pressure on the job
market and on social services. By this time a third of all
Puerto Ricans had some direct experience of life in the
United States. Studies were beginning to reveal complex
patterns of movement involving class sectors, extended
family groups, and individuals.[38] While most movement
seemed primarily to be a response to economic fluctuations in the United States, extra-economic factors were
also at work.

(2) The crystallization of several distinct patterns of
movement to and settlement in the United States made
the relationship among the overseas Puerto Rican communities, and between them and Puerto Rico, increasingly complex. Changes in class and culture on the Island
were closely connected to similar experiences of Puerto
Ricans in a wide range of settings in the United States.
Changes in class, language, generation, racial sentiment
and identity, as well as political experience and style,

realigned national forces in unprecedented and unpredictable ways.

(3) Post-revolution Cuban immigration to Puerto Rico brought home another facet of national vulnerability and powerlessness—the absence of any local voice in setting immigration policy.

A third contradiction was that declining birth rates only mildly eased the economic pressure of population increase. This was so despite the fact that by 1968 35 percent of the women between twenty and forty-nine years of age had been sterilized—a proportion several times larger than the closest comparable figure for any other country.[39]

Finally, evolving government and corporate strategies of development continued to require juridical and constitutional adjustments and clarifications, which meant that the status question remained open as further modifications to "perfect" or "culminate" the Commonwealth design became necessary.

This schematic summary has been intended to bring out the early appearance of these central contradictions and their roots in the strategies of industrial development mapped in the late 1930s and early 1940s, and to keep before the reader the interconnections among industrial expansion, migration, and the struggle over the status question. The mild setbacks of the early 1960s did not paralyze growth; on the contrary, even more impressive records in production and investment were achieved by 1970. Per capita consumption almost doubled (from $525 to $994 in constant 1954 dollars), and per capita gross national product broke the $1000 mark (from $634 to $1033, also in 1954 dollars).[40] Externally held investment more than tripled (from $1,772 million in 1961 to $6,861 million in 1970), and nearly tripled again to $18.6 billion by 1977. There were, however, a number of failures and "dysdevelopments," in the words of a recent officially sponsored reappraisal of the status question.[41] These included persistent unemployment, inflation reaching twice the U.S. rate, and a lag in migration after 1960 that helped renew population increase. Though the author cited also mentions "dependence" on foreign capital as a problem, one may wonder whether the term is appropriate in the presence of such a massive disproportion of external to local capital and the structural fusion of the labor, commodity, and capital markets.[42] This advanced economic integration has been accompanied by a restructuring and interpenetration of the Island and U.S. labor force and class formations that will now be briefly examined.

Migration, Changes in the Labor Force, and Class Realignments, 1960-1970

Puerto Ricans, then, are a population that has been dispersed, regrouped, and hammered into new configurations by the changing requirements of production and profit, and by the inability of its working sectors, in present circumstances, to survive disconnected from the contemporary process of U.S. capitalist expansion. Two quotations already cited are especially pertinent here. The first is Marx's discussion of the Irish migrations of the nineteenth century:

> But with modern compulsory emigration the case stands quite opposite. Here it is not the want of productive power which creates a surplus population; it is the increase of productive power which demands a diminution of population and drives away the surplus by famine or emigration. It is not the population that presses on productive power; it is productive power that presses on population.[43]

For Puerto Ricans, economic integration has been accompanied by the subordination and control of the total workforce evidenced, on the one hand, by the circulation of Puerto Rican workers within what is in effect a single labor market, and, on the other, by the reproduction on the Island of a labor force configuration increasingly similar to that in the United States. Table 4 in the appendix, drawn from the informative study by Miles Galvin, shows some of the major changes in the labor force in Puerto

Rico between 1940 and 1970. The labor force had grown
from 513,000 to 748,000, almost all of that growth occurring, as will be remembered, after the slackening of migration in the early 1960s, and estimates of the jobless and
marginally employed have clustered around 30 percent
in recent years. A substantial proportion of those without
jobs in 1970 and on into the present are young men and
women, not misfits crippled for industrial work by tra-
ditionalism; return migrants also figure disproportionately
among them. As the officially acknowledged unemployment edged upward in the 1970s, estimates for certain
sub-groups rose to 40 percent and even higher.[44] Moreover, in 1970 about three in five households were living in poverty. Larger families, whether a male head was
present or not, were almost all earning below Island poverty standards.[45] This situation has deteriorated steadily
since the early 1970s, with most poor families now subsisting on federally funded food stamps.

Within this persisting framework of forced idleness and
pauperism, dramatic changes have occurred in the active
workforce. Farmworkers have diminished from nearly
half the workforce to a little less than 10 percent. Manufacturing employment has nearly doubled since 1950,
and now comprises nearly 20 percent of the workforce.
Gains were most visible in metals and machinery, with
marked fluctuations over recent years in nondurables, except for drugs and medicines, petroleum refining, and
shoe production, which showed strong advances during
the 1960s. (This employment has not advanced from 1970
levels. However, there have been sharp declines in such
sectors as textiles and leather products, and marked gains
in chemicals, scientific instruments, and nonelectrical
machinery.) Jobs in construction and commerce have also
grown steadily over the past three decades, the first nearly
tripling to close to 12 percent of the workforce and the
second climbing from 10 to 19 percent. Services expanded
more slowly (from 14.3 to 16.7 percent of the workforce)
and changed in nature, with a shift from personal and
entertainment to professional and business services. The

most impressive growth sector, however, was government, which climbed steadily, from 2.5 percent of the workforce in 1940 to 15.4 percent in 1970. *Almost all of that growth occurred within the Commonwealth bureaucracy.*

Productivity, and therefore the share in the gross product of each of these sectors, varies considerably (see Table 8 in the appendix). For instance, the percentage of workers in services and in manufacturing in 1970 is fairly close (16.7 percent and 18.9 percent, respectively), but the gross product in manufacturing is twice that in services. On the other hand, there are seven times as many workers in services as in the financial sector, but the gross product in the two sectors is almost the same.[46]

Nine out of ten of those employed in 1970 were wage workers, while the mass of jobless or underemployed were of course by and large dependent on access to salaried work for any earnings. The self-employed, 86 percent of whom were male, were most heavily concentrated in the retail trades, with contingents of some size in farming, construction, and services. Of the 4 percent of the self-employed in manufacturing—about half in the production of durable goods—very few were likely to be in control of establishments of any size. The tendency in this sector is toward further denationalization and the elimination of small enterprises. The base for a national bourgeoisie, with independent control of a part of production, is slender indeed.

Female participation in the workforce has diminished since 1940 (24.5 percent versus 32.3 percent), probably largely because women have left numerous marginal forms of employment (needle and other piecework done in the home, much domestic service, and some farm work). Women have nevertheless maintained an important presence in key sectors: for instance, more than twice as many employed women as employed men are professionals (18.5 percent versus 8.8 percent). Men continue to dominate in such fields as accountancy, engineering, law, and the natural sciences, while women are typically nurses, health technicians, and social workers. But very substantial inroads have been made by women into university teaching, pharmacy, medicine, and some relatively new fields such as statistics and computer programming. Managerial, administrative, and selling occupations remain largely the domain of men, except for administration in education and managing and sales functions at the retail level.

The highest and lowest levels of industrial work remain in the hands of men. Women are outnumbered fifteen to one among craftsmen and shop supervisory personnel in industry (where they were primarily foreladies in light industry), and by nearly twenty to one among laborers. At the middle "operatives level," however, women outnumber men by five to four. Just over 25 percent of working women work at this level as assemblers, inspectors, packers, textile mill workers, and seamstresses.[47] Women similarly outnumber men among clerical and kindred workers (about five women for every three men), and over 20 percent of working women are in this sector as secretaries, typists, bookkeepers, and cashiers. The remaining large concentration of women (about 14 percent of all working women versus 10 percent of all working males) is in services, where women figure heavily in some personal services (beauticians) and as health aides, cooks, and domestics.[48]

The rapid expansion of the government bureaucracy and the centrality of the government as a chief employer parallel labor force changes in the United States and are crucial to an analysis of current political and economic trends. This brings us to the second pertinent quote from Marx, which points to the growth of unproductive labor in the British working class:

> What they assert—and partly rightly—is (firstly) that due to machinery and the development of the productivity of labour in general, the net revenue (profit and rent) grows to such an extent, that the bourgeois needs more menial servants than before; whereas previously he had to lay out more of his product in productive labor, he can now lay out

more in unproductive labor, [so that] servants and other workers living on the unproductive class increase in numbers. This progressive transformation of a section of workers into servants is a fine prospect. For the worker it is equally consoling that because of the growth in the net product, more spheres are opened up for unproductive workers, who live on his product and whose interest in his exploitation coincides more or less with that of the directly exploiting classes![49]

Marx saw these unproductive workers as dependent on the productive component of the workforce because they did not produce value themselves through labor, but only helped to realize or consume the surplus value produced by others. He regarded menial servants in his time as prototypical of this kind of worker. However, the forms of unproductive labor that are multiplying in Puerto Rico and elsewhere in the capitalist world today are extremely diverse and have complex relations both to capital and to the productive component of the workforce. This complexity calls for caution in imputing identity of class interests between all unproductive workers and the exploiting classes.

Just as in the sphere of productive labor, there are in unproductive activity persons in supervisory and control functions whose place in the social division of labor makes them objective allies of capital with a direct interest in the subordinate and oppressed situation of the workers. More to the point, in Puerto Rico and similar social formations, the expansion of the unproductive part of the workforce has been used to support allegations about the emergence of a new middle class and a spreading middle-class mentality. This interpretation seeks to advance the myth of social mobility in the colony and undercut demands for radical social change. However, the contradictions generated in the proliferation of such workers brings home their objective working-class placement. Losses in real income, the impact of inflation, repeated episodes of unemployment, and increasingly routinized work leave little room for doubt among such workers about the need to unite politically and ideologically with the rest of their class. At the same time, within the existing international division of labor unproductive workers may find that their jobs depend very much on the productivity of workers in the metropolis or at other points in the imperial chain. These are prickly issues urgently calling for close study.[50] In terms of our theme of changes in the labor force, migration, and the consequent realignment of classes, we can at this point suggest the following:

(1) The structure of the Puerto Rican workforce is now very close to that of a mature, monopolistic economy. It is no surprise, then, to find reproduced in the colony the class configurations, and attendant social and political tensions and contradictions, that are apparent in the metropolitan workforce. By 1976 the occupational distribution was very like that of the United States as a whole, with some predictable departures: gaps at the managerial and higher skill levels, a residual larger representation of farm workers, and a proliferation of nonproductive workers in clerical and service sectors that outpaced mainland trends in this direction (see Table 6 in the appendix).

(2) Economic activity in Puerto Rico has become an integral part of the operating system of the production and circulation of U.S. capital, though Puerto Rican workers have not caught up with even the poorest state in earnings per worker. The main economic difference between the colony and federated states lay in the privileged conditions for capital accumulation repeatedly guaranteed by federal and Commonwealth legislation.

(3) The fragments of a local bourgeoisie that have managed to survive within the constraints of U.S. colonialism have been successfully submerged within the overarching U.S. corporate apparatus of production and finance. There is no private-sector, local-business base from which the further consolidation of U.S. economic control can be effectively contested.[51] Ninety-one percent of the profits generated by industrial investment and 90 percent of industrial production in 1974 were tied to foreign capital. Fractions of the U.S. bourgeoisie and allied class sectors

in Puerto Rico have a stake in representing industrialization and other changes in Puerto Rico since 1940 as separate and sovereign rather than as a further appropriation by the United States of the resources, labor power, markets, and future options of Puerto Ricans.

(4) The Commonwealth design, conceived locally as a platform from which national economic development goals might be articulated by politicians and planners in the absence of an effective bourgeoisie, has been overwhelmed by the expansion of multinational corporate power. Commonwealth proponents in government are now incapable of advancing the expansion of local autonomy in any sphere except as such concessions expand their capacity to better meet the needs of their international corporate clientele. In other words, while the Commonwealth bureaucracy and the resources that pass through it have grown massively, its relative autonomy as an instrument of national articulation and defense seems feeble. The high-handed treatment received by Commonwealth representatives in attempted negotiations with the federal government in the course of the 1970s leaves no doubt on this point.

(5) The Commonwealth government has become the principal employer on the Island (employing three out of ten workers in 1976). As in the United States over the same period but in an even more intensive way, the number of workers being absorbed in the lowest, least stable levels of employment (e.g., clerical, sales, service) has grown rapidly (from less than three in ten to more than four in ten in 1976) as technology has advanced.[52]

(6) The reduction of the agricultural workforce to less than 3 percent of the labor force in 1976 means the liquidation of the rural proletariat and peasantry as political forces.

(7) Labor activity involves an ever smaller proportion of the population. Using 1976 data from the annual report to the governor, the unemployed (35.4 percent) and underemployed (14.6 percent) come to 50 percent of the available labor force. If housewives are included in this labor

reserve, the total unused workforce approximates 70 percent of the population fourteen years and older.[53] This is perhaps the principal problem for both the colonial bureaucracy and for the U.S. federal government, since resources must be found to support an increasing sector of the population that does not participate in the labor force. Federal costs in this connection are now approaching the profits withdrawn by private corporations.

(8) The growth and diversification of this labor force has been accomplished by restraining maximum wages in order to lure investors with the assurance of high profits. Workers and their organizations were until recently a party to this tacit pact, moderating wage demands with the hope of encouraging investment and more jobs. In recent years, however, it has become increasingly difficult to sustain the myth that low wages produce more jobs and not just more extravagant profits.[54] The 1970s brought a break in labor discipline, manifested in strikes and sabotage as well as in the workers' rejection of union leaders and organizations identified with the government and with U.S.-based internationals. Upward pressure on wages from within has thus been intensified at a time when U.S. employment levels are sagging and the competition from other low-labor-cost areas is becoming increasingly keen.

The compression of changes of this scale and complexity into such a short period would not have been possible without the massive circulation of people that took place at the same time. By the early 1970s the volume and diversity of these migration currents, the persistence and multiplication of the structural conditions impelling them, and the almost casual acceptance of repeated uprootings as a commonplace feature of national life made it questionable if the use of the word "migration" was descriptive of this aspect of the Puerto Rican experience.

With the diversification of the migration flows and of their composition, the dynamics of migration can no longer be predicted by simple correlation with U.S. employment levels. Each move is seen as enhancing the chances of another move.[55] Professionals and others alternate periods of work in the United States with their main occupations on the Island. A few become scheduled commuters. Others drift from having no fixed employment to having no fixed residence in a pattern of almost aimless search for small job advantages. Trends worth noting include:

(1) A sizeable flow of seasonal, government-contract, and self-directed farm labor that moves from the Island to U.S. farm areas and back every year. This traffic was estimated at 14,000 contract workers and 60,000 without contracts in 1973.[56] By 1977 the flow of workers under contract had declined to around 5,000 per year.

(2) Between 1964, when migration was at a low point after the great postwar surge, and 1973, net movement out of the Island totaled 66,829 as against 302,293 in the previous ten years. In three of these years there was a net *return*, and in 1972 and 1973 this net return came to 70,085 persons. The pace of net return was maintained between 1974 and 1976 at close to 40,000 per year.[57]

(3) In this same period, many of the migrants went elsewhere than New York, many directly from rural areas and small towns in Puerto Rico to other U.S. communities.[58]

It can be seen from this that within this process of differentiation and convergence, separation and return, there is both (1) an intensification of the relationships between Puerto Ricans on the Island and those with experience of life in the United States, and (2) an accentuation of the differences among Puerto Ricans as their experiences in other than Island settings become more prolonged and diverse.

Industrialization and migration have clearly absorbed local class formations more firmly than ever within the larger U.S. system of class relations, and have further consolidated command and control at the top, within the hegemonic power centers in the United States. Those local bourgeois who have some share in ownership and control of capital or who, through local political parties, compete for command of the Island's bureaucratic apparatus, enter into relations with U.S. power blocs as the weakest among many regional extensions and support groups.

After thirty-five years of industrialization, these Puerto Ricans, whether in or out of power locally, have far more influential patrons/clients/potential allies at the center, but these are double-edged relations that can be taken as much as evidence of greater dependency as of increased scope for action and efficacy. With rare exceptions, the characteristic mode of participation by Island politicians or political groups in U.S. class organizations at any level is as minor appendages or unconditional support groups—that is, as groups representative of specialized interests, whose support is devalued by the urgency of the need and desire to participate at any cost.[59]

The onesidedness of this relationship and the loss of local initiative is most visibly laid bare in the aftermath of the economic crisis of the early 1970s by the desperate and demeaning maneuvers by both autonomists and pro-statehood leaders and forces to wrest small concessions, adjustments, or even minor forms of recognition from their traditional allies in the United States. The collapse and apparent exhaustion of the combined strategies of industrialization and migration as a design for social development in the colony seemed to rouse little disposition in Washington to listen sympathetically or extend effective political support to Island politicians with ties to stateside parties. In fact, moderate *independentistas* were given a new and more respectful hearing in influential U.S. foreign policy circles.[60]

These events go beyond realignments of class fractions and political personalities and forces to a basic redefinition of superstructural issues. That is, a new formulation is being sought within the United States with respect to the diversity of political arrangements that will best accommodate the evolving high-technology, capital-intensive relations of production directed abroad by U.S.-based multinational corporations. At present, as

Hobsbawm points out, "The optimal strategy for a neocolonial transnational economy is precisely one in which the number of officially sovereign states is maximized and their average size and strength—i.e., their power effectively to impose the conditions under which foreign power and foreign capital will have to operate—is minimized."[61] President Ford's apparently casual pronouncements regarding statehood for Puerto Rico may thus be taken less as a signal for a concerted, immediate drive for annexation than as a fundamental shift in attitude toward the status question. This deliberate reappropriation and recasting of that question by the U.S. policy establishment comes as the political future of an emergent international economic order in which the United States expects to preserve a dominant role moves from low-visibility international forums to the center of U.S. politics.

This does not mean, of course, that the political future of Puerto Rico is at a single stroke placed beyond the minds and wills of Puerto Ricans, for it is the working-class majority of Puerto Ricans that has most directly suffered the ravages of the structural transformations that have occurred within the overall process of economic absorption. For this reason, this class is among the social forces historically placed for a direct confrontation with U.S. imperialism in its most advanced contemporary expression. And although the internal differentiation and cleavages among the working population (including its inactive components) mean that disunity and intraclass contention can be expected, it is now apparent that after the deployment of massive resources and considerable political ingenuity by the United States, this class has grown not only in size but in awareness that the present system cannot ameliorate the conditions in which the workers are now trapped, whether they remain in Puerto Rico or travel to the United States.

It should be no surprise, then, that political contention and class struggle on the Island remain at the center of attention in the United States, first, because of the magnitude of the economic interest to be protected; second, because of the consequent size and complexity of the local bureaucratic apparatus and the resources it now commands; and third, because of the sensitivity of the issues internationally and their crucial import for the future of capitalism in coming decades. For these reasons alone, the breakaway of the labor movement in Puerto Rico from the tutelage of the governing parties and of the U.S.-based internationals, as well as its growing politicalization, will be closely monitored and policed from the United States. Moves to organize the unemployed, militancy among government and other white-collar and service workers, the appearance of several Marxist-Leninist workers' parties—all of these are no longer issues for Puerto Ricans alone, but integral components of the class struggle in the larger system. The struggle for national liberation has become inextricably interlocked with the ongoing metropolitan process of class contention. Puerto Rico may negotiate some enlarged form of autonomy, but it is not likely to achieve independence, and certainly not an independence coupled with socialist objectives, without an upheaval in the United States on the scale of the crisis that shook France over Algeria and Portugal over its African possessions.

Puerto Ricans in the United States: Growth and Differentiation of a Community

The work of documenting the growth and the process of class differentiation of the Puerto Rican community in the United States itself is only beginning, and the theoretical and practical difficulties of presenting a clear delineation of classes and their components in a situation characterized by such movement and change counsel great caution in a preliminary statement of this kind.[62]

The work of historical reconstruction requires a refined understanding of the social composition of the successive migrant flows, the forces that set specific class sectors in motion, and the mode of their insertion into economic activity at their point of arrival in the United States. It also involves tracing the process of internal differentiation within the migrant community and the evolving diversity of ideological orientations and political practices within the immigrant group that shape relations between it and other forces on the Island and in the United States. This painstaking enterprise will take some years, and these few pages can only bring home to the reader how much remains to be done.

Puerto Rican migration has been characterized, here and elsewhere, as the massive displacement of members of a single class. Substantially correct though this is, it is only the point of departure and not a definition for all time of the social placement of an entire community. As has been made clear, the gradual consolidation and still emerging patterns of Puerto Rican communities in the United States have been paralleled by major changes in social organization and class structure in Puerto Rico. These changes have brought the relations of production and the configuration of the workforce in Puerto Rico into ever closer convergence with those prevailing in the United States. In both settings, parallel structural shifts in the economy have occurred and continue to advance with direct effects on the use of labor (e.g., the dissolution of the rural proletariat, the proliferation of unproductive workers, the expansion of public-sector employment, the grinding contradiction of unused and surplus human labor). In the constricted social space of the Island, these processes take on a particular intensity and compression, affecting the society at all levels. By contrast, for Puerto Rican workers in the United States, direct experience of these changes is narrowed by their place in the metropolitan workforce, where they form a mobile reserve with minimal participation above the ranks of unskilled and general-purpose workers, generally in the declining sectors and areas of the U.S. economy.

Although the 1930 census reported that Puerto Ricans

resided in all forty-eight states, in 1940 nearly 90 percent were in New York City, where 95 percent of the migrants in the following decade settled.[63] The Puerto Rican community had wrested a foothold for itself in the city in the 1920s, only to be plunged by the Depression into the most menial of factory and service jobs and onto the relief rolls. Many returned to the Island; others remained and took part in the political struggles of the Depression years. The first postwar wave of newcomers thus came into a community that had been lifted from a long siege of joblessness by the war, and yet had its own informal network of coping institutions for dealing with the larger society.

This organizational background is important, not only because it has largely been lost from sight, but because it demonstrates that from very early on, Puerto Ricans in the United States built organizations that had political objectives with a class and national content. Beginning in the early 1860s, Puerto Rican and Cuban patriots were involved in revolutionary activities on behalf of Cuban and Puerto Rican independence from Spain. This activity quickly spilled over into the labor movement and into related party ferment. The concentration of cigar makers in New York City (about 3,000 factories, 500 of which were owned by Hispanics, are reported for the turn of the century) brought a core of politically conscious, literate, and well-organized individuals to the forefront of the small but assertive Hispanic community. It was these men who carried political energies in new directions after the U.S. victory over Spain in 1898. Puerto Rican migration in the first decades of the century continued to include contingents of craftsmen and skilled workers, and numerous individuals seasoned in the labor struggles in Puerto Rico that followed U.S. occupation. The organizational ties between labor organizations in Puerto Rico and the American Federation of Labor and socialists in the United States also drew the community into politics.[64]

By the 1920s, when the Puerto Rican population in New York City shot up from a little over 8,500 to more than

45,000, there were organizations putting forward positions with a class and nationalist content in explicit terms. One of these, the Porto Rican Brotherhood of America (Hermandad Puertorriqueña), organized in 1923, articulated an orientation that characterizes many such groups to this day:

(1) Self-awareness concerning the working-class base of the membership or constituencies.

(2) A concern for mutual assistance and ethnic defense within the framework of the city's ethnic politics.

(3) Involvement in Island political issues and a commitment to the advancement within the United States of the cause of Puerto Rico.

(4) A special sensibility to issues connected with the U.S. role abroad, in Latin America and, most of all, in the Caribbean.

(5) Autonomy and self-reliance—an assertion that Puerto Ricans will define their own problems and needs and devise their own remedies.

This was a remarkably comprehensive program for a small, new community of workers, a fragment of a class torn loose from its moorings at home and engaging the imperial power on its home ground. In the very act of affirming the Puerto Rican right to self-determination, this class fragment was also expressing a primary contradiction of its existence, for it affirmed these rights on the basis of the citizenship it was implicitly repudiating as an imposed and watered-down version of full U.S. citizenship.

What kind of community base was there for organizations like the Hermandad? The migrant population of the 1920s included more males, more whites, more townsfolk and tradesmen, and more people with craft skills and experience of factory work than the Island average. Nevertheless, the community in New York was overwhelmingly working class, especially those living in the heart of *"la colonia"* (east and south central Harlem). Median earnings of Puerto Rican workers at the time were around $21 a week, although half that was not uncommon. There were, in addition, some five hundred small businessmen, mostly *bodega* and restaurant owners, and perhaps a hundred professionals.[65] There was no hesitation in organizations like the Hermandad to point to the class differences between Puerto Ricans clustered in East Harlem and the even poorer Brooklyn Navy Yard neighborhood and those few dispersed in higher income white neighborhoods around the city.

Partial tabulations for four Harlem assembly districts from an official but untabulated census of New York City provide additional perspectives on the community in 1925. Covering more than 7,000 persons in 1,535 households, the enumeration lists practically all those in the workforce as productive workers in light industry, with smaller contingents in unproductive commercial and service tasks, and a tiny fraction in public employment. Hispanics in the area were overwhelmingly Puerto Rican (nine in ten household heads were born in Puerto Rico), and lived in scattered enclaves among Italians, Russians, Irish, Jews, and the myriad nationalities that had substantial concentrations in one or another quarter of the polyglot neighborhood. There was a sprinkling of blacks in the area (a few enumerators classified all Puerto Ricans as Negroes), but the intermingling of the two groups in otherwise segregated ghettoes was not yet apparent. The Puerto Rican population was more heavily male than the U.S.-born black or West Indian populations registered in the same census, and only in those age groups over forty-five did women substantially outnumber men, reflecting in part the presence of grandmothers (there were ten times as many grandmothers as grandfathers).

The median household size (4.8 people) was strongly affected by the presence of lodgers and extended families. Barely 10 percent of the households were made up of persons living alone or sharing quarters with nonrelatives, while households with male and female adult heads formed the core of practically all others. Given a median time in the United States of about four years, these figures suggest a community built around cohesive family units that had been quickly reassembled in the new setting. In fact, the census column that gives the time of arrival for each individual gives a graphic sense of this reaggregation of families over a period of years (see Tables 13 and 14 in the appendix).

It was this family-grounded community that provided the base for diverse organizations—labor, cultural, and political—that was reflected in the Hermandad program. The community's assertiveness quickly provoked a reaction, and in the summer of 1926 there were the first organized armed assaults against Puerto Ricans and their small businesses. This in turn evoked a protest to police authorities in New York by the Puerto Rican Resident Commissioner in Washington and led to the formation of a civic defense organization, the Porto Rican and Spanish-American League for Civic Defense.

Similar political organizations and social activity continued into the Depression years, when local politicians began to seek more active links with Island leaders and to take stands on Puerto Rican issues as the presence of Puerto Ricans, especially in East Harlem, became more visible and insistent. In 1934 2,000 Puerto Ricans marched behind Antonio Barceló, a member of the Puerto Rico Senate, in support of a local candidate to the U.S. Congress, J. J. Lanzetta. The streets rang with the name of Don Pedro Albizu Campos, as another New York City figure, Congressman Vito Marcantonio, came to the defense of nationalists imprisoned for advocating armed resistance to the U.S. occupation of the Island, and won the backing of independence-minded Puerto Ricans.

Puerto Ricans in the thousands demonstrated during the Depression years in support of strikers in Puerto Rico, in protest against unemployment, against relief administration, and for the cause of Spanish Republicans. A Puerto Rican was elected to the New York state legislature in 1937; others were involved in the street violence that broke out during election campaigns in the tough, ethnically mixed district. The Marcantonio organization

provided a well-staffed service to Puerto Rican con-
stituents with job, relief, health, and other problems, a
service that Marcantonio closely monitored himself.[66]
Similar events and developments were taking place in
other political organizations and districts around the city,
especially in Brooklyn.

The first migrants to come after World War II, like those
already here, were mainly family people—young men and
women in their most productive years. Almost all were
literate and came from urban areas on the Island. A
majority came with some skills and work experience in
manufacturing or related activities. Only a few were unemployed on departure, and a sizeable majority reported
fulltime employment during the year before migration.
Their average schooling was around eight years, twice
that of the Island population as a whole. They were recruited largely from among the ranks of active workers
and the most ready reserve of the intermittently employed
in urban areas (Marx's "floating reserve"). Eighty-five
percent found work in blue-collar or service occupations.

The 1948 Mills study notes that most of these migrants
increased their earnings but took on work of lower status,
meaning that they did not find jobs to match the skill
levels they had attained on the Island.[67] At the end of the
1950s, 80 percent were in blue-collar and service jobs, and
fully 53 percent were semiskilled operatives;[68] official unemployment rates were already very close to Island levels
(9.5 percent for men and 11.0 percent for women). Over
the decade there had been a slight increase in white-collar
work (entirely within clerical and sales jobs) and a minis-
cule gain in the proportion at the crafts and supervisory
level in industry. Though fewer than 40 percent of the
women were in the labor force, their extreme concentration among operatives (61.9 percent) and clerical workers
(13 percent) meant that there were three women operatives for every four men in the factories and that men only
slightly outnumbered women among clerical workers. (It
will be remembered that in Puerto Rico, despite a smaller
relative number of women in the workforce, by 1970

females outnumbered males in both clerical work and among operatives.) In both categories, women earned less than men. The idea that Puerto Rican women have been at an advantage, either in access to the labor market, in job status, or in earnings, in ways that would undermine family relations or the manhood of male household heads thus seems to rest on a slim foundation. What these crude figures do convey is a sense that women have been migrating and taking jobs, not as occasional or privileged earners, but as a mobilizable reserve driven by the need to work shoulder to shoulder with men in factories and at clerical jobs at very low wages.

A marked change in the composition of the migrant flow appears to have occurred in the late 1950s and early 1960s. Migrants became younger and more rural, more diverse in skill levels, with heavy contingents of farm and service workers. There was at the same time a steady traffic of contract farmworkers, northward in the spring and southward in the fall, averaging about 13,000 per year between 1951 and 1964.[69] Uncounted numbers traveled this circuit on their own or made private arrangements with crew chiefs and recruiters hired directly by U.S. farm operators. This part of the migration flow seemed to be directly tapping the "latent" labor reserve in farm and other nonindustrial work. Though this population flowed mainly into the settlement clusters already established in various parts of the city, there was a quick fanning out from the core neighborhoods, and by 1950 at least a few Puerto Ricans were living in every health district but one in New York.[70] The community continued to build its organizations from the bottom up, as "hometown" and neighborhood clubs mushroomed, along with a sprinkling of more purposively oriented social service and political groupings, the latter at first dominated by Island political orientations and by neighborhood issues, not being drawn more directly into citywide politics until the 1950s.[71] The establishment in 1948 of an office of the migration division of the Island's Department of Labor provided a base from which citywide coordination of community activity could then be undertaken. The close links between Governor Muñoz Marin's *Populares* and the U.S. Democratic Party helped oil the wheels for gaining small concessions and token recognition of Puerto Rican interests in the scramble of the city's ethnic politics.

By the late 1950s, however, a breakaway from the dominance of the labor office, with its pattern of paternalistically dealing with the city administration over the heads of the community, was in full swing. Rival efforts to "federate" the grassroots, social, and hometown clubs began. Individuals and small groups started to build independent power bases in political clubs and to fight their way through the party structures into appointive jobs and a few elective positions in city and state government. A younger, college-trained group whose members had trickled through the city's high schools into higher education,[72] was trying to forge still another base of ethnic defense through organizations such as the Puerto Rican Forum, ASPIRA, and the Puerto Rican Association for Community Affairs (PRACA, first organized as the Hispanic Youth Association), emphasizing the reaffirmation of Puerto Rican identity. Vaguely modeled on agencies such as the NAACP and numerous Jewish service organizations, these groups were based on the premise that professional and technical talent could be trained within the community and effectively focused on issues and power relationships affecting it. They were in part a reaction to the self-seeking and subservience that marked much of the city's political life, especially within the party machines, as well as against a politics dominated by the question of the Island's status and by Island-based political organizations and rivalries.

These evolving modes of organization went through three critical periods in the 1960s. Each period reveals particular aspects of the seesawing struggle between formulas for controlled social reform organized from the top and the sustained protest and demand for autonomy constantly renewed by new leaders and new organizations arising directly from within the community. The first change was the militance and violence of the civil rights struggle and the subsequent mounting of a federal anti-poverty apparatus that deployed resources, programs, jobs, and new political opportunities and forces around the city. The anticipated outpouring of federal funds for local anti-poverty programs provided an opportunity to coordinate Puerto Rican organizations on a citywide basis with a resource base many times anything previously available. Two rival formulas for attacking poverty emerged, both starting from the premise that programs that would deal with the dispersed Puerto Rican population required centralized control. One plan, advanced by the Puerto Rican Forum, proposed to raise educational levels and strengthen family, cultural, and organizational life. The Forum proposed ten functional programs in eight neighborhoods to be administered through about sixteen existing organizations as well as others to be created as needed. Control was to lie in a citywide board of citizens drawn from the small circle of Puerto Rican professionals, politicians, city officials, clergy, and organizational leaders then prominent in the community.[73]

The counterproposal came from an *ad hoc* group, including numerous individuals who were originally behind the Forum proposal. The aim was to generate grassroots involvement and substantial decentralization through designating "block workers" and assigning a central role to neighborhood organizations and councils. "Programs and projects will only minimally emanate from the central organization," said the proposal. "The major portion of undertakings will be conducted on the most intimate community level." It was in effect a coup against some of the professionals and intellectuals in control of the Forum by the federations of local neighborhood organizations and hometown clubs, together with leaders who were more concerned with "practical politics," that is, with direct control of resources and jobs, votes, and political clout than grand strategies of social change.

The Puerto Rican Community Development Project, Inc. (PRCDP) proposal listed some 263 civic and social organizations registered in June 1965 at the Office of the Commonwealth. (Only a month later, the New York City Anti-Poverty Board registered 421 Puerto Rican organizations in five neighborhoods alone.) More than three-fifths of the 263 organizations were local or hometown clubs, 6 were citywide or borough federations of local clubs, 3 were sports clubs, 18 were religious groups, and 17 were political organizations. Fifteen were said to be "instrumental," i.e., issue-oriented, promoting rent strikes, voter registration drives, and similar actions. There were 10 professional and nine business associations. Seven thousand small businesses were estimated to be in operation, up from 500 in the 1920s. Forty-nine locals in the AFL-CIO Central Labor Council were reported to have significant Puerto Rican membership and 40 Puerto Ricans held elective union office. A third of the Catholic parishes in the city had Spanish-speaking clergy, as did about 15 percent of the Protestant and Orthodox churches. This did not include, however, the hundreds of Pentecostal and other storefront churches, many of which were moving into more solid quarters.[74]

Just as many of the anti-poverty programs were getting under way, the Republicans took control of the city, which involved a major reshuffling of the local Puerto Rican leadership. Under the Republicans, there was still another stocktaking of Puerto Rican "needs," along with a restructuring of the lines of communication and a reshaping of the "organization of organizations" that had emerged during the long years of Democratic-Popular collaboration.[75]

However, it was the youthful explosion of militancy in the colleges and neighborhoods only two years later that brought out in a most dramatic way the contradictions and divisions, as well as the bonds of continuity and unity, building up within the Puerto Rican community in New York and between it and Puerto Ricans on the Island. While on the surface this looked like just another youthful assault on U.S. institutions, mimicking on a far less threatening scale the actions of blacks a few years earlier, it had a deeper meaning for many Puerto Ricans. A generation of Puerto Ricans, the first completely formed in U.S. working-class communities, was laying its sense of crisis on the line for other Puerto Ricans. Something essential and valuable that they knew as a life-sustaining force and to which they felt a passionate attachment was seen to be slipping away. Yet it could not be recaptured or even known except by throwing into stark and angry relief all the cleavages of class, generation, language, race, and ideology that had come to divide Puerto Ricans as a consequence of colonization and migration.

Thus, the fight for control of institutions that has continued since the first takeovers of schools and churches in 1968 has been as much a contention for space in which to test the limits of national and class unity as for havens from which to strike back at oppression.[76] The movement of students and young workers and its collateral political expression have placed these issues squarely in the consciousness of Puerto Ricans in every context. The questions raised are fundamental: What remains of our nationality? What historical role lies ahead for us? What is it that we can ask and expect from one another?

That process of internal testing of self and each other and the testing of the community against encircling institutions lies at the heart of the national question as it confronts our people in daily living. As our numbers in the United States grow, do the complex forces that divide us become an insuperable obstacle to unity? According to the most recent estimates, there are now between 1.5 and 2 million Puerto Ricans in the United States. Seventy percent are still in New York and its environs, but that proportion is declining, and there are growing concentrations in New England, the Midwest, and California. Forty percent of those identified as Puerto Ricans are U.S.-born, but this part of the population is young, so that household heads are overwhelmingly Island-born. The average income of a Puerto Rican family in 1973 was a little more than half the average for all U.S. families, even though Puerto Rican women contributed more toward their own support and that of their families than did other women.

Unemployment in early 1974 was reported at 9 percent (8.6 percent for men, 9.8 percent for women), although, as on the Island, labor "maladjustment" (i.e., underemployment) is estimated at 33.3 percent in poverty areas and is higher still for some groups, especially youth.[77]

The most notable change in the U.S. Puerto Rican workforce, as on the Island, during the 1960s has been the continued growth of white-collar and service employment. Almost as many women work at white-collar occupations as work in factories, although there are as many male operatives (close to 50 percent) as service and white-collar workers together. Small gains in job status, income, and education are still being hailed as evidence of progress up the social ladder and advancing assimilation, but at the same time the degradation in function, in relative pay, in working conditions, and in job stability for white-collar and many service workers is being widely exposed. Similar questions arise as to the value of education in assessing employability or increased income. In a real sense, then, as new educational and work opportunities open up for a small number of Puerto Ricans, the material benefits and social conditions that once went with these are deteriorating.

Recent discussions of migration by specialists are less optimistic than those of the past, although they remain as barren as ever of critical reflection or theory. Kal Wagenheim, having noted the steady decimation of blue-collar jobs in New York City over recent years and the zero growth in real income among the U.S. poor between 1940 and 1970, concludes with what can only be called stale news: "All groups who now inhabit the inner cities will face a grim struggle for economic survival in the coming decade."[78] Jaffe and Carreras, counting on some further mobility gains among second generation Puerto Ricans if they can be induced to "disperse," cling to the hope that· time will show that migration was a solution: "Conceivably in another thirty years," they tell us (that is, in 2015), "increases in employment and population growth will become synchronized to the point where migration will diminish considerably."[79]

The Present Context of Struggle
for Puerto Ricans in the United States

The shallowness and ideological bias of such assessments should now be clear. Without over-reaching the data in hand or understating the difficulties that lie ahead in pursuing a scientific understanding of this situation, we feel a rather different set of statements needs to be made about the Puerto Rican migrant in the 1970s. The last few pages have sketched the growth, diversification, and increasing scope of political organization and practice as the migrant community in New York expanded in numbers, took on new economic roles, and established a significant presence in a broadening range of local institutions. These transformations have defined new needs, interests, and capabilities, as well as a new combativeness and resistance to assimilation based on a clearer understanding of national and class interests. The question before us is whether this community, or any part of it, constitutes a social force of any account within the overall framework of national and class domination from which it springs. The following summary observations, while not presented as inferences fully documented in the foregoing pages, flow logically from the data and theoretical underpinnings of the exposition to this point.

(1) The fluidity, circularity, and impermanence of migration give a particular cast to the Puerto Rican presence in U.S. territory. That fluidity is an indication of the advanced degree to which the Puerto Rican labor force is integrated into the U.S. economy. Within this movement, in New York and increasingly in other U.S. settings, there has been a sedimentation of experience that is reshaping the Puerto Rican nationality in complex ways. Unquestionably, some Puerto Ricans have come to regard them-

selves as "Americans." More importantly, being Puerto Rican in the United States, as in Puerto Rico, has produced cultural expressions that differ in complicated ways in terms of class, language, generation, racial sentiment and identity, as well as the recency and frequency of movement. Because these different expressions of "Puerto Ricanness" arise through the experience of dispersion but also enter into intense interaction with each other, an intricate dialectic of social forces results. The national status or definition of Puerto Ricans in the United States must, therefore, be viewed as problematic. The matter cannot be settled by theory alone, but only by the concrete unfolding of political practice growing out of the changing social formations in which Puerto Ricans are placed as actors, wherever they find themselves.

(2) Despite the diversity of cultural expressions, national identity and commitment are high among Puerto Ricans in the United States and are reinforced by the experience of new forms of economic, political, cultural, and racial domination encountered there. In contrast to the juridical genius and inventiveness lavished on developing the Commonwealth superstructure, it has not thus far been thought necessary to devise any specialized parallel structure for Puerto Ricans in the United States. Commonwealth representatives have at times assumed these functions informally, and Governor Hernández Colón recently proposed to U.S. foundations that a long-term plan be worked out in which the Commonwealth government would join with U.S. private and public agencies to "develop" and service areas of high Puerto Rican concentration in the United States.[80]

(3) Nearly half of all Puerto Rican workers in the United States are in blue-collar factory employment, while 15 percent are in the service sector, performing menial tasks such as cleaning, hauling, delivering, and so on. The 18 percent in white-collar work are heavily weighted with sales and clerical workers in the retail trades, notably in the mass, discount, and neighborhood stores. The social conditions of work and daily living are,

therefore, very similar for the mass of these workers, and while a small and very slowly growing number in professional, technical, or managerial jobs, as well as a few who are self-employed, may have an option of stepping out of the community, many forces combine to retain these individuals within the circle of "Puerto Ricanness" and direct their energies into the multitude of organizations defending Puerto Rican interests. In almost any workplace or institution where Puerto Ricans are present, the pressures, formal and informal, to participate in defensive organizations or movements remain very much alive.

(4) For all practical purposes, then, the Puerto Rican community remains a working-class community. It has generated a complex organizational life and political practice, but this has had only a very partial expression through the direct organization of workers at the workplace itself. The experience of Puerto Rican workers in major unions in the United States has been, if anything, more frustrating than that of Puerto Ricans dealing with unions—many of them U.S.-based internationals—on the Island.[81] Modes of participation within and outside the community are, of course, very much affected by the dominant patterns of manipulation, cooptation, selective inclusion, forced competition, and self-serving individualism promoted from the top in every sphere of action in the United States. These remain viable paths of accommodation and self-advancement for a few. But the contradictions of this process have operated to keep much potential leadership tied to and responsive to the community. The most committed part of this leadership has been projected outward by the community, increasingly in recent years from among the second generation. The movement ideology of the late 1960s, which reactualized many of the strands of national and class orientation with which the community surfaced politically in New York fifty years ago, has had diffuse effects. Despite frequent breakdowns, evasions, and violations of these ideals—which is a part of daily experience, familiar to all who move about in the community—some of those ideals of the

1960s, goals of unity, discipline, collectivism, accountability, and self-reliance, have become informally operative in a broad range of organizational settings. This is an important legacy of the movement in the colleges and *barrios* that is being carried, in modified form, into many areas of community life as these young people mature and move into new arenas of action. Key organizations that embodied the movement ethos disappear from view; the norms of political practice to which they gave life remain alive.

(5) In the established, liberal framework of ethnic competition and minority affirmation in the United States, the resolute national thrust and separatism of Puerto Rican claims, whether implicit or forthright, jars the sensibilities of dominant groups and other minorities, including some sectors of other Third World communities. People who can chime in sympathetically with cries of "Black Power" will gag on "Viva Puerto Rico Libre!" That is because in the United States today the liberation of Puerto Rico is an unambiguously revolutionary proposition, and concessions on small local matters may seem to legitimize ever larger claims. The national content of this thrust is nevertheless what carries Puerto Rican claims inexorably beyond simple appeals for increased participation and reform. The linkage of national and class goals to socialist objectives is an inevitable outcome of the conjunction of forces that define the present situation of Puerto Ricans.

(6) But what do revolution and socialism have to do with the concrete day-to-day struggles of this community, which seem to center on modest goals of recognition, inclusion, equity, and the winning of small spaces of relative autonomy in U.S. institutions? These goals do, after all, reflect only the secondary contradictions in the United States today, residual inequities in education, housing, health, and the sharing of all other values. The system holds out the hope of eventual equality in two forms: (1) the dispersal and assimilation of Puerto Ricans, and (2) under the new label of pluralism, a simulation within the

United States of the commonwealth idea. In this vaguely formulated corporatism, national and cultural minorities would be free to cultivate their languages, lifestyles, and institutional preferences within a common economic and political framework. To the extent that Puerto Ricans, in resisting assimilation and affirming their democratic rights, reject both these solutions, their movement inevitably takes on a revolutionary cast. The combination of national and class goals can find no resolution within the existing U.S. structure. Daily experience drives home this reality to Puerto Ricans in every sphere of activity, making it harder and harder to imagine a satisfactory state of the world without a socialist transformation. As Puerto Ricans become conscious that they do not wish to join forces with the oppressor, or to administer for them improvised imitations of their institutions, the revolutionary content of this struggle is revealed. The extraordinary surge of cultural production among young Puerto Ricans in New York in the visual arts, poetry, theater, and music conveys the excitement of this self-discovery, which is not merely the revival of a national tradition or a clinging to a faded identity, but the revelation of a potentially significant historical role for a submerged sector of workers in the United States who have only begun to make their presence felt.

This struggle, of course, unfolds within very real and institutional limitations. Revolutionary goals do not make a revolution, and the existence of root contradictions and local crises does not signal the collapse of a world system. For the moment, Puerto Ricans in the United States are practically invisible at the national level. It will take every ounce of political, professional, and community influence, for example, to get a single agency, the Census Bureau, to take the minimal steps to obtain an adequate count of Puerto Ricans in the 1980 census. Literally scores of such single-issue struggles engage Puerto Ricans at any given moment. The coming together of Puerto Ricans from various parts of the country to discuss issues from the perspective of their diverse settings has just begun. Many kinds of coordinated action, bringing together Puerto Ricans throughout the United States and the Island, will be required before any genuine engagement of other than localized issues can occur. In the meantime, defensive actions against established institutions will continue to be channeled through loose coalitions of organizations and individuals of many ideological positions that rally around issues as they arise. This is a mode of political action that takes a heavy toll on individuals and on the meager resources that the community controls. But no one who gets closer to the Puerto Rican community than the census can really believe that it is a nationality on the path to self-liquidation.

The foregoing sketch has stressed the elements of continuity in the national and class content of the ideological orientations and political action of Puerto Ricans in the United States over the last several decades. At the same time, an attempt has been made to bring out how the growing size, dispersal, occupational diversity, and the range of institutional involvements of that community have progressively projected its political action from a neighborhood to a citywide and then to a national level. Earlier sections sought to place these changes within the larger context of the design for development applied in Puerto Rico since 1940, in which industrialization and migration have been coupled as central strategies. The main difference for Puerto Ricans in the two settings is the construction over this period of a very specialized political-bureaucratic superstructure on the Island that is as yet absent in the United States. The total process, is, of course, far from played out. As it advances, the historical importance of the Puerto Rican case is more and more forcefully brought home. Central questions of theory and practice, with import extending far beyond a narrow national interest, flow from this analysis and from the concrete situations in which Puerto Ricans now find themselves. The political struggles of Puerto Ricans have been propelled to a higher level because the material conditions of our insertion into the main economic and political structures of U.S. capitalism have advanced beyond those of any other colonized nationality.

Through a double process of colonialism and migration, the Puerto Rican working class has become a central protagonist of transformations in national and transnational class configurations that are beginning to occur on a world scale. On the one hand, the complete scale of capitalist relations is being reproduced in Puerto Rico and other industrializing nations. At the same time, the sustained circulation and presence of Puerto Rican workers in the United States recreate there the colonial relations formerly screened from metropolitan society through confinement to territorial extensions abroad, or to tribal reservations at home. Today Puerto Rico not only exports surplus workers but is beginning to import labor power from less developed entities in the world capitalist network, thus beginning on a lesser scale to generate multinational class formations internally. Part of that imported labor power includes the offspring of Puerto Ricans whose work experience has been primarily or totally in various regions of the United States. They bring to Puerto Rico new patterns of response to conditions in the labor market and new experiences and modes of class struggle. At the same time, there is an intensification of migration flows, legal and illegal, into the United States from countries pursuing industrialization in modes that ever more closely approximate the Puerto Rican "model." As a consequence, what seem to be new, objective conditions for a broad multinational movement of working-class unity are taking shape in numerous cities around the country.

These new conditions and opportunities propel the political and intellectual work of Puerto Ricans and others caught up in these changes into uncharted areas. Can there be a unity among workers when internal differentiation among them is becoming increasingly complex? What role can language and culture play in the struggle for liberation of a nation so deeply penetrated and a nationality so widely dispersed within the territory of the dominant power? What is the role of youth and of future generations in further resistance to colonial and class oppression? Sound and factually supported analysis of these questions does not exist and cannot be improvised. This is indeed a worthy intellectual and political agenda.

Notes

1. On this period, see Gordon K. Lewis, *Puerto Rico: Freedom and Power in the Caribbean* (New York: Monthly Review Press, 1963); Thomas G. Mathews, *Puerto Rican Politics and the New Deal* (Gainesville: University of Florida Press, 1960). The quote is from the introduction to that volume by Rexford G. Tugwell, p. ix. Gerardo Navas Dávila, in an unpublished dissertation, traces the connections between the New Deal and postwar years ("The Dialectic of National Development: The Case of Puerto Rico," University of California at Berkeley, 1972). Angel Quintero Rivera sets out to trace the economic and class shifts behind the political combination of forces pushing forward what was to become the development project of the *Populares* in the 1940s in "Bases sociales de la transformación ideológica del PPD, 1940-1950," *Cuadernos* 6 (1975).
2. These threats were given substance in the successive bills proposing independence for Puerto Rico by Sen. Millard E. Tydings of Maryland.
3. Details of these events are given in Mathews, *Puerto Rican Politics and the New Deal*; see especially pp. 274ff.
4. Frederic P. Bartlett and Brandon Howell, *The Population Problem in Puerto Rico* (San Juan: Planning, Urbanizing, and Zoning Board, 1944).
5. Puerto Rico Planning, Urbanizing, and Zoning Board, *A Development Plan for Puerto Rico* (San Juan, 1944).
6. See Stanley Friedlander, *Labor, Migration, and Economic Growth* (Cambridge, Mass.: MIT Press, 1965), and Charles T. Goodsell, *Administration of a Revolution* (Cambridge, Mass.: Harvard University Press, 1965), for a review of social conditions around 1940.

7. The last figure dropped to some 36 million tons in 1940, but the general scale of change is what is pertinent here. See Harvey Perloff, *Puerto Rico's Economic Future* (Chicago: University of Chicago Press, 1950), p. 137.

   Data in this section are drawn primarily from Esteban Bird, "The Sugar Industry in Relation to the Social and Economic System of Puerto Rico," Senate Document No. 1, San Juan, 1941. This study originated in the planning division of the Puerto Rican Resources Administration. Bird himself draws extensively on Victor Clark, *et al.*, *Porto Rico and Its Problems* (Washington, D.C.: The Brookings Institute, 1930). The study by Arthur D. Gayer, Paul T. Homan, and Earle K. James, *The Sugar Economy of Puerto Rico* (New York: Columbia University Press, 1938), financed by two of the major U.S. producers of sugar on the Island, concludes that on balance the industry showed "accomplishment along all lines essential to Puerto Rican well-being" (p. 273). Shortly after, in the preamble to the 1941 land reform law, the sugar industry is described in the following terms: "The sugar latifundia has [sic] spread it tentacles within the vast area of its dominions to the operation of commercial and industrial establishments and of grocery and general stores; has limited the circulation of money, has caused the annihilation of communal life in many of the urban centers; has made it impossible for thousands of human beings to be the owners of even the lot where their homes are situated, all to the consequent unbalancing of the economic structure of the Island and to the grave endangering of the peace, the tranquility, the dignity, and the economic and social freedom of the people of Puerto Rico." Cited from Land Authority of Puerto Rico, *Land Law of Puerto Rico* (San Juan: Insular Procurement Office, 1943), p. 4.

8. Rexford G. Tugwell, *The Stricken Land* (Garden City, N.Y.: Doubleday and Co., 1947), p. 8.

9. Bird, "The Sugar Industry in Relation to the Social and Economic System of Puerto Rico," p. 49.

10. Gayer, *et al.*, *The Sugar Economy of Puerto Rico*, p. 283.

11. Cited in Mathews, *Puerto Rican Politics and the New Deal*, p. 146.

12. See George L. Cowgill, "On Causes and Consequences of

Ancient and Modern Population Change," *American Anthropologist* 77, no. 3 (1975).

13. Gayer, *et al.*, *The Sugar Economy of Puerto Rico*, describes in some detail the beginning operations of the Asociación Azucarera Cooperativa Lafayette.

14. Comments on the state of the labor force in 1940 are based principally on a review of census materials, as well as on data summarized in a dissertation by Miles Eugene Galvin, "Collective Bargaining in the Public Sector in Puerto Rico," University of Wisconsin, 1972. The pertinent tables are shown in the appendix to this chapter.

15. See Appendix A in Bartlett and Howell, *The Population Problem in Puerto Rico*.

16. This struggle is described in some detail by Blanca Silvestrini Pacheco, "Puerto Rican Workers and the Socialist Party, 1932-40," Ph.D. diss., State University of New York at Albany, 1973.

17. Some of the appeals to Puerto Ricans from Gov. Rexford G. Tugwell are collected in *Changing the Colonial Climate* (New York: Arno Press, 1970).

18. Tugwell, *The Stricken Land*.

19. Goodsell, *Administration of a Revolution*, p. 21. Unemployment remained at these levels to the end of the war. See also Enrique Lugo-Silva, *The Tugwell Administration in Puerto Rico* (Mexico: Editorial Cultura, 1955).

20. See Clarence Senior, *Puerto Rican Emigration* (Río Piedras: Social Science Research Center, University of Puerto Rico, 1947), and Julia Henderson, "Foreign Labor in the U.S. During the War," *International Labor Review*, December 1945. Mexicans, West Indians, and Hondurans were the most numerous among contract workers entering the United States; only Newfoundlanders were allowed to bring whole families into the country.

As has been seen, Puerto Rican migration to the United States in the decades before 1940 was moderate and selective in its composition. This fact has been invoked as further evidence of the rationality of migration, since "push" factors were presumably most acute in this period. Be that as it may, until this flow was cut off by adverse legislation in the 1920s, these early years were also a time of heavy European immigration. It was also a period marked by substantial return migration to Europe (notably during depressions) *and* considerable movement of workers across state lines. Puerto Ricans behaved no differently in these respects than other migrants. As a new group just gaining a toehold, Puerto Ricans were hard hit by the 1930s depression, and many returned to the Island or moved from New York further into the United States in search of solutions.

21. Jay R. Mandle, "The Plantation Economy and Its Aftermath," *Review of Radical Political Economics,* Spring 1974.

22. W. J. Woytinsky, "Postwar Economic Perspectives," *Social Security Bulletin* 9, no. 1 (January 1946).

23. Tugwell's *Stricken Land* continues to provide instructive reading on the inner workings of liberal colonialism. Goodsell, *Administration of a Revolution,* gives considerable detail on the bureaucratic overhaul. Though his volume is optimistically titled, he observes that ten years later the bureaucracy was back in a "straitjacket of orthodoxy" (p. 205).

24. Gerardo Navas Dávila ponders this issue at some length. A highly idealized account of the New Deal background to this economic and political restructuring is given by Earl Parker Hansen, *Puerto Rico: Ally for Progress* (New York: D. Van Nostrand Co., 1962). Both Hansen and Mathews allude to the suppression by PRRA of its own internal studies of Island economic conditions.

25. Lewis, *Puerto Rico.*

26. The following discussion draws substantially on two studies: Lloyd G. Reynolds and Peter Gregory, *Wages, Productivity, and Industrialization in Puerto Rico* (Homewood, Ill.: Richard D. Irwin, 1965), and Stanley L. Friedlander, *Labor, Migration, and Economic Growth* (Cambridge, Mass.: MIT Press, 1965). Both organize data in valuable ways and challenge assumptions of planners and government publicists. Both show the same stubborn optimism in the face of negative findings that, as has been noted, characterizes less technical research.

27. It is important, however, to keep clear that we are talking generally of low-skilled, assembly work in apparel or light consumer goods production. The work investors bring to the Island is engineered to the specifications of the human resources that have been generated there by the productive process itself. Reynolds and Gregory (p. 105) give an exam-

ple of a brassiere factory where production is broken down
into twenty-eight operations, exclusive of cutting. Training
is required for only one or two of these.

28. Corporación de Fomento, *The Industrial Development Program, 1942-1960* (San Juan: December 1959).

29. Reynolds and Gregory also remark that "there have been
virtually no losses among the most highly educated or professional classes" (p. 31).

30. The only negative effect of migration that Friedlander concedes is a slight lowering of average education on the Island.
Hernández Alvarez, dealing more carefully with return migration, distinguishes parallel flows of actively successful
and failed migrants in the return flow. More careful study of
migration patterns should permit the identification of the
class base of such multiple flows and changes in them over
time. We need to understand not just the effects of the displacement of workers as a class but also the consequences of
the admixture of other class elements in the current of migration.

31. Friedlander, *Labor, Migration, and Economic Growth*, p.
128. This aspect of migration takes on importance as the
difference between what a Puerto Rican worker can earn on
the Island and in the United States diminishes. In 1970, the
average hourly earnings in manufacturing in Puerto Rico
were just over half the equivalent earnings in the United
States, but since Puerto Ricans on the mainland seem to
earn three-fifths to three-fourths of the average for their
occupations, this differential is substantially reduced. Taking three-fifths as the norm in 1970, the difference would be
about $.25 an hour; in 1963 it was about $.35 an hour (see
Table 12 in the appendix to this chapter).

32. U.S.-Puerto Rico Commission on the Status of Puerto Rico,
Status of Puerto Rico (August 1966), p. 56.

33. "Indeed, the degree of access to private marketing and distribution channels enjoyed by products made in Puerto Rico
indicates that at the present time *the Puerto Rican
economy, although industrialized, is more dependent
rather than autonomous as an economic unit.* Failure to
recognize this basic and unique fact might precipitate policy
errors which could significantly reduce the essential flow of
mainland private capital. The consequences of this in terms

of employment, infrastructure development, and continued economic growth need not be belabored." Ibid., p. 84; italics added.

34. Ibid., p. 71.
35. Ibid., p. 62.
36. See the articles by Morris Morley, "Dependence and Development in Puerto Rico," and by Mary K. Vaughan, "Tourism in Puerto Rico," in Adalberto López and James Petras, eds., *Puerto Rico and Puerto Ricans* (New York: Schenkman Publishing Co., 1974).
37. Light manufacturing assembly plants concentrated on the Mexican border are decamping from those sites. Wages there have crept up toward a dollar an hour, and producers affirm they can get equivalent labor elsewhere in Central America for less than fifty cents an hour (*New York Times*, May 26, 1975, p. 21). See also *NACLA's Latin American and Empire Report* 9, no. 5 (July-August 1975). This issue is titled "Hit and Run: U.S. Runaway Shops on the Mexican Border."
38. Return migration had, of course, been going on continuously for decades. John P. Augelli, "San Lorenzo: A Case Study of Recent Migrations in Interior Puerto Rico," *American Journal of Economics and Sociology* (1952), notes the presence of many returnees in his study of a small rural town in the late 1940s. Reynolds and Gregory found that about one-eighth of their sample of workers taken in the mid-1950s had lived on the mainland. José Hernández Alvarez, in *Return Migration to Puerto Rico* (Berkeley: University of California Press, 1967), makes the first serious attempt to measure return flows and characterize their main currents.
39. Sterilization usually occurs after at least two live births. See José Vázquez Calzada, "La esterilización feminina en Puerto Rico," mimeo. (San Juan: Escuela de Medicina, Universidad de Puerto Rico, 1973).
40. Manuel M. Jaramillo-Yañez, *Factores sociales en el desarrollo económico: El caso de Puerto Rico, 1960-1970* (San Juan: Junta de Planificación, 1974), p. 8. This study is mainly of interest for the data series of economic and social variables that it contains.
41. Michael N. Reisman, *Puerto Rico and the International Process: New Roles in Association* (Washington, D.C.:

American Society of International Law, 1975), pp. 28-31 and Appendix 8. This volume also contains the texts of Public Law 600, the Federal Relations Act, and the Constitution of the Commonwealth of Puerto Rico. The 18 billion figure for 1977 is from the Planning Board report to the governor for 1976-1977. See Junta de Planificación, *Informe económico al gobernador, 1977* (San Juan, 1978).

42. Reisman, *Puerto Rico and the International Process*, p. 31.

43. Karl Marx and Frederick Engels, *Ireland and the Irish Question* (Moscow: Progress Publishers, 1971), pp. 54-59. In *Capital,* vol. I, p. 704, Marx comments: "The Irish famine of 1846 killed more than 1,000,000 people, but it killed poor devils only. To the wealth of the country it did not the slightest damage. . . . Irish genius discovered an altogether new way of spiriting a poor people thousands of miles away from the scene of its misery. The exiles transplanted to the United States send home sums of money every year as travelling expenses for those left behind. Every troop that emigrates one year, draws another after it the next. What were the consequences for the Irish labourers left behind and freed from the surplus population? That the relative surplus population is today as great as before 1846; that wages are just as low, that the oppression of the labourers has increased, that misery is forcing the country towards a new crisis."

44. It is impossible in this brief account to sift the voluminous data on unemployment and occupational distributions or to evaluate the several approaches to obtaining these estimates. The broad trends discussed are based on the summary account in Galvin, "Collective Bargaining and the Public Sector in Puerto Rico," and Bureau of the Census, *Census of Population: 1970, Detailed Characteristics, Puerto Rico* PCCD, D 53 Puerto Rico (Washington, D.C.: U.S. Government Printing Office, 1973). See also Planning Board, *Puerto Rican Migrants: A Socio-Economic Study* (San Juan, 1972). Additional materials are cited in Ricardo Campos and Frank Bonilla, "Industrialization and Migration: Some Effects on the Puerto Rican Working Class," *Latin American Perspectives* 3, no. 3 (1976).

45. The standard applied by the Census Bureau for a nonfarming family of four with a male head was $3,745. Poverty

thresholds ranged from $1,487 (for a female nonrelated individual 65 years and over living on a farm) to $6,116 (for a nonfarming family with a male head and seven or more members).

46. This analysis cannot be taken very far here. The important point to understand is that differences in the quality of the workforce, in roles in production, and in efficiency shape the relations of production and class orientations of workers at every level. An intensive analysis, probing far beyond these surface modifications in the configuration of the workforce, will have to be carried out before serious answers can be given to the many pressing questions concerning the political class implications of the reorganization of production still in progress. Some of the more crucial transformations seem to have been crystallizing in the course of the 1970s and will be difficult to assess before 1980 census returns become available.

47. Interestingly, there are some two hundred female bricklayers and plasterers and about half that many auto mechanics, mechanics on heavy equipment, and carpenters.

48. The recent recession has served to bring out the precarious situation of women in the workforce. Job slashes, especially in manufacturing, where women have been present in strong numbers for decades, hit women far more severely than men. Though women comprised less than a third of the total workforce, they constituted 42 percent of those receiving unemployment compensation in 1974. Seven out of ten "discouraged" job seekers were said to be women. Nearly three-fourths of the households headed by females were living in poverty. See Isabel Picó Vidal, "La mujer puertorriqueña y la recesión económica," *Avance* 3, no. 145 (May 1975). On the basis of similar findings concerning female servitude as clerical workers in the United States, Martin Oppenheimer of Rutgers University has characterized women as a "hidden proletariat." See *Transaction* 12, no. 4 (May-June 1975), p. 12.

49. Karl Marx, *Theories of Surplus-Value* (Moscow: Progress Publishers, 1967), pt. II, p. 571.

50. We have gone into this in more detail in Campos and Bonilla, "Industrialization and Migration," and in Campos

and Bonilla, "La economía política de la relación colonial: La experiencia puertorriqueña," mimeo. (New York: Centro de Estudios Puertorriqueños, 1977).

51. That consolidation is, in any case, already very advanced. Manufacturing, banking, retail sales, industrial exports, transport, and total nongovernment employment are overwhelmingly in the control of U.S. investors.

52. As has been noted, the status of these middle sectors of salaried workers who live off surplus value and join capital in the realization process requires close study. The proliferation of non-work and no-work, and the radicalization of these "noncommodity" sectors implies, as Claus Offe notes, further pressure toward the *"non-capitalist* allocation of capitalist produced surplus value." The attendant disturbances and political realignments will be difficult to unravel but are readily visible in San Juan, to say nothing of New York and Washington. See Claus Offe, "The Abolition of Market Control and the Problem of Legitimacy," *Kapitalstate* 1, no. 1 (May 1973).

53. Junta de Planificación, *Informe económico al gobernador, 1976* (San Juan, 1977). See also the monthly reports of the Bureau of Labor, *Empleo y desempleo en Puerto Rico.*

54. A valuable account of these events is in Galvin, "Collective Bargaining and the Public Sector in Puerto Rico." According to Labor Department figures, about a fourth of the salaried workforce (175,000 persons) were in unions in 1973.

55. See Planning Board, *Puerto Rican Migrants: A Socio-Economic Study*, pt. IV, "Some Selected Data-Oriented Topics of Migration," p. 97.

56. See Felipe Rivera, "The Puerto Rican Migrant Farmworker: From Exploitation to Unionization," in this volume. See also "Puerto Ricans on Contract," *NACLA* 11, no. 8 (1977).

57. See Table 9 in the appendix to this chapter. That table is taken from a recent Planning Board study. Net passenger figures are not satisfactory as close estimates of this movement and are used only to give a sense of the shift in trends.

58. Jaffe and Carreras place two out of ten Puerto Ricans in the United States in six states (Massachusetts, Connecticut, Pennsylvania, Illinois, California, and Florida). See A. J. Jaffe and Zaida Carreras Carleton, *Some Demographic and*

Economic Characteristics of the Puerto Rican Population Living on the Mainland, USA (New York: Bureau of Applied Social Research, Columbia University, 1974).

59. Though no formal class analysis is attempted here, this sketch draws substantially on concepts and terms from Nicos Poulantzas, *Political Power and Social Classes* (London: Sheed and Ward, 1973). See also the article by Poulantzas and the commentary by Manuel Castells in *Las clases sociales en América Latina* (Mexico: Siglo XXI, 1973).

60. Rubén Berríos, "Independence for Puerto Rico: The Only Solution," *Foreign Affairs* 55, no. 3 (April 1977).

61. Eric Hobsbawm, "Some Reflections on The Break-Up of Britain," *New Left Review* 105, (1977).

62. The recent appearance of extensive reports of 1970 census data and 1974 population survey figures on the Spanish-origin population in the United States will help in rounding out the preliminary analysis that has been undertaken here.

    For an extended analysis of the census undercount of the Spanish-origin population in 1970, see U.S. Commission on Civil Rights, *Counting the Forgotten*, April 1974. The New York City Health Population Survey has attempted corrected estimates for Puerto Ricans in the city; see Morey J. Wantman, Morton Israel, and Leonard S. Kagan, *Population Health Survey* (New York: Center for Social Research, City University of New York, 1972). The Bureau of the Census in 1975 formed a committee in which Chicanos, Puerto Ricans, and Cubans are represented to advise it on the 1980 census. Whether this group can have any impact in improving census performance remains to be seen. Legislation has also been proposed calling for federal agencies to regularly report statistics on the Spanish-origin population, especially with regard to unemployment. The 1970 data on Puerto Ricans in the United States is presented in considerable detail in Jaffe and Carreras, *Some Demographic and Economic Characteristics of the Puerto Rican Population Living on the Mainland, USA*, and Kal Wagenheim, *A Survey of Puerto Ricans in the U.S. Mainland in the 1970s* (New York: Praeger Publishers, 1975). See also Bureau of the Census, *Current Population Survey: Persons of Spanish Origin in the United States, March 1974*

(Washington, D.C.: U.S. Government Printing Office, 1974).

63. Commonwealth of Puerto Rico, Migration Division, *A Summary in Facts and Figures* (New York, January 1959).

64. César Andreu Iglesias' posthumously published *Memorias de Bernardo Vega* (Río Piedras: Editorial Huracán, 1977) is the first politically informed account of these formative years of the Puerto Rican community in the United States. It provides innumerable leads for the factual reconstitution of the period. The information that follows on the Hermandad is taken from a May 1926 souvenir dance program of the Puerto Rican Brotherhood of America. At that time the Brotherhood estimated the Puerto Rican population in the city at 100,000 (i.e., over twice the 1930 census count). They claimed that 5,000 Puerto Ricans had registered and voted in the 1926 elections. The dance program contains advertisements by the Caribe Democratic Club and the Club Estrella de Borinquen (a unit of the Juventud Nacionalista Puertorriqueña de Nueva York). It also mentions an Alianza Obrera Puertorriqueña. The Brotherhood states: "It is our duty to expose the injuries suffered by our colony so that they may be aired in a purifying atmosphere and be healed by the remedy that we ourselves . . . and no one but ourselves . . . may apply to them."

65. Lawrence R. Chenault, *The Puerto Rican Migrant in New York City* (New York: Columbia University Press, 1938). Chenault notes that the largest employers of Puerto Ricans in the 1920s were a biscuit and a pencil factory and numerous laundries. Domestic service and home needlework were the main occupations for women, as they were in Puerto Rico during those years.

66. The political flavor of the district in this period is well captured in Alan Schaffer, *Vito Marcantonio: Radical in Congress* (Syracuse, N.Y.: Syracuse University Press, 1966). The Marcantonio papers, held at the New York Public Library, are an unmined source on the Puerto Rican community between 1930 and 1950. An unpublished document by George Charney ("Puerto Rico Revisited") also brings to life some of the political activity of the time.

67. Rose Goldsen, C. Wright Mills, and Clarence Senior, *Puerto Rican Journey: New York's Newest Migrant* (New York: Harper, 1950), p. 71. See also Commonwealth of Puerto

Rico, *A Summary in Facts and Figures*. The data given on migrant characteristics were for 1948 and 1950.

68. United States-Puerto Rico Commission on the Status of Puerto Rico, *Status of Puerto Rico,* esp. pp. 176-78.

69. Clarence Senior and Donald Watkins, "Toward a Balance Sheet of Puerto Rican Migration," in U.S.-Puerto Rico Commission on the Status of Puerto Rico, *Status of Puerto Rico: Selected Background Studies* (Washington, D.C.: U.S. Government Printing Office, 1966).

70. Welfare and Health Council of New York City, *Population of Puerto Rican Birth or Parentage, New York City: 1950* (New York, September 1952). The district without Puerto Ricans was Bay Ridge in Brooklyn.

71. The postwar resurgence of *independentista* and nationalist activity, expressed, on the one hand, by the 1946 constitution of the Partido Independentista Puertorriqueño and, on the other hand, by the Nationalist insurrection of 1950, had very concrete ramifications in New York politics. In 1945, for example, it was Vito Marcantonio who sponsored a House bill providing for Puerto Rican independence and incorporating amendments to the Tydings Bill that were proposed by the Congreso Pro Independencia (the CPI was the forerunner of the PIP in Puerto Rico). These events led up to the Popular Democratic Party's break with its more resolutely independence-minded wing. The strong repression of Nationalists, and of radical activity generally, in the 1950s has shrouded this aspect of the community's political history from general view. A compact account of events in Puerto Rico at this time is given in Robert W. Anderson, *Party Politics in Puerto Rico* (Stanford: Stanford University Press, 1965), ch. 6.

72. This group brought together second and "bridge" generation individuals. Bridge generation persons, as defined by Joseph Monserrat, are Puerto Ricans with some education and real life experience in Puerto Rico but who are U.S.-trained and comfortable in English and in U.S. organizational modes. In the Puerto Rican case, of course, these "generations" are continuously renewed and straddle broad age groups. Joseph Monserrat, "Symposium on Puerto Rico in the Year 2000," *Harvard Law Journal* 15, no. 1 (Fall 1968), pp. 12-27.

73. These proposals constitute the first attempts substantially controlled by Puerto Ricans to formulate comprehensive programs for the community, based on extensive analysis of the state of the population and its needs and resources. They were produced under great pressure and tailored to the ideological and program requirements of the city's Anti-Poverty Operations Board, but they are rich in information and insights into the political and ideological trends of that moment. See an unpublished article by the Puerto Rican Forum, "The Puerto Rican Community Development Project," 1964.

74. Ibid. See especially the chapter on organizations. The breakdown was gathered by PRCDP to demonstrate the vitality and enterprise of Puerto Ricans and their ability to respond to opportunities for self-help. "The Puerto Rican middle class," the proposal stated, "has been created and has risen like the phoenix during the past twenty years out of the very contradictions of an emerging new automated and cybernetic world." It is unclear how seriously this assertion about the rising Puerto Rican middle class was meant to be taken. In any case, such a class had little to do with the concrete struggles into which the managers of the poverty war plunged with their locally recruited forces and, sometimes, in opposition to them. By most accounts, the energy, drive, and leadership in the contention that was to mark the 1960s came directly from the streets and tenements.

75. *Puerto Ricans Confront Problems of the Complex Urban Society: A Design for Change*, proceedings of a community conference sponsored by the Hon. John V. Lindsay, April 15-16, 1967. One of the few studies of local Puerto Rican leaders was made around this time (John W. Gotsch, "Puerto Rican Leadership in New York," M.A. thesis, New York University, 1966). Gotsch remarks on this leadership's dependence on recognition from outside the community and a lack of projection to state or national levels. He saw most of the few people he studied as bent largely on self-advancement. In this connection, see also Rosa Estades, "Patterns of Political Participation of Puerto Ricans in New York City," Ph.D. diss., New School for Social Research, 1974.

76. Alfredo López sets out to tell this story from the perspective of a young participant in *The Puerto Rican Papers* (New

York: Bobbs Merrill, 1973). López subtitles his volume "Notes on the Re-emergence of a Nation."

77. In 1974, official unemployment figures for New York City were set at just over 12 percent (the highest in twenty-five years) and in Puerto Rico at 18 percent. The estimates of labor maladjustment are from the works cited in note 44.

78. Kal Wagenheim, *A Survey of Puerto Ricans in the U.S. Mainland in the 1970s,* pp. 69-70.

79. Jaffe and Carreras, *Some Demographic and Economic Characteristics of the Puerto Rican Population Living on the Mainland, USA,* p. 55.

80. This plan is detailed in the *Congressional Record* 120, no. 130, August 22, 1974. James Jennings, in *Puerto Rican Politics in New York City* (Washington, D.C.: University Press of America, 1977), notes that all attempts from the top to construct manageable structures of leadership for Puerto Ricans in the city (e.g., by political parties, by Commonwealth officials, by municipal administrators and social agencies) have been to no avail. The community continually generates leadership and organizational bases to challenge externally mounted structures of control.

81. See Herbert Hill, "Guardians of the Sweatshop: The Trade Union, Racism, and the Garment Industry," in López and Petras, eds., *Puerto Rico and Puerto Ricans.* Additional discussion of labor market shifts in New York City can be found in Clara Rodríguez' piece in this volume and in New York City Council on Economic Education, *Fact Book on the New York Metropolitan Region* (New York: Pace University, 1976).

Appendix

Table 1
Puerto Rico:
Employment Status by Sex and Place of Residence, 1940

	Puerto Rico	Urban			Rural		
		Total	Male	Female	Total	Male	Female
Population	1,869,255	566,357	264,672	301,685	1,302,898	673,608	629,290
Percent of population 14 years and older	61.7	68.2	66.2	70.0	58.9	59.5	58.3
Percent of population 14 years and older in labor force	52.1	51.7	75.2	32.3	52.3	81.2	20.8
Percent of labor force in employment	85.1	81.0	77.4	88.0	87.1	86.5	89.6
Percent of labor force in public emergency work	4.0	5.0	7.1	1.0	3.5	4.3	0.3
Percent of labor force seeking work	10.9	14.0	15.5	11.0	9.4	9.2	10.1

Source: U.S. Bureau of the Census, *Sixteenth Census of the United States, 1940;* Puerto Rico Population, Bulletin No. 2, "Characteristics of the Population " (Washington, D.C.: U.S. Government Printing Office, 1943).

Table 2
Puerto Rico:
Employment Status by Sex and Place of Residence, 1950

	Puerto Rico	Urban			Rural		
		Total	*Male*	*Female*	*Total*	*Male*	*Female*
Population	2,210,703	894,813	429,578	465,235	1,315,890	681,368	634,522
Percent of population 14 years and older	58.85	64.26	62.62	65.76	55.18	55.83	54.49
Percent of population 14 years and older in civilian labor force	45.49	44.83	65.59	26.58	46.01	72.83	16.51
Percent of civilian labor force in employment	94.65	92.13	90.93	94.72	96.60	96.91	95.11
Percent of civilian labor force unemployed	5.34	7.87	9.07	5.28	3.40	3.09	4.89

Source: U.S. Bureau of the Census, *U.S. Census of Population, 1950* (Washington, D.C.: U.S. Government Printing Office, 1953), vol. II, "Characteristics of the Population," pt. 53, "Puerto Rico."

Table 3
Puerto Rico:
Employment Status by Sex and Place of Residence, 1960

	Puerto Rico	Urban			Rural		
		Total	Male	Female	Total	Male	Female
Population	2,349,544	1,039,301	498,236	541,065	1,310,243	664,528	645,715
Percent of population 14 years and older	59.86	64.35	62.55	65.99	56.30	56.19	56.42
Percent of population 14 years and older in civilian labor force	41.64	44.64	65.08	26.80	38.92	63.93	13.29
Percent of civilian labor force in employment	94.36	93.89	93.47	94.78	94.52	95.17	91.31
Percent of civilian labor force unemployed	5.80	6.11	6.53	5.22	5.48	4.83	8.69

Source: U.S. Bureau of the Census, *U.S. Census of Population, 1960* (Washington, D.C.: U.S. Government Printing Office, 1960–1964), "Puerto Rico." Final Reports PC (1)–53B, C, D.

Table 4
Changes in Occupational Composition of Employed
Workers in Puerto Rico, 1940–1970
(in percent)

Occupation	1940	1950	1960	1970
Nonfarm laborers	5.1	5.8	8.2	8.4
Farmers, farm laborers	44.1	35.9	22.7	10.2
Craftsmen, foremen, operatives	23.3	25.0	26.4	32.8
Service workers	11.3	10.8	11.1	13.0
Other white-collar workers	12.9	19.6	25.2	26.3
Professional and technical workers	3.0	2.9	6.4	9.3
Total	99.7	100.0	100.0	100.0

Source: Miles E. Galvin, "Collective Bargaining in the Public Sector in Puerto Rico," Ph.D. diss., University of Wisconsin, 1972, p. 82. The 1940 figures have been taken from the census for that year and added to Galvin's table.

Table 6
Percent Employed by Occupation, 1976

	Puerto Rico	United States
Professional and technical	12.5	15.2
Managerial, administrative (except farm)	8.4	10.4
Salespeople, clerical workers	20.8	23.8
Craft and kindred workers	12.1	12.9
Operatives	20.0	15.3
Nonfarm laborers	6.4	4.9
Service workers*	13.7	13.8
Farmworkers (salaried)	2.7	1.4
Farm managers	2.4	2.3
Government	29.6	17.0

Sources: U.S. Department of Labor, *Monthly Labor Review,* September 1976. Department of Labor, *Empleo y desempleo en Puerto Rico,* September 1976.
*Only 0.8 percent of these are in domestic services.

Table 5

Employed Labor Force of Puerto Rico by Major Industrial Sector, 1940–1970
(in thousands)

Sector	1940		1950		1960		1970	
	Number	%	Number	%	Number	%	Number	%
Agriculture, forestry, fishing, mining	231	45.0	217	36.4	126	23.2	72	9.6
Manufacturing	56	10.9	55	9.2	82	15.1	141	18.9
Home needlework	45	8.8	51	8.6	10	1.7	—	—
Construction	16	3.1	27	4.5	45	8.3	85	11.4
Trade	53	10.4	90	15.1	97	17.9	141	18.8
Transportation, communications, public utilities	20	3.9	30	5.0	39	7.2	51	6.8
Services	73	14.3	77	12.9	76	14.0	125	16.7
Public administration	13	2.5	45	7.6	63	11.6	115	15.4
Other industries, including finance, insurance, real estate	6	1.2	4	0.7	6	1.1	17	2.3
Total employed labor force	513	100.1	596	100.0	544	100.1	747	99.9

Sources: Lloyd D. Reynolds and Peter Gregory, *Wages, Productivity, and Industrialization in Puerto Rico* (Homewood, Ill.: Richard D. Irwin, 1965), p. 10, and Bureau of Labor Statistics, Department of Labor, Commonwealth of Puerto Rico, *Special Labor Force Report Number 70-2E.*

Table 7

Median Weekly Earnings of Wage and Salary Workers by Industry Group in Puerto Rico, October 1952–October 1971

Industry group	October			Percent change 1952–1971
	1952	*1960*	*1971*	
Agriculture	$ 6.50	$ 9.40	$24.20	272
Construction	15.60	31.30	63.50	307
Manufacturing	13.60	32.10	63.80	369
Trade	15.50	29.90	64.80	318
Finance, insurance, real estate	38.20	51.30	94.30	147
Transportation, communications, public utilities	20.20	38.20	81.40	303
Services	8.60	22.30	64.90	655
Public administration	21.10	42.30	82.60	166
All industries				261

Source: Galvin, "Collective Bargaining in the Public Sector in Puerto Rico," p. 298.

Table 8
Gross Product by Major Sector in Puerto Rico, 1950–1970
(in millions of constant dollars)

Sector	1950	1960	1970
Agriculture	132.1	164.0	161.8
Manufacturing	119.7	366.3	1,160.1
Construction and mining	30.4	·101.1	388.9
Transportation and other public utilities	59.7	151.6	451.5
Trade	144.2	321.5	939.7
Finance, insurance, and real estate	74.5	201.3	571.2
Services	46.2	146.6	575.7
Government, commonwealth and municipal	75.1	187.1	638.5
Government, federal	45.7	79.2	158.3
Nonresidents	−15.1	−91.3	−414.1
Statistical discrepancy	41.9	54.0	−29.8
Total	754.4	1,681.4	4,601.8

Source: Galvin, "Collective Bargaining in the Public Sector in Puerto Rico," p. 48.

Table 9
Puerto Rico Passenger Traffic for Fiscal Years 1940 to 1976
(number of persons)

Fiscal years	Departures	Arrivals	Net balance
1940	24,932	23,924	− 1,008
1941	30,916	30,416	− 500
1942	29,480	28,552	− 928
1943	19,367	16,766	− 2,601
1944	27,586	19,498	− 8,088
1945	33,740	22,737	−11,003

1946	70,618	45,997	−24,621
1947	136,259	101,115	−35,144
1948	132,523	104,492	−28,031
1949	157,338	124,252	−33,086
1950	170,727	136,572	−34,155
1951	188,898	146,978	−41,920
1952	258,884	197,226	−61,658
1953	304,910	230,307	−74,603
1954	303,007	258,798	−44,209
1955	315,491	284,309	−31,182
1956	380,950	319,303	−61,647
1957	439,656	391,372	−48,284
1958	467,987	442,031	−25,956
1959	557,701	520,489	−37,212
1960	666,756	643,014	−23,742
1961	681,982	668,182	−13,800
1962	807,549	796,186	−11,363
1963	930,666	925,868	− 4,798
1964	1,076,403	1,072,037	− 4,366
1965	1,265,096	1,254,338	−10,758
1966	1,475,228	1,445,139	−30,089
1967	1,628,909	1,594,735	−34,174
1968	1,858,151	1,839,470	−18,681
1969	2,105,217	2,112,264	+ 7,047
1970	2,076,710	2,032,628	−44,082
1971	2,115,147	2,113,336	− 1,811
1972	2,286,765	2,328,429	+41,664
1973	2,476,567	2,504,988	+28,421
1974	2,539,783	2,575,900	+36,117
1975	2,363,375	2,402,559	+39,184
1976	2,316,122	2,354,880	+38,758

Source: Puerto Rican Planning Board, *A Comparative Study of the Labor Market Characteristics of Return Migrants and Non-Migrants in Puerto Rico* (San Juan, 1973), p. 257. Data for 1974–1976 are from Junta de Planificación de Puerto Rico, *Informe económico al gobernador, 1976* (San Juan, 1977).

Table 10

Employment Status and Major Occupation Group of the Total and Spanish-Origin Population Sixteen Years Old and Over by Sex and Type of Spanish Origin, for the United States, March 1974

Employment status and occupation	Both sexes			Male			Female		
	Total population	Spanish origin		Total population	Spanish origin		Total population	Spanish origin	
		Total	Puerto Rican		Total	Puerto Rican		Total	Puerto Rican
Persons sixteen years old and over (in thousands)	148,875	6,344	877	70,767	3,019	394	78,108	3,325	483
Number in civilian labor force (in thousands)	89,633	3,808	459	54,312	2,408	296	35,321	1,400	163
Percent unemployed	*5.3*	*8.1*	*9.0*	*4.8*	*7.2*	*8.6*	*6.0*	*9.8*	*9.8*
Number employed (in thousands)	84,878	3,498	417	51,678.	2,236	271	33,200	1,262	147

Percent:

Professional, technical, and kindred workers	14.7	6.5	5.8	14.1	6.7	4.4	15.5	6.0	8.8
Managers and administrators (except farm)	10.5	5.7	7.9	14.1	7.3	9.6	4.9	2.9	4.8
Sales workers	6.4	3.4	3.6	6.1	3.0	4.1	6.7	4.0	2.0
Clerical and kindred workers	17.6	14.7	18.5	6.6	7.0	13.7	34.9	28.3	26.5
Craft and kindred workers	13.4	12.1	8.6	20.9	17.6	10.7	1.7	2.1	4.8
Operatives, including transport	16.0	28.2	33.8	17.9	27.0	31.4	12.9	30.2	38.1
Laborers (excluding farm)	4.8	7.7	5.5	7.3	11.4	7.7	0.9	1.1	1.4
Farmers and farm managers	1.9	0.2	—*	3.0	0.4	—	0.3	—	—
Farm laborers and supervisors	1.5	5.7	1.4	1.8	7.4	1.1	1.0	2.6	2.0
Service workers	13.3	15.9	14.9	8.2	12.0	16.6	21.2	22.9	10.9
	100.1	100.1	100.0	100.0	99.8	99.3	100.0	100.1	99.3

Source: U.S. Bureau of the Census, *Current Population Survey: Persons of Spanish Origin in the United States, March 1974* (Washington, D.C.: U.S. Government Printing Office, 1974).

*— represents zero or rounds to zero.

Table 11
Summary of Employment Status of the Civilian Non-Institutional
Puerto Rican Population Fourteen Years of Age and Older,
Average for FY 1950–1951 through 1972–1973
(thousands of persons)

Fiscal year	Total persons employed	Participation rate (%)	Unemployment rate (%)
1950–51	605	55.5	15.4
1951–52	571	53.5	16.0
1952–53	550	50.9	14.8
1953–54	540	50.1	14.5
1954–55	539	49.0	15.3
1955–56	558	48.3	13.2
1956–57	552	47.5	13.2
1957–58	555	47.2	12.8
1958–59	546	46.3	14.2
1959–60	542	45.4	13.3
1960–61	573	46.0	11.9
1961–62	590	46.4	12.8
1962–63	601	45.8	13.1
1963–64	635	45.9	11.3
1964–65	657	46.2	11.6
1965–66	677	47.0	12.1
1966–67	684	47.1	12.7
1967–68	701	46.8	12.0
1968–69	722	46.7	10.7
1969–70	738	46.4	10.8
1970–71	755	46.4	11.6
1971–72	783	47.0	12.3
1972–73	810	46.6	12.1

Source: Puerto Rican Planning Board, *A Comparative Study of Labor Market Characteristics of Return Migrants and Non-Migrants in Puerto Rico* (San Juan, 1973), p. 248.

Table 12

Average Hourly Earnings of Production Workers in All
Manufacturing Industries, Puerto Rico and United States, 1950–1970

Year	All manufacturing Puerto Rico	All manufacturing United States	Ratio of earnings, Puerto Rico to U.S.
1950	$0.42	$1.44	.292
1951	0.45	1.56	.288
1952	0.47	1.65	.285
1953	0.48	1.74	.276
1954	0.50	1.78	.281
1955	0.56	1.86	.301
1956	0.66	1.95	.338
1957	0.77	2.05	.376
1958	0.83	2.11	.393
1959	0.87	2.19	.397
1960	0.92	2.26	.407
1961	0.99	2.32	.427
1962	1.06	2.39	.444
1963	1.12	2.46	.459
1964	1.18	2.53	.466
1965	1.24	2.61	.475
1966	1.30	2.72	.478
1967	1.39	2.83	.491
1968	1.55	3.01	.515
1969	1.66	3.19	.520
1970	1.76	3.36	.524
Absolute increase			
1950–70	$1.34	$1.92	
Percentage increase			
1950–70	319.0	133.3	

Source: The United States data are from the Bureau of Labor Statistics, U.S. Department of Labor, *Handbook of Labor Statistics.* The Puerto Rican data are from the Bureau of Labor Statistics, Department of Labor, Commonwealth of Puerto Rico (averages for calendar years).

Table 13
Age and Sex Distribution of New York City Puerto Ricans,
U.S.-Born Blacks, and West Indians, 1925
(in percent)

Age	Puerto Ricans		U.S.-Born Blacks		West Indians	
	Male	*Female*	*Male*	*Female*	*Male*	*Female*
Under 15	20	23	21	20	4	5
15–24	30	29	15	18	18	26
25–44	42	36	48	48	68	59
45 and over	8	12	16	14	10	10
Number	3,185	3,496	21,180	23,442	6,053	5,833
No data	2	3	52	75	26	33

Sex Ratios by Age for New York City Puerto Ricans,
U.S.-Born Blacks, and West Indians, 1925
(Female = 100)

Age	Puerto Ricans	U.S.-Born Blacks	West Indians
Under 15	93	95	83
15–24	113	75	77
25–44	130	92	117
45 and over	70	99	104
15 and over	114	85	105

Source: Data for U.S.-born blacks and West Indians come from Table A–40 in H. G. Gutman, *The Black Family in Slavery and Freedom, 1750–1925* (New York: Pantheon, 1976). Puerto Ricans were separately tabulated for Assembly Districts 16, 17, 18, and 19 in Manhattan by the Centro de Estudios Puerto-rriqueños, CUNY.

Table 14
Types of Puerto Rican and Black Households,
New York City, 1925
(in percent)

	Black	*Puerto Rican*
Single person	7	6
Irregular non-kin	7	4

Irregular kin
    without husband or wife,
    or parent or child
	3	2

Kin-related household with core nuclear group	83	88
Total	12,987	1,535

Source: See Table 13.

PART III

Selected Topics

CHAPTER 6

Economic Factors Affecting Puerto Ricans in New York
Clara E. Rodríguez

Introduction

The migration of Puerto Ricans to the United States is a phenomenon that must be seen within its historical context in order to understand more fully its present-day significance. Because of the particular historical and material conditions affecting Puerto Ricans and the United States, Puerto Rican migration differs from that of previous groups in certain very important respects. Yet because of the particular dialectic at work between the successive waves of immigrants and the development of capitalism in the United States, there are unavoidable and pronounced similarities. Let us first review the similarities and then the differences between Puerto Rican migration and that of previous groups.

The historical role of immigrants in the United States has been that of low-wage laborers whose exploitation has tended to increase the surplus value of capitalists while maintaining general wage levels in depressed conditions. Immigrants have become members of the industrial reserve army, intermittently employed, underemployed, and unemployed—as economic fluctuations allow. These conditions of low wage levels and surplus labor have tended to favor extensive and rapid capitalist development in the United States. The presence of large numbers of immigrants, arriving successively, has contributed to the persistence of these conditions.[1]

Puerto Ricans have, to a large extent, assumed the role

The author is Dean of the School of General Studies, Fordham University, in the Bronx.

of previous immigrant groups—that of depressing wage levels and increasing the ranks of the industrial reserve army. Belton Fleisher and Herbert Hill have both pointed out that it was the presence of Puerto Ricans that kept the general wages in New York so low during the 1950s and early 1960s.[2] Hill points out, more specifically, that in the International Ladies Garment Workers Union (ILGWU), a union with a high proportion of Puerto Ricans, wages actually fell within the period of peak Puerto Rican migration, 1950-1960.[3]

Early in the development of capitalism in the United States, the ranks of the industrial reserve army were quite fluid. The opportunities open to early proletarians to become owners of their own labor power—for example, as farmers, artisans, and storeowners—were considerable. This meant that workers were constantly needed to replace laborers leaving industrial employment. Thus, the waves of successive immigrants took the place in the industrial reserve army of earlier immigrants and their children.

In the case of Puerto Ricans (and blacks), these conditions of early capitalist development in the United States no longer exist. Thus, despite the assumption of a similar role in the workforce by Puerto Ricans, the outcome of the dialectic between Puerto Ricans and the economic system in the United States will be different by virtue of the differences in material conditions. In short, there is no place to go and no one to queue up after the Puerto Ricans. Instead, there is a scramble for the bottom rungs by blacks and Puerto Ricans.

Moreover, we must look at both the colonial relationship existing between Puerto Rico and the United States, and the stage of capitalism when Puerto Ricans migrated. An analysis of these conditions will yield an historical view of the forces that have affected the migration of Puerto Ricans. A brief overview of these conditions will precede the study in more depth of the experience of Puerto Ricans who have migrated to New York.

The Colonial Relationship Between
Puerto Rico and the United States

Most analyses of Puerto Rican migration to the United States have pointed up the significant relationship between the growth of national income and the decrease in unemployment in the United States and increased Puerto Rican migration. These "pull forces" have been generally acknowledged in the literature. Other studies have noted the relationship between increased unemployment in Puerto Rico and Puerto Rican migration to the United States—the "push forces." What have not been generally treated, however, are the roots of those push and pull forces in the colonial relationship.

Of what significance to migration would these changes in employment and national income be if the colonial ties were not present? Would an increase in national income in the United States provoke migration from Puerto Rico but for the colonial ties? Would those factors that have generally been seen as facilitating the Puerto Rican migration (such as accessibility of air travel, the military service experience, increased mass communication) have existed but for the colonial relationship? Why weren't cheap and easy airfares established to nearby cheap labor pools of French Canadians, Cubans, or Appalachians? Would military service and the radio have been similarly experienced by Puerto Ricans but for the colonial tie? But for the colonial relationship, would the "pull forces" have been perceived, responded to, or perhaps even generated? Put very bluntly, would Mayor Wagner of New York have gone to Puerto Rico to tell Puerto Ricans about the jobs available in New York?[4]

Since U.S. domination (1898), Puerto Rico has gone from a semifeudal society, to a one-crop agricultural society dominated by colonial absentee sugar interests, to an industrializing society that is still dominated by the colonial power. The Puerto Rican class structure has correspondingly changed from one with minor and major agricultural interests (indigenous and Spanish colonial), to one with the predominance of an agricultural proletariat and then to one with a surplus population of urban and rural laborers.[5] It is this surplus population that could not be integrated into the capital-intensive industrializing economy of Puerto Rico who became, in the main, the Puerto Rican migrants to the United States.[6]

Stage of Capitalism When
Puerto Ricans Migrated

Monopoly capital characterized the mode of production in the United States when Puerto Ricans began to arrive in significant numbers. The change in the mode of production, from competitive capital to monopoly capital, was accompanied by a change in the forces of production—increased automation, which meant an increasingly capital-intensive industrial sector, with greater numbers of low-wage, low-skilled people out of work, and with decreasing low-skilled jobs available in the labor market.[7] A change in the location of productive firms (suburbanization) was another characteristic of this particular stage of capitalism. (Many firms left, ostensibly, to implement an even higher degree of automation. Thus, changes in the forces of production affected the location of productive firms.) This change in the location of firms also meant a decrease in the number of productive plants or firms within a certain region. The effect of all this on migrants to urban areas was considerable.

The growth of highways—as contrasted with the lack of growth in mass transport—made these jobs and residences inaccessible to poor, black, urban residents (read urban migrants).[8] Suburban jobs were known and accessible to those with more money . . . and to those who were white. Racism and ethnic exclusion, as manifested in real estate practices, zoning, government restrictive covenants, and social-psychological pressures, generally kept out nonwhites and minority ethnic groups. The United States at this particular stage of capitalism was moving to its present urban, demographic form—white suburbs and increasing concentrations of nonwhites in the inner cities. The change in the location of productive firms, in combination with the exclusionary practices cited above, perpetuated the class-racial divisions that have historically been present in the United States.

There are other characteristics of this stage of capitalism that have changed only slightly, but that are significant in the analysis of migration. These are the cyclical nature of capitalism and the ideology of the ruling class.

The cyclical nature of capitalism has persisted at this more mature stage of capitalist development. The upswing of the New York City economy during 1950-1967 masked the sectoral decline discussed above. Thus, Puerto Ricans entered at a time of cyclical prosperity and were soon after to suffer from a cyclical and secular decline in relevant economic activity. The relationship between the industrial reserve army and cyclical fluctuations appears to have altered somewhat. It could be that, given the changes in the forces of production—higher automation, higher skill-level requirements—the industrial reserve army is less affected by fluctuations. Hence, it may be more likely to remain unemployed or underemployed permanently or for long periods.

The ideology supporting this economic structure continued to legitimize class divisions and the system under which exploitation occurs. The educational policies fostered, incorporated, and taught this ideology. The schools persisted in their historically evolved methods: they attempted to de-ethnicize, Americanize, and inferiorize students. They instilled in the immigrant ethnic groups the view that hard work and individual effort would release them from oppression. Yet educational inequality persisted and oppressed students went on to become oppressed workers.

A major assault on this ideology was made by blacks during the 1960s. In dialectical fashion, a "white backlash" occurred. This picked up considerable momentum from the depressed economic situation of the country and its inflationary condition in the late 1960s and early 1970s. Thus, material conditions again created an ideological force inimical to the situation of nonwhites in this country.

It is vitally important that this essay be seen as only the first step in a systematic and scientific exploration of the position and role of Puerto Ricans in the New York City economy. Among the very important questions that are not considered are the following: Is the rate of capitalist profit falling more rapidly in New York City than in other parts of the United States? If so, what effect has this had on the ability of the New York economy to absorb the surplus it has extracted from Puerto Rican and other workers? What effect has this had on the situation of Puerto Ricans in the New York City labor market? How will Puerto Ricans, who are largely a surplus population in the eyes of the ruling class, be dealt with or absorbed? Through makework? Or paraprofessional positions? Or induced migration to other areas of the United States (including Puerto Rico)?

Post-Migration Effects

Many of the myriad aspects of the Puerto Rican community in New York have been examined, discussed, deplored, or excused without sufficient attention being paid to the effects of the New York economy on Puerto Ricans. Generally, the economy has been superficially analyzed and then only as a push or pull factor in the migration of Puerto Ricans to New York.[9] The role of the economy in determining what happened after Puerto Ricans migrated to New York has yet to be fully examined in the growing body of literature on Puerto Ricans.

It is clear from available data that Puerto Ricans have not been evenly integrated into the New York economy.[10] Comparing the occupational distribution of Puerto Ricans between 1950 and 1970 (Table 6.1), we see that relative to blacks and whites, Puerto Ricans have been, and are, disproportionately represented in the blue-collar occupations. This disproportionate concentration vis-à-vis other groups held constant between 1950 and 1970—despite a significant decrease (from 61.0 percent to 51.3 percent) in the proportion of Puerto Ricans in the blue-collar jobs between 1960 and 1970.[11] That is, although the proportion of Puerto Rican blue-collar workers decreased, the proportion of black and white blue-collar workers still remains significantly lower.

This decrease in blue-collar workers between 1960 and 1970 seems to be accounted for by an increase in service-sector workers rather than by significant gains in white-collar employment. Thus, with respect to white-collar jobs, Puerto Ricans have the smallest proportion of white-collar workers of all three groups: 27.2 percent compared to 32.5 percent for blacks and 51 percent for the total population. When we look at the figures in more detail, we see that there has been greater mobility of Puerto Rican females into white-collar occupations than of Puerto Rican males.[12] The mere analysis of the proportions of blue-collar and white-collar workers in the labor force is not itself sufficient to indicate what has been the relative success of Puerto Rican economic integration, for some blue-collar workers earn more than many white-collar workers. Thus, it is necessary to look at income differentials by occupation.

Looking at Table 6.2, we see that within each occupational group Puerto Rican males and females are paid less than black or white males or females. No data are available by specific occupations—for example, doctors or plumbers—but the figures indicate fairly clearly that Puerto Ricans have only marginally been integrated into the New York economy.

If we look at unemployment rates for Puerto Rican

Table 6.1
Percent Employed by Ethnic Group in White-Collar,
Blue-Collar, and Service Occupations, 1950, 1960, 1970

Percent

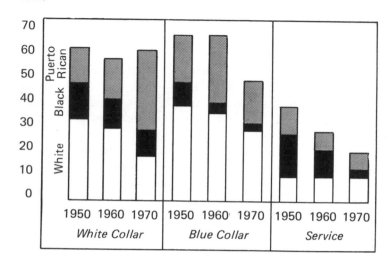

Table 6.2

Median Earnings in 1960 by Major Occupational Groups of Males and Females with Earnings, Sixteen Years and Over, by Race and Ethnic Group, New York City

	Total	White	Black	Puerto Rican
Male				
Professional, managerial, and kindred workers	$10,995	$11,400	$8,046	$7,040
Craftsmen, foremen, and kindred workers	8,174	8,520	6,770	6,238
Operatives, including transport	6,556	6,767	6,187	5,148
Laborers, except farm	6,577	6,986	5,816	5,051
Total male experienced labor force	7,679	8,140	6,241	5,430
Female				
Clerical and kindred workers	5,360	5,464	4,867	4,563
Operatives, including transport	3,741	3,715	3,854	3,651
Total female experienced labor force	4,978	5,131	4,572	3,861

Sources: "Summary Manpower Indicators for New York City," *1970 Census of Population.*

males between 1950 and 1970, we see the same lack of integration. In each year the unemployment rate for Puerto Rican males in New York was about double that of whites and higher than that of blacks. For the years 1950, 1960, and 1970 respectively, unemployment among Puerto Rican males was 10.6, 9.9, and 6.2 percent, while among "nonwhites," it was 8.4, 6.9, and 5.4 percent, and among "others," it was 5.1, 4.3, and 3.9 percent. Had the labor-force participation rates of Puerto Rican males in the New York Standard Metropolitan Statistical Area (SMSA) not declined substantially between 1960 and 1970, the unemployment rate would have been even higher.

Since the labor market is the prime determinant of income in the United States it is not surprising to find that Puerto Ricans are poorer than either whites or blacks. The proportion of families with incomes below $7,000 (the low-income budget line) is 64 percent for Puerto Ricans, as compared with 29 percent for whites and 49 percent for blacks, while the proportion of families in poverty (under $3,700) was similarly skewed, with 30 percent of Puerto Rican families being thus classified in 1970, compared with 12 percent of all races and 21 percent of blacks. The median family income of Puerto Ricans has also lagged a considerable distance behind that of other groups since 1950: in New York City in 1970 it was $5,575, compared to $10,424 for whites and $7,150 for blacks.

Determinant Factors Affecting the Socioeconomic Position of Puerto Ricans

What are the root causes of Puerto Rican high unemployment, skewed occupational distribution, and low income? If we examine the economy and its relation to Puerto Ricans, we find a number of factors that, combined, account for these phenomena. These include automation, sectoral decline, blue-collar structural unemployment, racial and ethnic prejudice, restrictive union policies, inadequate educational opportunities, and the restriction of Puerto Ricans from government employment.

In a nutshell, here is how these factors operate and interact. Automation and the movement of surviving blue-collar jobs to the suburbs, the South, and to other countries have caused a sectoral decline in the number of manufacturing jobs available in New York City. Since these trends occurred more rapidly than out-migration or the retraining of blue-collar workers to fill white-collar jobs, a severe problem of blue-collar structural unemployment arose. Because of racial and ethnic prejudice,

restrictive union policies, inadequate educational opportunities, and the restriction of Puerto Ricans from government employment, Puerto Ricans bore the brunt of this
blue-collar structural unemployment. The indices cited
above are but manifestations of the problems of the
economy vis-à-vis Puerto Ricans.

Automation. Automation is one of the more significant
changes the economy was undergoing during the Puerto
Rican migration. The effects of automation upon the black
labor force have already been discussed and examined
fairly closely.[13] Given the similarities of the black and
Puerto Rican labor forces, the same line of analysis is
applicable to Puerto Ricans. Thus, it is argued that the
effects of automation are and were very dramatically felt
in the blue-collar workforce, and since a large proportion
of black (and an even larger proportion of Puerto Rican)
workers are blue collar, the black labor force has been
more affected by automation than the white labor force.

Since Puerto Ricans have the highest proportion of
blue-collar laborers in New York City, they have been the
most affected.

Suburbanization. Paralleling automation was a trend
toward increased suburbanization of industry which
placed many blue-collar jobs in the suburbs. If Puerto
Ricans came to know about suburban job openings, transportation to the jobs, if present, was expensive in terms of
money and time—adding one or two hours to each workday.[14] In addition, the industries in the suburbs already
had a substantial pool of labor among the suburbanites
who had moved nearby or would soon flee the city to get
those jobs. Thus the jobs in the suburbs were fairly unat-
tainable to Puerto Ricans, while the attainable jobs in the
city were few. Moreover, the numbers of city jobs held by
suburbanites who commute into the city is very high. Although many of the jobs held by commuters are white
collar and thus may not be immediately open to many
Puerto Ricans, they do further delimit the opportunity
structure for Puerto Ricans.

The effect that suburbanization of industry and people

had on Puerto Ricans was not just limited to employment. It depleted the tax base of the cities. With a shrinking middle class, the revenues collected proved insufficient to cover the services usually provided. At the same time, the city, with its younger, poorer population had greater demands put on its services. Thus, while the Puerto Ricans had greater needs, the city had less money.

Sectoral decline. Automation and suburbanization combined to cause sectoral decline. Sectoral decline is not a recent phenomenon in New York. Vernon and Hoover found that between 1929 and 1939, and between 1947 and 1956, New York City lost ground with respect to its growing industries, while it held on to its declining ones.[15] However, the problem has become more acute in recent years, thereby adversely and significantly affecting Puerto Ricans. A dramatic example can be seen in manufacturing. In 1960, manufacturing employed 60 percent of the Puerto Rican workforce. In the decade that followed, manufacturing jobs in the city decreased by 173,000.[16] This loss was not offset by an increase in low-level service jobs, the other major area of Puerto Rican workforce concentration. Thus, as would be expected and as the Commission on Civil Rights of Puerto Ricans found, sectoral decline became an important contributory cause of high unemployment amongst Puerto Ricans.[17]

Even in 1970, those sectors of decline were where the majority of Puerto Ricans were to be found, while those sectors of growth had few Puerto Ricans employed. Despite the decline in jobs in manufacturing, this area has continued to hold significant proportions of the Puerto Rican labor force. Even in 1968-1969, as the U.S. Commission on Civil Rights noted, Puerto Ricans in poor neighborhoods were still found in overwhelming numbers in manufacturing. In 1970, 60 percent of the manufacturing jobs paid less than was required to sustain a decent, minimum standard of living as determined by the Bureau of Labor Statistics.[18]

Blue-Collar Structural Unemployment. Sectoral decline combined with insufficient educational opportunities and retraining of blue-collar workers to produce blue-collar structural unemployment, which has been an almost chronic condition of the economy for about a decade. In simplest terms, the problem is an excess of blue-collar workers over blue-collar jobs and a scarcity of white-collar workers for excess white-collar jobs. The Regional Plan Association finds this to be one of the main problems of the regional economy. Puerto Ricans, again because of the labor force composition, have been and are bearing the brunt of this structural problem.

The trends in this area indicate a further deterioration of the situation. When you compare the labor force composition of Puerto Ricans (and blacks) against the present and projected job demand for blue- and white-collar jobs and service jobs, you see that blacks and Puerto Ricans do and will suffer the most from the problem of blue-collar structural unemployment.[19] The unemployment could be diminished if more Puerto Ricans (and blacks) entered the white-collar rather than the blue-collar labor force. "However," as the Regional Plan Association states, "it appears that public schools in the regions' older cities and manpower training programmes both tend to channel blacks and Puerto Ricans into blue collar work."[20] Thus, it appears that New York's educational institutions and even its manpower agencies contribute to the problem.

Trade Unions. The environment in which these trends have been occurring has been strongly affected by the unions. Formerly a vehicle of minority mobility, they now function to keep out minorities. Having battled the older entrenched ethnic groups for an occupational niche, the newer ethnic groups now use the unions as a means of securing their positions. Although data on unions are very difficult to come by, it is fairly clear that with the exception of low-level jobs in garment factories and food services, most skilled or craft unions are closed to Puerto Ricans.[21] Thus, many Puerto Ricans' benefits and pay raises may be inferior to those of other workers doing the same job. (This may account, to some extent, for the income discrepancies by occupation noted previously for

Puerto Ricans, blacks, and whites.) The result of union blockages has been the growth of freelance, nonunionized, and therefore lower paid, Puerto Rican plumbers, painters, plasterers, electricians, etc.

The net effect of the unions' role on the economy may turn out to be a negative one, for the unions have functioned to limit the supply of semiskilled and skilled labor in order to have a better bargaining position on wage demands. This tactic, however, may have hampered growth and possibly expansion of the economy; the growth of other lower-skilled, but complementary, job openings may also have been hampered in this way. (For example, the prohibitively high labor costs of construction were a definite factor in curtailing housing construction during the 1960s.) The net effect has been higher wages and benefits for union members, but fewer jobs. These few jobs did not go to unknown, unconnected, colored Puerto Ricans.

Racial and Ethnic Prejudice. Also influencing the effects of these trends on Puerto Ricans were racial barriers. Although ethnic differences often presented a barrier to previous immigrant groups, Puerto Ricans have had to contend with institutionalized racism, as well as institutionalized hostility to ethnic differences. For although, officially, only 9 percent of Puerto Ricans are categorized as black (according to census self-classification), a much larger proportion appears racially nonwhite to Americans and will thus experience racial discrimination.[22] Thus, racism is an important factor affecting the labor market for Puerto Ricans and accounts significantly for the severe distortions in resource allocation to which Puerto Ricans have been subject.

The more "objective" economic factors which have adversely influenced the economic integration of Puerto Ricans into New York City were automation, suburbanization, sectoral decline, and restrictive union policies, factors which were not present to any significant degree during the migrations of previous immigrant groups. Yet these factors have typified the regional New York economy (and to some extent the U.S. economy) in the last decades. When Puerto Ricans and southern blacks were arriving in great numbers, these factors interacted with each other and with racial and ethnic prejudice to create an economic environment inimical to Puerto Rican economic integration.

Inadequate Educational Opportunities. Although it must be admitted that there are educational differentials between Puerto Ricans, blacks, and whites in New York City, these are not sufficient by themselves to explain the occupational patterning, income differentials by occupation, and the extremely high unemployment rates to which Puerto Ricans are subject. This is to say nothing of the causes of these educational differentials, such as the inferior schooling Puerto Ricans receive in the New York City schools, and received as a result of U.S. imperialistic educational policies in Puerto Rico.[23]

Furthermore, if we compare the educational attainments of the New York City population in 1970, we see that although there are differences between ethnic groups, they are not as great as the above figures on income and occupation would lead us to expect. For example, close to 53 percent of the white population in New York City twenty-five years and over are not high school graduates, compared to 80 percent of Puerto Ricans within this age group. Does this justify a median income about two times as large?[24]

Government Employment as a Last Resort. Wilhelm notes that the government has assumed an increasingly larger role as an employer of blacks.[25] Because of this, black unemployment has been kept from increasing too dramatically. Government, however, has not intervened in the same way with respect to the Puerto Rican community, for in 1970 only 12 percent of Puerto Ricans were employed by government, compared to 23 percent of blacks, while local government employed only 7 percent of Puerto Ricans as compared with 15 percent of blacks.[26] Thus, government has not served as an employer of last resort to Puerto Ricans.

A recent extensive survey of municipal government was so appalled at the high under-representation of Puerto Ricans in New York City government that it specifically recommended that, "Utmost priority should be given by the Department of Personnel and all agencies to recruiting members of the Puerto Rican community."[27] No other ethnic group was so "honored."

Summary. In summary, though Mayor Wagner went to San Juan to tell Puerto Ricans that the mainland needed migrants to fill jobs, Puerto Ricans were to meet the sad realities of job placement in New York. This job market had a decreasing demand, for low-skilled jobs were being eliminated by automation, others were protected by unions, others were moving to the suburbs, while suburbanites were taking many jobs in the city. Thus, Puerto Ricans moved into the only jobs available: low-wage work in the service sector (as waiters, kitchen help, porters, and hospital workers), and in light manufacturing (as sewing machine operators). In short, the jobs nobody else wanted. These tended to be low paying and the sectors in which they were found tended to be declining or unstable.

Not only were jobs few, low paying, and often insecure, but once a job was secured mobility was also bad. Where could you go from being a sewing machine operator? Perhaps to the post of supervisor, earning $10 more a week. Similarly, in the food trades the ladder to success started with dishwasher and usually ended with waiter. The few chef positions available were usually reserved for people who had more to offer in the way of "public relations"—as, for example, French chefs did. Most jobs were deadend jobs.

Migration Dividends to the Economy

Despite the depressed position of Puerto Ricans in the New York economy, Puerto Ricans were and are crucial to its proper functioning. Even though the jobs do not pay much, they are important. Someone has to serve the table and wash the dishes of the white-collar workers. It is in this context that we must see the exploited, yet crucial, position of Puerto Ricans. The textile industry provides one example of the crucial role Puerto Ricans played in an industry vital to New York's economy.

New York accounts for 70 percent of all dollar sales of clothing in the United States at the wholesale level.[28] Garment manufacturers produce and sell more than $7 billion in apparel each year. Although the total number of garment firms has declined over the years, the total dollar volume of business has risen. As with industrialization in farming, the remaining firms are larger and financially stronger.

Some scholars contend that but for the Puerto Rican migration, New York City would not have been able to hold on to this very important industry.[29] Puerto Ricans have, in a sense, provided a "positive tipping point." Without this source of cheap labor many more firms would have left the city; those that stayed would have had to reduce their production. In this sense, New York's claim to be the garment capital of the world rests upon Puerto Rican shoulders.

The Harvard study of the New York metropolitan region took note of this role in the 1950s:

> The rate of Puerto Rican migration to New York is one of the factors that determine how long and how successfully the New York metropolitan region will retain industries which are under competitive pressure from other areas. To the extent that some of these industries have hung on in the area, they have depended on recently arrived Puerto Rican workers, who have entered the job market of the New York area at the rate of about 13,000 each year.[30]

Puerto Rican migration was not at a consistently high level in the 1960s, and this may affect the numbers entering the job market. However, the rate of second-generation entry into the job market and the rate of non-Puerto Rican migration to the suburbs may compensate for decreased Puerto Rican migration. Thus, Puerto Ricans may retain their role as "tippers" who enable or encourage firms to stay or to grow. Low wages for Puerto Ricans continue and thus provide a main incentive in this respect.

Although figures are not available for the hotel and restaurant industry, it would seem that a similar phenomenon has occurred, and is occurring, there. If anything, the role of "tippers" would be accentuated because Puerto Ricans make up a greater percentage of employees in this field.[31] To some extent, the growing numbers of blacks and Puerto Ricans in the health and hospitals services might be seen to be a forthcoming, and parallel, phenomenon. In this case, however, government intervenes sufficiently to ensure that blacks and Puerto Ricans are recruited into these occupations. These services can be seen to be almost public utilities that do not have the option of leaving the city, but of growing or deteriorating.

Although at present unresearched, Puerto Rican migration has also undoubtedly had a large role in moving previous immigrant groups up the economic ladder. Twenty-five years ago garment workers were predominantly Jewish and Italian; now Puerto Ricans and other new immigrants have taken their place. Although mortality accounts for a large part of the decline of Jewish and Italian employees, their children are seldom found as workers in the garment trades. Nor are they usually to be found in similar low-paying occupations. The question, of course, is whether a larger proportion of them would have had to take these low-paying jobs despite probable increased education and language skills. This question remains unanswered. But the fact remains that Puerto Ricans took these jobs and that the sons of previous immigrant groups in the garment trades took better jobs and perhaps became owners and managers in expanded firms. Whatever the causes, the ethnic queuing occurred.[32]

The significance of the manufacturing industries to the welfare of the city cannot be overemphasized. There is a renewed awareness of the importance of the garment industry as the largest employer in the city. (The garment industry employs more people than any other type of manufacturing, providing a total annual payroll of $1.5 billion.)[33] And as important as manufacturing is to the city, Puerto Ricans are to manufacturing. Despite the imposed marginality of the Puerto Rican community in decision-making, if there were an exodus of Puerto Ricans, the city would be in serious straits. Puerto Ricans provide the unacknowledged, but indispensable, role of perhaps all previous immigrant groups and blacks—that of workers supporting the base of the economic system. Although the number of Puerto Rican workers is not sufficient to allow us to speak of their being the major part of the workforce, their placement and concentration make for a strategically very significant position.

Welfare: The Economy's Response

Given the low incomes, high unemployment, and insecure jobs held by Puerto Ricans, we would expect to see an extremely high rate of welfare recipients among the Puerto Rican population in New York. In fact, it is not as high as might be expected given the parameters of Puerto Rican poverty. In 1970, 30 percent of Puerto Rican families in New York were on welfare; that is, fully 70 percent were completely self-supporting. Of those families eligible for welfare, that is, with incomes less than poverty level, only 56 percent were on welfare.[34] But the whole issue must be seen within a wider context in order to grasp the full significance of the role the economy has played in placing Puerto Ricans on welfare.

Soon after the large migration of Puerto Ricans to New York, there began to be heard the thesis that Puerto Ricans migrate to New York in order to go on welfare. In other words, the thesis was that welfare in New York was the Puerto Ricans' response to adverse economic conditions in Puerto Rico. This was coupled with claims of astronomically high rates of public assistance to Puerto Ricans. Both these points have been effectively rebutted by Valdivieso, who shows that there has been a significant time lag between migration and welfare assistance.[35] During the 1950s when the great bulk of the Puerto Rican migrants arrived and qualified for public assistance payments, there was a very low rise in such payments. In the 1960s, when welfare rolls expanded, the proportion of Puerto Ricans on welfare rose. Factors other than ethnic propensity must account for this rise: Puerto Ricans did not migrate to get on welfare. It was not a pull factor.

Welfare can be seen to be a contracting economy's response to structural and sectoral unemployment.[36] In addition to taking up the slack in the economy, it also provides jobs for clerical and higher skilled workers—the welfare establishment—while it cools out what may otherwise be an unbearable and explosive situation for the unemployed. At the same time, it tends to subsidize the low-wage industrial sector and the landlord class, which is a direct beneficiary of welfare rent payments.[37] Given the fears associated with color in this country, it is not surprising that welfare has come to be used as an economic policy. That is to say, to some extent individuals are encouraged by the system to apply for welfare; this is done as a means of handling the more difficult structural economic problems.

The system encourages this through the economic factors already noted, for example, unemployment, low incomes, low-status jobs. But it also encourages it directly through the liberalization of welfare policy. Note, for example, those measures that were instituted between 1960 and 1970 when the welfare rolls swelled: doing away with "need" or proof of eligibility, investigator visits, and the man-in-the-home clause; rising rates of support; and support for drug addicts. The fact that welfare funds are mainly federal (50 percent) and state (25 percent) gives added incentive for the city government to cope with its economic problems in this way.[38]

In this period of economic contraction, Puerto Ricans, as the poorest of the poor, have been shunted into welfare—but not more than in proportion to income. Their resistance has been substantial, however, for 70 percent have managed to sustain their families without welfare on extremely low wages, and much higher percentages managed to do so prior to 1960.[39] But for increasing proportions, the only way to survive is welfare. It is in the dilution of alternatives that the system forces Puerto Ricans into welfare.

Notes

1. The extent to which immigrant labor was deliberately recruited so as to control the workforce, and to keep wages low and profits high, has not received sufficient attention. Charlotte Erickson, in *American Industry and the European Immigrant, 1860-1885* (Cambridge, Mass.: Harvard University Press, 1957), concludes that there was little direct recruitment between those years. However, the role immigrants played *after* their arrival in depressing wage levels is often illustrated in analyses of strike behavior, where immigrants and blacks were used as "scabs."
2. See Belton H. Fleisher, "Some Economic Aspects of Puerto Rican Migration to the United States," Ph.D. diss., Stanford University, 1961; and Herbert Hill, "Guardians of the Sweat-Shops: The Trade Union, Racism, and the Garment Industry," in Adalberto López and James Petras, eds., *Puerto Rico and Puerto Ricans* (New York: Schenkman Publishing, 1974).
3. Actual wage rates fell; however, rising costs of living made for an even more dramatic decrease in *real* wages.
4. *New York Times*, June 27, 1954.
5. The surplus population was also the result of a declining death rate, which may have been one of the benefits of a higher per capita income.
6. Adalberto López attributes a great degree of deliberate intention in the attitude of the government to Puerto Rican migration. See "The Puerto Rican Diaspora," in López and Petras, eds., *Puerto Rico and Puerto Ricans*.
7. This change in the forces of production was also accom-

panied by an expansion in the service and government sectors, where some of the low-skilled workers were absorbed.

8. The growth of highways was a direct result of the interests of monopoly capital in collusion with government. See Larry Sawyers, "Urban Form and the Mode of Production," *Review of Radical Political Economics* 8, no. 1 (1975).

9. On this, see Stanley Friedlander, *Labor, Migration, and Economic Growth* (Cambridge, Mass.: MIT Press, 1965); Fleisher, "Some Economic Aspects of Puerto Rican Migration to the United States"; Antonia Pantoja, "Puerto Rican Migration," *Preliminary Report to the U.S. Commission on the Civil Rights of Puerto Ricans,* 1972; Nathan Glazer and Daniel Moynihan, *Beyond the Melting Pot* (Cambridge, Mass.: MIT Press, 1970); Clarence Senior and Donald Watkins, "Toward a Balance Sheet of Puerto Rican Migration," in U.S.-Puerto Rican Commission on the Status of Puerto Rico, *Status of Puerto Rico: Selected Background Studies* (Washington, D.C.: U.S. Government Printing Office, 1966).

10. The following figures are, in the main, census figures. There is a great deal of truth in the charges made against the Census Bureau with regard to undercounting and miscounting, and resulting inaccuracies. The actual number of Puerto Ricans in New York may be closer to 1.2 million, a full 50 percent more than the 800,000 estimated by the census. Despite the very valid objections to the census figures, they are unfortunately the only ones available for the present analysis. They are used mainly to indicate relationships, not exact representations, thus avoiding to some degree the objections raised. However, they probably understate what will be seen to be fairly significant contrasts between blacks, Puerto Ricans, and whites.

11. See Clara Rodríguez, *The Ethnic Queue in the United States: The Case of Puerto Ricans* (San Francisco: R&E Research Associates, 1973).

12. The effect this is having on the traditionally strong patriarchal Puerto Rican family structure is an important issue that has not been given sufficient attention in the literature.

13. See Sidney M. Wilhelm, *Who Needs the Negro?* (New York: Doubleday-Anchor, 1971).

14. The American Transit Authority estimated the nationwide average cost for an inner-city resident to travel to the suburbs for his or her job to be $15 per month in 1968. In New

York, the estimate for transportation from Harlem to Farmingdale, L.I., was $40 per month in the same year. See Robert Will and Harold Vatter, eds., *Poverty in Affluence* (New York: Harcourt, Brace & World, 1970). This does not take into account waiting time, and schedules are usually geared to facilitate the mass of suburbanites coming into the city for work and not vice versa.

15. Raymond Vernon and Edgar M. Hoover, *Anatomy of a Metropolis* (New York: Doubleday-Anchor, 1962).
16. U.S. Department of Labor, Bureau of Labor Statistics, "The New York Puerto Rican: Patterns of Work Experience," *Regional Report No. 19,* Poverty Area Profiles, 1972.
17. U.S. Commission on Civil Rights, "Demographic, Social, and Economic Characteristics of New York City and the New York Metropolitan Area," *Hearings on the Civil Rights of Puerto Ricans,* staff report, February 1972.
18. *New York Times,* November 5, 1972, p. 43.
19. Regional Plan Association, "Linking Skills, Jobs, and Housing in the New York Urban Region" (New York, 1972).
20. Ibid., p. 3.
21. William Tabb presents data (limited to referral unions) that bears out the contention that Puerto Ricans are vastly under-represented in certain unions, especially the craft unions. See an unpublished report by William K. Tabb, "Puerto Ricans in New York City: A Study of Economic and Social Conditions," Bureau of Labor Statistics, New York Regional Office, 1972.
22. State Charter Revision Commission for New York City, "New York City Today: Demographic and Economic Background Information," staff report, December 1973.
23. See Clara Rodríguez, "Puerto Ricans and the New York City School System," *Urban Review* (June 1974); and Ismael Rodríguez Bou, "Significant Factors in the Development of Education in Puerto Rico," in U.S.-Puerto Rico Commission on the Status of Puerto Rico, *Status of Puerto Rico: Selected Background Studies* (Washington, D.C.: U.S. Government Printing Office, 1965).
24. New York City Manpower Area Planning Council, *Comprehensive Manpower Plan for New York City, Fiscal Year 1974* (New York: Office of the Mayor).
25. Wilhelm, *Who Needs the Negro?*
26. U.S. Bureau of the Census, *U.S. Census of Population:*

1970, General Social and Economic Characteristics (Washington, D.C.: U.S. Government Printing Office, 1973), PC (1)-C34, Tables 88, 92, 98, 25.

27. New York City Commission on Human Rights, "The Employment of Minorities, Women, and the Handicapped in City Government," 1973.

28. *New York Times*, November 26, 1972, Business and Finance Section, p.1.

29. See, for example, Senior and Watkins, "Toward a Balance Sheet of Puerto Rican Migration," pp. 689-765; Roy B. Helfgott, *et al.*, *Made in New York* (Cambridge, Mass.: Harvard University Press, 1959); and Raymond Vernon, *Metropolis, 1985* (Cambridge Mass.: Harvard University Press, 1960).

30. Vernon, *Metropolis, 1985.*

31. For exact numbers of Spanish-surnamed by industry and by occupation within industry, see Economic Equal Opportunities Commission, *Job Patterns for Minorities and Women in Private Industry,* 1966.

32. The owners of garment industries remain predominantly Jewish, with a sprinking of Italians. See *New York Times,* November 26, 1972, Section 3, p. 2.

33. Ibid., p. 1.

34. According to former social services employees, many non-Puerto Rican Spanish-speaking people pass as Puerto Ricans in order to get on welfare. This to some extent inflates the figures.

35. Rafael Valdivieso, "Why Puerto Ricans Came to New York," unpublished ms., 1971.

36. This conception of welfare has a number of antecedents. See Marx's analysis of public concessions to workers and the poor in "The Struggle for the Normal Working-Day. Compulsory Limitation by Law of the Working-Time," *Capital,* vol. I (New York: International Publishers, 1970), pp. 278-97. For historical evidence supporting the relationship between welfare and fluctuations in the economy, see Frances Fox Piven and Richard Cloward, *Regulating the Poor* (New York: Vintage Books, 1971) and David M. Gordon, "Income and Welfare in New York City," *The Public Interest* 16 (1969).

37. See Charles Valentine, "Black Studies and Anthropology:

Scholarly and Political Interests in Afro-American Culture," *Addison Wesley Modular Publications*, Module 15 (1972).

38. State Charter Revision Commission for New York City, "New York City Today: Demographic and Background Information," December 1973.
39. U.S. Bureau of the Census, *U.S. Census of Population: 1970*, Tables 90, 95, and 101. These figures are for the whole year, and so the figures at any one time during the year will be less.

CHAPTER 7

Demographic Aspects of Migration
José L. Vázquez Calzada

Migration has been one of the population topics that has received the least attention from demographers and other social scientists. A few general statements based on common sense constitute what are called "theories of migration." There are very few countries in the world for which reliable information about this phenomenon exists.

Puerto Rico is no exception. The few facts available are incomplete and inaccurate in spite of the fact that today migration is the most important variable of the population equation on the Island. Very little is known about the volume or the social, economic, and cultural effects of the immigration currents of North Americans, Cubans, and other foreigners, or about the massive return of migrants and their children to Puerto Rico.

This work only intends to put together the accumulated knowledge about this important variable. In this way, the existing flaws will be detected and research efforts will be facilitated.

Historical Facts

The political relations that resulted from the invasion and conquest of Puerto Rico by U.S. troops in 1898 propitiated the movement of Islanders to the United States. It is estimated that from the date in which the United States took possession of the Island to 1944, around 90,000 persons migrated to the mainland. During that forty-five-year period, the greatest movement occurred during the decade of the 1920s, when more than 40,000 Puerto Ricans mi-

The author is a demographer at the School of Medicine, University of Puerto Rico.

grated. The Depression in the 1930s not only reduced this exodus considerably, but during some years the current was reversed. Between 1930 and 1934 there was a return migration of almost 10,000 people, which is equivalent to 20 percent of the Puerto Rican population in the United States at that time.

Once World War II was over, one of the greatest population exoduses registered in contemporary history began. It has been said that the abundance of employment opportunities in the United States, as well as the expansion of air transportation and the reduction in the cost of the trip, were factors that gave impulse to this movement.

Thus, during the decade of the 1940s more than 150,000 Puerto Ricans abandoned their native land, and more than 400,000 more did so during the 1950s. According to the data derived from the census, net migration diminished during the last decade (1960-1970), but even then the figure was over 250,000.

Until 1950, the population movement between Puerto Rico and the United States was primarily in one direction. The return of migrants, as well as the immigration of North Americans and of other foreigners, was insignificant. Since that date the migratory balance, referred to in previous paragraphs, only represents the net result of a series of population movements. Hernández Alvarez estimates that approximately 50,000 Puerto Rican migrants returned to the Island during the 1950s, and that the immigration of people of Puerto Rican origin (migrants and children of migrants) reached 283,000 during the 1960s.[1] In addition, around 50,000 North Americans moved to Puerto Rico during that period. Taking all these figures into consideration, it can be concluded that the migration of Puerto Ricans to the United States increased to more than half a million people during the last decade.

In these estimates the immigration of Cubans and other foreigners has not been taken into consideration, which according to the 1970 census amounted to about 45,000 people.[2]

Table 7.1
Net Migration of Puerto Ricans to the United States, 1900–1969

Period	Number	Annual average	Rate
1900–09	2,000	200	0.0
1910–19	11,000	1,100	0.1
1920–29	42,000	4,200	0.3
1930–39	18,000	1,800	0.1
1940–49	151,000	15,100	0.7
1950–59	430,000	4,300	1.9
1960–69	253,000	25,300	1.0

Sources: For 1900–1950: José L. Vázquez Calzada, "Las causas y efectos de la emigración puertorriqueña," mimeo. (San Juan: Escuela de Medicina, Universidad de Puerto Rico, 1968). For 1960–1969: Estimates by José Hernández Alvarez, Sociology Department, University of Arizona, mimeo.

Place of Origin and Destination of Migrants

In the great majority of cases the migrants came from rural zones of Puerto Rico—more than 60 percent in the last decade.[3] In contrast, the great majority established themselves in urban areas in the United States. According to the 1970 census, 98 percent of the Puerto Rican migrants lived in U.S. urban areas,[4] and this has been so at least since the previous census.

In geographic terms, the most populated municipalities on the Island (San Juan, Ponce, and Mayagüez) were the ones that contributed the most to the migration in absolute quantities, that is, in numbers. But if the migration is considered as a percentage of the population of the municipality, no geographic pattern is distinguishable from the 1950s on. (There are no figures before this.) The municipalities with the highest and lowest rates (as per-

Table 7.2
Migratory Movements Between 1960 and 1970

Immigration to Puerto Rico	333,424
Return of migrants	148,974
Children of migrants	134,450
North Americans	50,000
Emigration of Puerto Ricans	586,636
Net balance of emigration	253,212

Source: Estimates prepared by José Hernández Alvarez, Sociology Department, University of Arizona, mimeo.

centage of total migration) are dispersed throughout the Island.[5]

At the beginning of the century, Puerto Ricans were dispersed throughout various regions of the United States, although New York City held most of them. Since then the city gained increasing importance as a place of residence for Puerto Rican migrants, and in 1940 it accommodated 88 percent of the total number. From that date on, a tendency toward a greater dispersion has been observed, and according to the 1970 census only 58 percent of *boricuas* lived in New York City.

While New York City and state have lost importance in this respect, other states, such as New Jersey and Illinois, have increased significantly in their Puerto Rican migrant population. In spite of the tendency toward dispersion throughout the United States, more than 90 percent of all Puerto Ricans are still concentrated in seven states. Here I am speaking only of Puerto Rican migrants; I do not include the migrants' children.

In terms of the location of immigrants on the Island—those migrants who returned, as well as Cubans and North Americans—the picture is totally different. The majority of the immigrants established themselves in urban zones, especially in the San Juan metropolitan area. This is a well-known fact. The great majority of the migrants who returned to the Island during the 1955-1959

Table 7.3
Percentage of the Total Population Born in Puerto Rico and Residing in New York State and New York City, 1910–1970
(by percent)

Year	New York City	New York State
1910	36.6	42.4
1920	62.3	65.4
1930	84.0	87.1
1940	87.8	90.4
1950	82.9	84.6
1960	69.8	72.9
1970	58.4	62.5

Sources: U.S. Bureau of the Census, *Censuses of Population, 1960* and *Census of Population, 1970*; U.S. Bureau of the Census, *Puerto Ricans in the United States,* 1960 and 1970.

Table 7.4
Distribution of Puerto Rican Migrants According to the State of Residence, 1960–1970
(by percent)

	1960	*1970*
New York	72.9	62.5
New Jersey	6.5	10.3
Illinois	4.2	6.6
Pennsylvania	2.4	3.1
Connecticut	1.8	3.0
California	2.5	2.9
Florida	2.3	2.3
Other states	7.4	9.3
Total	100.0	100.0

Source: U.S. Bureau of the Census, *Puerto Ricans in the United States,* 1960 and 1970.

period established themselves in urban areas—Hernández estimated this at 70 percent. For the North Americans and foreigners, as well as the children of the migrants, the proportion that established itself in urban areas was even larger.

Characteristics of the Migrants

In spite of various attempts, the government of Puerto Rico has been unable to obtain reliable information about the sociodemographic characteristics of the migrants. Not even simple facts like age and sex have been obtained on a continuous basis. The facts that are analyzed in this section have been derived from the censuses or taken directly from them.

Sex and Age of the Migrants. According to the data derived from the census, migration does not seem to be too selective in terms of sex. Males and females tend to move to the United States in more or less the same proportion. It should be pointed out that since 1950 a slight predominance of males seems to exist: between 1950 and 1959, there were 118 male migrants for every 100 female migrants, while in the last decade the proportion was 123 males for every 100 females.

In terms of age, the migrants are mainly young adults. During the 1950-1959 decade, 70 percent of those who left the Island were between the ages of fifteen and thirty-nine, and only 18 percent were under fifteen. These proportions contrast sharply with those of the Island's population, clearly showing that migration is selective in terms of age.[6] As shown in Table 7.5, the migrants are on the average older than the general population of the Island. Due to the impossibility of separating the facts of both migratory currents—that is, the out-migration current and the in-migration current—the corresponding computation of the 1960-1969 decade has not been made. It should be pointed out, though, that the average migrant residing in

Table 7.5
Distribution of the Population Residing in Puerto Rico
and of the Migrants by Age Group
(in percent)

Age	Percentage of migrants 1950–1960	Percentage of population 1960
Under 15	18	43
15–39	70	35
40 and older	12	22
Total	100	100
Median age	24	18

the United States was thirty years old in 1970, as compared to twenty years old for the population residing on the Island.

Level of Instruction. The migrant, contrary to what was believed in the past, has on the average a much higher level of education than that of the population residing on the Island (see Table 7.6). This was demonstrated in the data obtained by the Department of Labor during the 1950s and also by the census. In 1960, the adult Puerto Rican (twenty-five years and older) residing on the Island had an average of five completed years in school, compared with an average of eight years for the migrant

Table 7.6
Median Number of Years of School Completed for the Population
Twenty-Five Years and Older Residing in the Island and for
the Migrant Population Residing in the United States, 1960–1970

Year	Residing in Puerto Rico	Migrants
1960	4.8	7.9
1970	6.9	8.4

residing in the United States. According to the 1970 census, the corresponding figures were 6.9 years in Puerto Rico and 8.4 years in the United States. However, this does not seem to be the case among the younger age groups (twenty to twenty-four years old and fifteen to nineteen years old). In other words, people between the ages of fifteen and nineteen, and twenty and twenty-four, who reside on the Island have a higher level of education than the migrants in the same age groups.

Occupations. No information exists of the occupational skills of the migrants at the moment of departure. Only the kinds of jobs they undertake in the United States are known. Obviously, the kind of job has a lot to do with skills and capabilities, but it is also influenced by language limitations, by prejudice, and by many other problems known to everyone. In spite of these limitations, the census figures can shed some light on this matter.

According to the 1970 census, almost 40 percent of the *boricuas* employed in the United States were "operators." This proportion is double the corresponding figure for people employed in Puerto Rico. In general, Puerto Rican migrants have occupations of less status and prestige than Puerto Ricans on the Island, in spite of the fact that they have a higher level of education. So, for instance, while in Puerto Rico the percentage of professionals among the employed population is 12 percent, among the migrants it is only 5 percent. A similar situation occurs with managerial and clerical occupations. An outstanding fact is the high proportion of salesmen among the migrant population as compared to the population residing in Puerto Rico.

Implications of Migration

Migration has been considered by some social scientists, as well as by the majority of our government leaders, as the best solution to the demographic problem of the Is-

Table 7.7
Distribution of the Population of Puerto Rico and of the Migrants
Residing in the United States by Occupational Groups, 1970
(by percent)

	Puerto Rico	Migrants
Agricultural	7.4	1.2
White collar	39.0	25.8
Professionals, etc.	12.0	4.6
Managers, etc.	7.2	3.2
Clerical, etc.	12.3	3.8
Salespeople	7.5	14.2
Manual	41.0	50.5
Artisans, etc.	15.0	11.7
Operators, etc.	19.4	38.8
Nonagricultural workers	6.6	5.9
Service workers	12.6	16.6
All occupations	100.0	100.0

land. Although publicly it was indicated that the government of Puerto Rico was not fostering migration, its actions showed just the opposite. In the population projections prepared by the Planning Board, one of the first variables always included was massive migration. In private conversations I was told that migration, as a solution to the population problem, was less controversial than family planning. Some even publicly proposed a planned massive migration to Brazil and to the islands of the Caribbean.

There is no doubt that mass migration has been a great escape valve for population pressures in Puerto Rico. It is hard to imagine how things would be on the Island if we added the 1.5 million Puerto Ricans in the United States to the present population. Puerto Rico is not the paradise that some want us to believe. In spite of this massive exodus of *boricuas* and the frantic industrialization programs that have placed in the hands of foreign absentee ownership all

Table 7.8
Rate of Unemployment According to Age and Sex, 1970

	Male	*Female*
14–19	28.7	29.2
20–24	20.4	16.5
25–34	9.3	8.5
35–44	7.5	6.5
45–54	6.7	—
55–64	7.3	—
65 and older	—	—

Source: Puerto Rico Department of Labor. Where there are no data, it is because there were too few cases in the sample.

of our industrial and economic life, Puerto Rico still suffers from many of the same problems of the 1940s, and others have deepened.

Unemployment, one of the most serious problems of the Island, continues to be as high as three decades ago. Official estimates place the figure at 12 percent, although some economists believe that it really reaches more than 20 percent. Hubert Barton, an economist and one of the former government consultants on industrial development, has presented some figures that bring it to 30 percent.

Even according to official figures, unemployment is a critical problem among our youth. Almost 30 percent of the young people between fourteen and nineteen who want to work are unemployed, as are almost 20 percent of those between the ages of twenty and twenty-four.

Another problem that is hardly ever mentioned in Puerto Rico is the extraordinarily high incidence of what has been called voluntary idleness—in other words, laziness. While the unemployed person is searching for a job, the voluntarily idle one is neither in school, at work, or looking for a job. According to the figures obtained from

Table 7.9

Rate of Economic Activity of the Male Population in
Puerto Rico and Three Categories of Countries

Categories	Rate
Industrialized	60.5
Semi-industrialized	62.8
Agricultural	65.1
Puerto Rico	51.0

Source: United Nations, *Demographic Aspects of Manual Labor* (New York, 1963). For Puerto Rico, the figures were computed from figures from the Puerto Rico Department of Labor. The rate is figured by taking the total of males that are active as percentage of the total male population, adjusted according to age. That is, the differences in the age structure of different countries have been considered.

United Nations publications, where figures for all countries can be found, Puerto Rico stands out as the country with the highest proportion of idleness in the world. Its rate of economic activity—that is, the proportion of the population that participates in the production of goods and services—is the lowest among countries for which this information exists in the United Nations yearbook. This situation is much more serious among the male population.

The levels of income of the average Puerto Rican are still very low. In spite of the economic growth, government leaders feel so proud of, the real per capita income is still around $500, as it was in 1940—and the dollar today has the buying power of $.30 then. Neither have we advanced when compared to the poorest state in the United States, Mississippi. In 1940, the per capita income in Mississippi was 80 percent higher than that in Puerto Rico; in 1970, it was 81 percent higher. If we have achieved anything, it has been only a worsening of the situation, if compared with Mississippi. In relation to the economic objectives our political leaders drew up for themselves back in the

1940s, that is, to reach the level of the poorest state of the United States, the failure has been complete.

In addition, income distribution has worsened significantly.[7] It is enough to say that, according to the 1970 census, 64 percent of our families lived on the threshold of poverty. For the rural population, this proportion reached to more than 80 percent and in some municipalities, like Maricao, it surpassed 90 percent.

And to achieve an economic growth that has not yet been able to reduce the grave problems of idleness and low income levels, Puerto Rico has been mortgaged and most of our economic life has been placed in the hands of huge U.S. corporations with absentee owners. Absenteeism, another ill that, it was said in the 1940s, was to be eradicated, today dominates almost all of our industries, banking, and commerce. Puerto Ricans have become errand boys in their own land.

Migration is, then, only the symptom of a critical socioeconomic situation. It is the escape valve for those who have seen their aspirations frustrated in their own land. Many Puerto Ricans migrate with the hope that things cannot be worse in the United States than they are on the Island. But migration is not, and cannot be, the solution to the problem of an imbalance between resources and population. It could be used to give an initial impulse to socioeconomic development since it relieves demographic pressure, and thus a greater proportion of resources can be dedicated to nondemographic (i.e., social, economic) investment. What cannot be done is to structure a people's development and economy on the premise, implicit or explicit, of mass migration on a continuing basis. To do such a thing is dangerous, inefficient, and questionable.

It is a dangerous recourse because the volume and direction of these movements are out of our control, out of the control of the people of Puerto Rico. Migration seems to be closely linked to the conditions of the job market in the United States, as well as the economic situation in that country. Any economic disturbance in the United

States will be felt in Puerto Rico in all its intensity. Examples of this close association are the economic crisis of the 1930s, the small recessions in the 1950s, and the situation that we are going through at this moment.

Migration tends to decrease during periods of crisis in the United States and sometimes, as I said before, the current has reversed itself; more than 280,000 people of Puerto Rican extraction have returned to Puerto Rico, and the current of returning migrants seems to have increased considerably since 1970. An economy which depends on its ability to get rid of its excess population by means of migration cannot be expected to have great stability and finds itself on a very unsound base.

Furthermore, migration turns out to be a very costly solution. In the long run, these movements represent a great loss in terms of the economic and social investment made by our society, by our community. This is a very unfortunate situation in a country with such scarce resources. Our migrants are young people, at the age of greatest economic productivity; they have a level of education which is higher than that of the average Puerto Rican, and they apparently have a better disposition toward work.

Migration has also been questioned from a moral and human point of view. It is inhuman and unjust to think of the migrants as simple statistics. Their suffering, their dreams, their aspirations and frustrations cannot be, nor should they be, ignored by those who see migration as the solution to the demographic problem and who would like this exodus to continue so that they can accommodate themselves better in Puerto Rico.

It is pitiful and incredible how little importance and attention population movements have received from our government. Even more incredible has been the position that many of our social scientists have assumed. The relative passivity of our intellectuals in the face of the exodus of Puerto Ricans is disturbing and exasperating, more so when, in the last few years, it has been accompanied by a massive immigration of North Americans and other foreigners. I do not think, though, that we should act simply out of prejudice or guided by emotions. It is necessary that we first understand the nature and magnitude of these movements, as well as their causes and consequences. This is one of the real challenges for the Puerto Rican social scientist.

Notes

1. José Hernández Alvarez, *Return Migration to Puerto Rico* (Berkeley: University of California Press, 1967), p. 16.
2. This number is somewhat doubtful and has been questioned by many experts in the field.
3. Estimates done by the demographic studies section of the School of Public Health, University of Puerto Rico.
4. U.S. Bureau of the Census, *Puerto Ricans in the United States, 1970*, Table 2.
5. José L. Vázquez Calzada, "Las causas y efectos de la emigración puertorriqueña," mimeo. (San Juan: Escuela de Medicina, Universidad de Puerto Rico, 1968).
6. Hernández Alvarez, *Return Migration to Puerto Rico*.
7. José L. Vázquez Calzada, "El desbalance entre recursos y población en Puerto Rico," mimeo. (San Juan: Escuela de Medicina, Universidad de Puerto Rico, 1966).

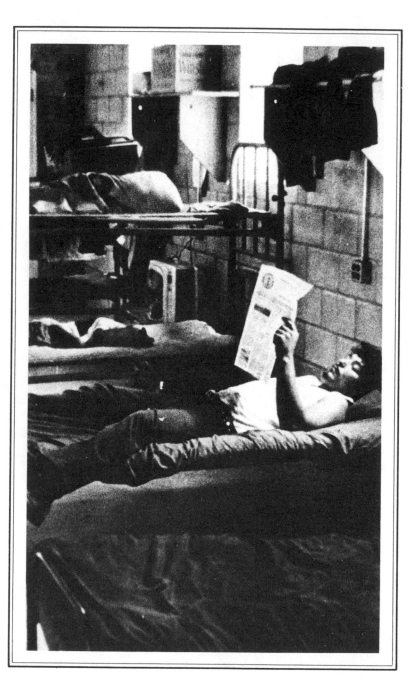

CHAPTER 8

The Puerto Rican Farmworker: From Exploitation to Unionization
Felipe Rivera

> "It is only the organization and resoluteness of the working class which protects it from the natural tendency of the capitalist to exploit to the utmost. That is why in all colonial territories . . . when workers realized the necessity for trade union solidarity numerous obstacles were placed in their paths by the colonial regimes."
>
> —Walter Rodney, *How Europe Underdeveloped Africa*

The situation of the Puerto Rican migrant farmworker is in many respects no different from that of the other migrant farmworker groups in the United States. The conditions which they confront, whether legal, financial, or social, are all symptomatic of a lifestyle created by an economic system that requires the exploitation of certain sectors of the population in order to benefit others. What makes the Puerto Rican migrant farmworker unique, however, is the unresolved question of the political status of the Island. Puerto Rico remains a colonial territory of the United States, and that relationship defines all contact between the two entities. Specifically, it is the definition of the relationship of the United States agricultural industry and laws to Puerto Rico and the Puerto Rican migrant farmworker that will be discussed here.

The author was chairman of the ATA Support Committee (Asociación de Trabajadores Agrícolas). He has an MBA in corporate and labor relations.

Exploitation:
What the Puerto Rican Farmworker Comes to

The U.S. agricultural industry in 1973 had the highest income growth rate (32.5 percent) of any industry in the country. Agricultural lobbies, which have long been able to influence labor laws, trespass laws, and tax exemption status, and to shift elsewhere the cost of workers' benefits, continue to do so today with basically the same arguments: that farming is a small family business. But farming is big business earning millions of dollars in profits for powerful corporations that are the beneficiaries of this windfall. As of 1969, 10 percent of all the farms in the United States accounted for nearly 66 percent of total sales, and the trend continues. Yet the myth of the small family farm is exploited by agribusinesses to deny farmworkers the basic protection that belongs to all workers—the right to organize and bargain collectively.

The farmworker is the lowest paid and least protected of all laboring groups in the United States, and it is those states in which a reduction in the number of farms is not anticipated—Delaware, New Jersey, West Virginia, and Pennsylvania—that use the services of the Puerto Rican migrant farmworker.

In farm work there are no federal labor laws governing employer-employee relations: the definition of "employee" in the National Labor Relations Act (NLRA) does not include any individual employed as an "agricultural laborer," while the Fair Labor Standards Act's provisions on minimum wages (Sec. 206) and maximum hours (Sec. 207) do not apply to "any employee employed in agriculture" by a farmer who uses less than 500 person-days in any *calendar quarter,* or to any employee employed as a "hand harvest laborer" and paid at piece rates. The first provision means that a farmer must use at least seven people six days a week for twelve weeks in order to make his farm laborers eligible, a highly unlikely prospect.

The political strength of farm organizations in the U.S.

Congress made exclusion of the farmworker from the National Labor Relations Act a precondition for its passage thirty-nine years ago. The NLRA has been amended twice since then, but the agribusinesses' lobbying power has stopped Congress from changing that status. Legislation regulating migrant farm work is, therefore, left up to the states, and here the powerful farm lobbies do much to influence the manner in which these laws and regulations are drawn up.

Economic power is translated into political clout in local, state, and federal legislatures. That is why farmworker minimum wages are $1.60 an hour. That is why farmworkers are excluded from the protections provided under the NLRA. That is why farmworkers are not eligible for overtime pay, workmen's compensation, unemployment insurance, and, by extension, a decent education, adequate health care, good housing, and the respect which should be accorded the men and women who harvest much of the food America eats. The agribusiness interests of New Jersey, Connecticut, Delaware, Massachusetts, New York, and Pennsylvania, all states that employ Puerto Rican migrant farmworkers, maintain a strong hold on the local legislatures, cry poverty while reaping huge profits, depress costs at the expense of the farm laborer, and impose social costs they themselves generate on the surrounding communities.

• It was not until recently that a trespass law in New Jersey, which did not allow the farmworkers visitors of any kind, was knocked down by the courts. The farmers are still fighting the decision.

• The national trend regarding farm size holds true regionally. While total farm acreage is decreasing, farm size is increasing as fewer owners come to hold larger tracts of land. Taking into consideration the inflated prices of farm products, today's grower is making a financial killing.

• In Connecticut, for example, farm land was assessed for tax purposes at $198 per acre in 1973. Urban sprawl and development means the land is worth over $7000 an acre in the open market, but the grower gets his land assessed as farm land by maintaining what land he has left unsowed. To increase profits on the farm land he must keep costs down. Tax costs and planting costs are fixed. What he can play with are labor costs . . . and the lives of the laborers.

• The communities surrounding the farm areas are economically affected by the grower's practices in two ways. In the first place, the low wages cause the surrounding communities to subsidize the incomes of the local workers, either day-haulers or walk-ins, who are underemployed, underpaid, and either chronically or seasonally unemployed. (A day-hauler is someone who lives in the area near the farms and is hired on a day-by-day basis; a walk-in is someone who approaches the grower independently and makes arrangements for wages, conditions, etc.)

In the second place, growers recruit Puerto Rican migrant farmworkers (from 50,000 to 60,000 a year) to, in effect, maintain a larger, easily accessible labor pool which they can treat and pay poorly. As much as 65 percent of that labor force remains in the region after the harvest is over and the growers have pocketed their profits. It is the communities in which these now unemployed farmworkers live that have to provide them with jobs or subsidize them—not the growers, who are exempt from unemployment insurance laws.

• The Puerto Rican migrant farmworker, whether under contract or not, is one of the farm laborers most adversely affected by the political/social/economic exploitation perpetrated by those who have been a party in the encouragement of this migration. A 1968 study entitled *Seasonal Farm Workers in the State of New Jersey*, commissioned by the state, revealed the following general characteristics:

Age: The typical contract worker is thirty years old. The typical noncontract worker is thirty-four years old. (These age levels have since been lowered to an average of about twenty-two.)

Sex: Ninety-eight percent were male; 2 percent were female.

Education and language: The contract and noncontract workers have similar backgrounds. They have both completed the fourth grade and neither can speak English.

Illnesses: Over 70 percent of the workers reported some illness that had interfered with their work (i.e., virus infections, arthritis, stomach pains, bad ankles, backaches, etc.), which were probably due to the type of work they were doing.

Deaths and causes of deaths: The average life expectancy of the Puerto Rican and black farmworker was fifty-five years, in contrast to the average U.S. citizen's life expectancy of 70.2 years in 1965. *The evidence suggests that Puerto Rican and black workers may be unwittingly losing ten to fifteen years of their lives if they remain employed as migrant labor.* Forty-seven percent of the deaths are due to circulatory problems, such as heart attacks and strokes.

Skill: The typical contract and noncontract worker is skilled in agriculture, the contract worker having five years of seasonal farm-work experience and the noncontract worker about six years; both are, however, inexperienced and unskilled in other employment. (The experience level has decreased, as with age above.)

Marital status: Both the contract and noncontract worker are married and leave their families behind in Puerto Rico when they come to the United States.

Earnings: Both the contract and noncontract worker will earn about $1.75 an hour (in 1973). Over a year period, including the earnings of the whole family, both workers will earn slightly under $3,000 per year. (Earnings for 1974 will probably average around $2.05 per hour for a forty-hour week, giving a migrant $1,968 for six months. Total average family earnings will, of course, depend on an additional income in Puerto Rico.)

Given these above conditions, the question which must

be answered is why these farmworkers come to the U.S. farms to work.

The Contract . . . Mechanism for Exploitation

A key measure of the success of a secretary of labor or a government is a low unemployment rate. What better way to keep unemployment low than by deporting it? The history of the contract negotiated between the growers and the Department of Labor of the Commonwealth of Puerto Rico dates from 1948, when 4,906 Puerto Ricans came to the United States to work. The number of workers covered by the contract continued to increase, reaching a high in 1968, when 22,902 came to fourteen states. In 1973 the number had decreased to slightly over 14,000, but the number of noncontract workers had increased to approximately 60,000 and some Puerto Ricans suspect that the figures may be as high as 200,000 if winter migrations to Florida farms are included.

The Commonwealth government was never in a position to "negotiate" a contract. It approached the bargaining table with the need to (1) reduce chronic unemployment, (2) attract U.S. corporate interests using unprotected labor as bait, and, at the same time, (3) protect those it was sending to work for the same U.S. corporations it was seeking to attract to the Island. The contract offered the migrant farmworker each year for the last twenty-six years shows clearly the winner and loser in this obvious conflict of interest (see "Contract Comparative Analysis," Appendix 2 in this chapter). Although it is a tripartite agreement between the grower, the Commonwealth, and the farmworker, *to date the farmworker has not participated in any of the negotiations, either directly or through workers' representatives.* The contract itself lacks all basic protection for workers. It does not provide for overtime pay, nutritional meals, or a grievance procedure; it does not protect the worker from arbitrary firing, poor housing, inadequate health care, usury, violence, or loss of property. Contract enforcement is usually nonexistent, with only fifteen field representatives in fourteen states to cover thousands of farms.

But the contract's greatest shortcomings lie in the present "representatives" inability or unwillingness to enforce the contract and in the continued nonrepresentation of the workers themselves in the agreement's negotiations.

The Puerto Rican Migrant Farmworker . . .
Unionization

Economic conditions on the Island have been worsening for the wage earner, and for the agricultural worker in particular. The cost of living has been growing at a rate of approximately 22 percent per year, whereas salaries have been increasing at a lesser annual rate. These figures are superimposed on an unemployment rate which has hovered around 30 percent, with a figure of almost double that for the sixteen to twenty-three age group, the largest age grouping in Puerto Rico. The agricultural labor force of the Island has decreased 78 percent, from about 200,000 workers in 1940 to an estimated 35,000 today. These farmworkers cannot be, and are not, completely absorbed by the industries that have been attracted to Puerto Rico. Many of the firms originally induced to invest and locate in Puerto Rico, if labor intensive, were geared toward the employment of women (needle trades). The more recent investors have provided capital-intensive industries (for example, the petrochemical industry), *which requires a degree of technical skill not yet developed in Puerto Rico.* The result is that unskilled workers who cannot function in an increasingly technical work environment, and who must compete with better educated or better trained North Americans or Cubans, are left unemployed or with the option to migrate to the farms or cities of the United States to work for wages which, though higher than those received by agricultural workers on the Island, do not meet their economic needs, force them to withstand adverse housing, health, and social conditions, and keep many underemployed or seasonally unemployed. They will receive $2.00 to $2.15 per hour for agricultural work for six months. This income, if sent to the farm-worker's family, will be sent into an economy with a cost-of-living index that has been growing at twice the rate of that in the United States.

A major condition to be contended with on the United States mainland is that of labor supply. Considerations include its availability, the determination of that availability, and the consequent effect on wages for both the migrant farmworker and the surrounding com-munities.

Before the contracts are signed each year between the growers and the Commonwealth government, Rural Manpower Services is required (in accordance with 20 CRF, Sec. 602.8) to determine whether or not there is enough local labor available to warrant the importation of an outside labor force. Quite apart from doubting whether any such determination is ever made, the fact is that for the past twenty-five years it has been announced that there were not sufficient local laborers available. The re-sult is that farm laborers from extremely depressed areas are shipped to farms to work for very low wages in an industry unprotected by national labor laws. This has an enormous effect on the income and wage levels of the communities surrounding these farms:

(1) Any segment of the local labor force seeking to make a living in the agricultural section is prevented from doing so by the importation of Puerto Rican farmworkers, who either come from an area with unemployment rates as high as 40 percent and/or are paid only $1.30 an hour for their labor.

(2) The farmer can use the foreign labor to prevent unionization. Presently, the Commonwealth of Puerto Rico government is negotiating contracts with Florida growers. It reasons as follows: (a) In previous years con-

tracts were not negotiated because it was believed that discriminatory practices in the South would make working conditions for the Puerto Rican migrant unsupportable. The Puerto Rican Department of Labor apparently feels that these conditions no longer exist. (b) A great deal of publicity has been given to the almost slavelike movement of Puerto Rican migrant farm labor to Florida under intolerable conditions. The situation first came to light when several cases of typhoid were detected among the workers. (c) A third reason surfaces as to why there is suddenly a move to sign contracts with the Florida growers. The United Farm Workers (UFW) of America recently organized the largest grower in Florida, and it is only a question of time before the other growers are affected. By using Puerto Rican labor, the growers hope to forestall this movement and deal with the Commonwealth, whose contract is less stringent than that of the UFW.

The actions of the Commonwealth government, as well as those of Rural Manpower Services, act to depress wages in those areas to which Puerto Rican migrant farmworkers are sent, contrary to the claim that the contract negotiated by the Puerto Rican Department of Labor is a wage model for the remainder of the nation. As can be seen by the contract comparisons in the appendix, the contract negotiated by the UFW in Salinas, California, *in 1970* contains a higher wage rate than that of the Commonwealth contract negotiated *in 1973*.

Another way to look at wages is to consider the number of day-haul workers used in areas where the Puerto Rican migrant worker has a contract. In southern New Jersey, approximately 10,000 day-haul workers are used daily during peak season. There are also contracts for walk-ins and specialists. All of these workers come from the areas surrounding the camps. Because of the better wage arrangements found where the UFW contract is in force, fewer work crews are coming from the south or southwest to work in the New England or Middle Atlantic fields. Farmers are fully aware of the fact that they would be unable to pay $2.05 an hour if they were only able to rely on local labor. In addition, a labor force which lives close to its place of work is easier to organize than transients who travel 1,800 miles initially to get to the work area, and can then be shifted from farm to farm at the whim of the grower.

Finally, the number of workers "ordered" by the growers who sign the contracts with the Commonwealth is always larger than that actually needed to do the work. Growers reason that they must protect themselves, given the large numbers of workers who "break" their contracts. Leaving aside, for the moment, the reasons why contracts are "broken" so often (six out of seven workers break their contracts), the growers are in the enviable position of creating, and being able to maintain, a buyers' market. By flooding the market with cheaply acquired labor, and being assured of the source, they can maintain low wage levels to the detriment of the local labor pool, and can also decrease the possibility of unionization.

The Need to Organize

The conditions delineated both on the Island and in the United States, along with the additional factor of UFW efforts to organize migrant farmworkers in the South and Southwest, have all played a significant role in the present efforts to organize the Puerto Rican migrant farmworker. In addition, there is a growing demand on the part of the Puerto Rican agricultural workers themselves to negotiate their own contracts and a call for the passage of agrarian reform laws on the Island.

These demands have manifested themselves in the following forms. First, many contract workers have become increasingly restive and have been involved in several work stoppages, primarily resulting from contract violations and nonenforcement. Second, an increasing number of workers come to the U.S. farms to work without contracts. And third, growing pressure is being placed on the

Island government to seek ways to decrease importation of foodstuffs that could be grown on the Island.

Studies begun in Puerto Rico to ascertain the need and feasibility of organizing agricultural workers on the Island soon determined that any organizational efforts would have to take place in the United States, primarily because workers there are more concentrated and more susceptible to organizing. The group doing the study in Puerto Rico, the Comité de Apoyo Migrante Puertorriqueño (CAMP), sent representatives to Connecticut and southern New Jersey to create the Ministerio Ecuménico de Trabajadores Agrícolas (META). It was through the efforts of META that the Asociación de Trabajadores Agrícolas (ATA) was founded in August 1973. This organization is primarily composed of, and presided over, by Puerto Rican migrant workers and is registered in Connecticut, Massachusetts, and New Jersey. It is the only group presently working toward the unionization of the Puerto Rican migrant farmworker and has been recognized as such by the UFW, which wrote a letter to the governor of Puerto Rico to that effect. ATA has also received recognition from the Movimiento Obrero Unido (MOU) in Puerto Rico.

ATA is taking a threefold approach to its organizational efforts. (1) Alleviate poor work and wage conditions for the Puerto Rican migrant farmworkers. (2) Infuse self-respect as well as demand the respect of others for workers who contribute to society. (3) Raise political awareness in terms of the basis for migration and its relation to Puerto Rico's socioeconomic status.

In referring to the above in reverse order:

(1) The educational process of expanding awareness of the basic issues is one that begins the moment contact is made with the worker and is continued indefinitely as part of ATA's role. This is already evident in the fliers and other materials given out by ATA to members and prospective members.

(2) A thrust of the ATA literature to its members emphasizes the theme of self- and mutual respect. This theme is particularly relevant to labor, and especially to

the minority worker in U.S. society. This was, for example, the point around which the Rev. Dr. Martin Luther King, Jr., and the striking sanitation workers of Atlanta, Georgia, rallied in the conflict which cost Dr. King his life.

(3) The changes in wages and work conditions sought by ATA from the U.S. growers are best understood through their contract demands: (a) A $3.00 per hour guaranteed minimum wage with a forty-hour work week. (b) That the growers voluntarily accept the respective state regulations regarding unemployment insurance and overtime pay. (c) Hot and more nutritional meals at lower cost. (d) Better health care; noncamp diets for hospital patients, with a doctor and nurse available twenty-four hours a day; and workmen's compensation for the first four days of hospitalization. (e) No deductions from wages for the cost of the fare to the United States.

All of the above demands are, of course, predicated upon the growers' recognition of ATA as the exclusive bargaining agent for the Puerto Rican migrant farmworker.

As a direct consequence of its membership's actions, ATA is making four basic demands of the Commonwealth government: (1) Commonwealth government support, in writing, for all migrant legal action. (2) Immediate agrarian reform legislation for the Island. (3) An end to the Department of Labor's promotion of farm labor migration to the United States. (4) No discrimination due to race, religion, or political belief.

The obstacles to be overcome in any attempt to organize the Puerto Rican migrant farmworker are great. Some are obvious: grower opposition and legislative aid in this opposition; mechanization; and the use of the present contract as a bar by taking the position that the farmworkers are already being represented by the Commonwealth of Puerto Rico government. This last, as indicated earlier, is an obstacle of particular interest and one which raises the question of conflict of interest in the Commonwealth of Puerto Rico's posture with respect to contract negotiation and enforcement. The conflict of interest theory has validity. One cannot cater to corporate interests, particularly in labor-intensive industries, and at the same time fully protect the interests of the workers, either in Puerto Rico or in the United States.

Other obstacles which must be confronted by any cohesive attempt at solving the Puerto Rican migrant farmworker's problems will include: (1) the continual change of personnel (due to poor wages and conditions), (2) the distance between permanent residence and place of work, and (3) the increased use of local labor (day-haulers and walk-ins) to replace the Puerto Rican migrant. It is because of the latter that any remedial or protective measures should also incorporate into any organization being established that segment of the local labor force that is presently available to work in the fields.

Appendix 1: Legalized Exploitation, or the 1974 Migrant Farmworker Contract Between U.S. Growers and the Puerto Rican Commonwealth Government

The very first sentence of the new agreement between the two negotiators immediately sets the tone for the "new" contract:

> The grower and the worker that subscribe to this contract for the present agree that all the terms and conditions of the "Agricultural Contract Between [the grower] and Puerto Rican Farm Worker—1973" governs and will continue to apply, with all its force and effect, during the calendar year of 1974 with the following modifications.

The modifications go on to demonstrate a mockery of collective bargaining agreements.

1973	1974
1. Article 1(b) provided for a $25.00 bonus for working to the end of the contract (twenty-four weeks) and another $50.00 for working more than twenty-six weeks. No limit was mentioned beyond the twenty-six week period, but the bonus was a part of the contract.	1. Modification of the contract *excluded* the bonus. Result: Loss of at least $25.00, and as much as $75.00, for 1974.
2. Article 3(a) provided for a 120-hour work guarantee for each successive three-week period during the length of the contract. This would conceivably allow the employer to demand sixty or seventy hours of work in the third week if the worker had only worked sixty or fifty hours respec-	2. The basic flaw of this clause was not removed. Although it was reduced to an eighty-hour guarantee for each successive two-week period, the employer can still demand long hours for the second week given a short first week.

1973	1974

tively in the first two weeks of the 120-hour guarantee.

3. Article 4(c) provided for contract wage rate of $1.90 per hour.

3. Hourly pay has increased to $2.15 an hour for 1974. This is $.25 per hour increase, or a six-month increase of $240.00.

4. Article 4(d) on piece rates provided that if a contract worker who worked for piece rates received less in a week than comparable time rates under the contract, the employer was to make up the difference the following week.

4. The new contract, while maintaining the guarantee of comparable wages, removes the guarantee of having the difference made up the following week. How long can the employer hold onto the difference?

5. Article 4(j) is a penalty clause to the grower and/or association for improper record maintenance.

5. Although there were some word changes, the clause remains the same. What should be remembered, though, is that in the twenty-six years of the contract the Commonwealth government has never once brought a grower and/or association to court.

6. Article 5(b) protected the worker from discrimination in employment or housing because of race, color, creed, or membership in or activity on behalf of a labor organization.

6. To its credit, the 1974 agreement has added sex, nationality, political affiliation, and "any attempt to form, join, or help a labor union." ATA can take credit for bringing these issues to the fore by making them a part of its initial demands.

1973	1974
	The growers (specifically the Shade Tobacco Growers Agricultural Association) allowed the inclusion of a phrase about joining a labor union that was already fact by virtue of a 1974 court decision won against them, giving ATA free access to Shade camps. (Civil No. 117 U.S.D.C., Hartford, Conn.)

7. Article 6(a2) gave joint responsibility for camp and living quarter cleanliness to the grower and worker, and attempted to provide for cooperative efforts toward improvement.

Article 8(c) made the worker responsible for maintenance of living quarters. Failure to do so could cause the employer to make necessary (or unnecessary) changes and charge the worker.

7. The new clause makes the worker responsible specifically for the cleanliness of the immediate living quarters occupied by the worker (Shade and Glassboro have barracks), while the cleanliness of the camp and living quarters in general are the responsibility of the growers.

The modification of 8(c) has continued this policy while allowing for normal deterioration as before.

8. Article 6(c) provided for three hot meals (nutritional value not stipulated). The hot portion of the lunch was to be something other than soup or drink. Cost per week was $17.50 or cost, whichever was less. (Routine deduction: $17.50.)

8. Nutritional value has not been defined, the hot portion of something other than soup and drink still only applies to lunch, and the cost has gone up to $21.00 per week or cost, whichever is less. Extra cost yearly: $72.00.

1973

9. Article 7(a) stipulated that migrants would pay their own fares as well as land transportation from airport to farm. The employer would make arrangements for, and procure, the transportation. When the contract was concluded, the worker was to have only the airfare money returned, as well as a ticket back to Puerto Rico.

Article 7(c) of the 1973 contract called for the return of all airfare deductions made from the workers' wages, plus the responsibility of the employer to make return land and air transportation arrangements and pay the costs.

The formula for deductions made from the workers' wages for advances for transportation or any other advances was as follows: $5.00 deduction from the first $25.00 of weekly salary, $2.00 deduction from each additional $5.00 in such weeks. A weekly statement was to be given the worker.

1974

9. Under the modified clause the worker still pays the airfare but the land transportation costs section was changed and the employer is made responsible for land travel arrangements and costs. The obvious flaw in this clause continues to be the deduction made from the worker's meager salary. A basic ATA demand is the removal of the deduction clause.

The 1973 clause was broken up into two separate clauses, 7(c1) and 7(c2). In the first section, the employer will begin paying back at the rate of $10.00 a week, beginning midway through the contract, the money deducted from the workers' wages for transportation. The full sum is to be returned if the contract ends before full reimbursement is made. The second section provides for the last employer to pay transportation back to the place of recruitment, including land transportation to the airport. Commencement of repayment for airfare deductions midway through the contract has

1973	1974
	been instituted because of repeated accusations that the growers had been forcing workers to break the contract so as not to return what was due upon completion.

The new contract has the same provisions. Given that all contracts have required the deductions, there is not now nor has there ever been any mention of the cost per worker for air and land transportation. The employers make arrangements with the carriers and then make deductions. How does one verify that costs equal deductions?

10. A section 9(i) has been added to the new contract providing for rapid transportation to adequate medical facilities in all emergency cases. The historical grievance has been that it is the employer who determines degree of illness and that their criteria leave much to be desired.

11. Article 10(d1) placed the grower under the jurisdiction of the Puerto Rican courts for purposes of enforcement or litigation, and

11. The notice or process is not considered served, under the new contract, until the grower receives said summons. This may

1973	1974
the forwarding of notice or process constituted the serving of same.	now become a question of being able to serve a summons to someone who may be attempting to evade it.

12. The first sentence of Article 11(b) allowed an employer to designate a worker as elected to accept a non-negotiable return ticket to the place of recruitment and the employer would give it to him. The article said nothing about whether the worker could disagree. The designation of physical unfitness was a unilateral determination.

12. In the new contract the word "employer" has been changed to read "association." The substance is unchanged, in what can amount to unjustified arbitrariness which can give any employer a ready-made mechanism to get rid of "troublemakers."

13. Section 11(c) of the 1973 contract provided for a non-negotiable ticket to be given a worker in case of the death of a spouse, child, or parent, along with $15.00 subsistence. If notice and verification were delayed, the cash equivalent would be given anyway.

13. A positive step taken in the 1974 modification has been the inclusion of the words "or the occurrence of grave illness."

14. A new section 11(d) added to the contract reads: "Organizations providing legally permitted services to the worker have the right to visit the workers during reasonable hours. Provided that the period of visitation is established by law or

1973	1974
	court decision, that period being considered reasonable." The inclusion of this clause is in recognition of the U.S. District Court decision against the Shade Tobacco Growers Association, which allowed ATA access to its camps. This was not a concession won by the Commonwealth negotiations but by ATA.
15. Section 11(f) of the contract provided for the worker to receive $15 or more (depending on agreement) for travel expenses at the end of the contract period.	15. Section 11(f) of the 1973 contract has been eliminated from the new contract. This is an additional monetary loss.

New Clauses

16. Again as a result of the demands made public by ATA, a new clause Section 11(i) has been added to the contract, and once again it is a poor substitute for what should be provided, and what ATA would like to see. Trying to pass itself off as a grievance procedure, this clause provides a free telephone to the Migration Division Regional Office so that workers can make complaints regarding application, interpretation, or violation of the contract. (This, of course, assumes that the workers know what the contract covers, and past experience has shown that they do not.) Action is to be taken within five days, whether it be to resolve the issue or pass it on to the central office in New York City, which can either resolve the complaint or send it on to the Commonwealth's secretary of labor, who can resolve the issue or take it to court.

What must be kept in mind is that the Migration Division has been continuously accused of not enforcing the contract and is presently being sued in court (Vázquez *v.* Ferré) for nonenforcement. Also, the Commonwealth in twenty-five years of being a "representative" of the workers *has never taken a grower to court for noncompliance.* Simply by establishing free telephone service, it is unlikely that this history of neglect and inefficiency will be corrected. In southern New Jersey, the Glassboro Farm Growers Service Association has hundreds of grower members. Do they, or will they, provide telephones in the shacks that the workers live in? If not, will the growers let the workers use the telephones in their homes? Will the Migration Division have more than two field investigators covering up to six-hundred farms in southern New Jersey? Will the Commonwealth be concerned about losing future contracts if they actively enforce the contract which they negotiate and which is supposed to protect the Puerto Rican migrant farmworker? If past practice is any indication of future performance, only Bell Telephone will benefit from the new clause.

17. Another new clause 11(j) requires that the worker be able to produce proof of being eighteen years of age or older upon signing the contract.

This completes the analysis of the 1974 contract negotiated by the Commonwealth of Puerto Rico government representatives and the North American growers. A monetary tally of the new changes shapes up as follows:

Salary increase for six months:	$240.00
Less: no bonus	75.00
no travel expenses	15.00
increased food cost for six months	72.00
Losses in 1974 contract	$162.00
Income change under new contract	$ 78.00

If this figure is broken down to reflect hourly gain, the *real increase in salary is not $.25 per hour but $.08 per hour*. This is only a 4 percent salary increase, whereas the cost of living in Puerto Rico rose from 12 to 15 percent; moreover, the prices of necessities and convenience articles in the camps are determined by the growers.

The 1974 contract inherits all the deficiencies of the 1973 contract, including no overtime pay, no job security, no unemployment insurance benefits, and no definition of a crew chief or foreperson's role. It is expressly because of these great continuing deficiencies that the Puerto Rican migrant farmworker has created the Asociación de Trabajadores Agrícolas de Puerto Rico . . . ATA.

Appendix 2: Comparison of Conditions and Contracts in the Salinas Valley and the General Agreement Between Independent Employers and the Commonwealth of Puerto Rico

I Before UFW (before 1970)	II Under UFW contracts (1970)
$1.65 an hour prevailing wage[1]	$2.00 an hour minimum[2] (3-year contract)
Hiring through labor contractors or foremen	Union hiring hall
No seniority system	Seniority system
No pesticide control	Pesticide control
No limit on hours	Nine-hour limit
No overtime pay	Overtime pay after nine hours
No grievances allowed	Grievance procedure
No elected representatives	Elected representatives and committees on crews
No medical benefits	Medical benefits[3]
No control on layoffs due to mechanization	Control on layoffs due to mechanization[5]
No paid holidays	Paid holidays
No worker bargaining rights	Collective bargaining rights handled by elected representatives
No pension plan	Pension plan[6]

262

III Under Teamster contracts (1970)	IV Under Commonwealth contracts (1973)
$1.85 an hour prevailing wage (5-year contract)	$1.85 an hour minimum (1-year contract)
Hiring through labor contractors or foremen	Hiring through recruitment offices in Puerto Rico under auspices of Rural Manpower Services
No seniority system	No seniority system
No pesticide control	Pesticide control
No limit on hours	No limit on hours
No overtime pay	No overtime pay
No effective grievance procedure	No grievance procedure
No elected representatives	No elected representatives
Medical plan but no known cases of it being paid	Medical benefits[4]
No mechanization control	No control on layoffs due to mechanization
No paid holidays	No paid holidays
Bargaining by paid officials behind closed doors	No worker bargaining rights
Phoney pension plan	No pension plan

Source: Columns I, II, and III: *Si Se Puede*, July 1973, p. 6.

Notes

1. Rate of unskilled nursery work is $1.90 per hour minimum.
2. Interharvest 1972 contract, $2.27 per hour; UFW strawberry contract with PictRipe, $2.40 per hour; Teamster 1973 contract, $2.30 per hour (increased to compete with UFW).
3. UFW medical plan: $500 maternity; dental; hospitalization; four union medical clinics.
4. Farmworkers must pay $.65 per week. Under UFWOC contract the employer pays $.10 per hour worked to the Robert F. Kennedy Insurance Plan. Of those benefits in note 3 above, only hospitalization is provided.
5. Almaden and Paul Masson UFW contracts; no layoffs due to mechanization.
6. UFW 1973 strawberry contract, $.12 per hour for pension fund; Teamster 1973 contract, $.05 per hour—money often used to finance luxury hotels and gambling casinos.

Bibliography

Books

Abad, José Ramón. *Puerto Rico en la Feria—Exposición de Ponce en 1882.* Ponce: Establecimiento Tipográfico "El Comercio," 1885.

Acosta, J. J.; Quiñones, F. M.; Ruiz Belvis, S. *et al. Proyecto para la abolición de la esclavitud en Puerto Rico.* San Juan: Instituto de Cultura Puertorriqueña, 1969.

Anderson, Robert W. *Party Politics in Puerto Rico.* Stanford: Stanford University Press, 1965.

Araujo, Isidoro. *Derechos de importación en la península sobre los azúcares de Cuba y Puerto Rico.* Madrid: Imprenta de Antonio Andés Babi, 1855.

Asenjo y Arteaga, Federico. *El catastro de Puerto Rico. Necesidad de su formación y posibilidad de llevarlo a cabo.* Puerto Rico: Editorial Don Carlos B. Meltz, 1890.

Barbosa de Rosario, Pilar. *La Comisión Autonomista de 1896.* San Juan, 1957.

Bartlett, Frederic P. and Howell, Brandon. *The Population Problem in Puerto Rico.* San Juan: Puerto Rico Planning, Urbanizing, and Zoning Board, 1944.

Bermejo García, Juana Gil. *Panorama histórico de la agricultura en Puerto Rico.* Seville: Instituto de Cultura Puertorriqueña—Escuela de Estudios Hispano-Americanos, 1970.

Bloch, Maurice, ed. *Marxist Analyses and Social Anthropology.* London: Malary Press, 1975.

Boletín Histórico de Puerto Rico. 14 vols. Compiled by Cayetano Coll y Toste. San Juan: Tipografía Cantero y Fernández, 1914-1926.

Braverman, Harry. *Labor and Monopoly Capital: The Degradation of Work in the Twentieth Century.* New York: Monthly Review Press, 1974.

Bukarin, Nicolai I. *Imperialism and World Economy.* New York: Monthly Review Press, 1973.

Carroll, Henry K. *Report on the Island of Porto Rico.* Study done for the U.S. War Department. Washington, D.C.: U.S. Government Printing Office, 1899.

Chenault, Lawrence R. *The Puerto Rican Migrant in New York City.* New York: Columbia University Press, 1938.

Cifré de Loubriel, Estela. *Catálogo de extranjeros residentes en Puerto Rico en el siglo XIV.* Río Piedras: Editorial Universidad de Puerto Rico, 1962.

————. *La inmigración a Puerto Rico durante el siglo XIX.* San Juan: Instituto de Cultura Puertorriqueña, 1964.

Clark, Victor, *et al. Porto Rico and Its Problems.* Washington, D.C.: The Brookings Institution, 1930.

Cruz Monclova, Lidio. *Historia de Puerto Rico. Siglo XIX.* 6 vols. Río Piedras: Editorial Universidad de Puerto Rico, 1970.

Davis, George W. *Report on the Civil Affairs of Puerto Rico.* Study done for the U.S. War Department. Washington, D.C.: U.S. Government Printing Office, 1899.

————. *Report on Industrial and Economic Conditions of Puerto Rico: 1899.* Report for the U.S. War Department, Division of Insular Affairs. Washington, D.C.: U.S. Government Printing Office, 1900.

De Diego, José. *Nuevas campañas.* San Juan: Editorial Cordillera, 1966.

————. *El plebiscito.* San Juan: Editorial Cordillera, 1960.

Díaz Soler, Luis. *Rosendo Matienzo Cintrón. Orientador y guardián de una cultura.* San Juan: Ediciones del Instituto de Literatura Puertorriqueña, 1960.

Economic Equal Opportunities Commission, *Job Patterns for Minorities and Women in Private Industry.* 1966.

Erickson, Charlotte. *American Industry and the European Immigrant, 1860-1885.* Cambridge, Mass.: Harvard University Press, 1957.

Fernández de Cintron, Celia, and Vales, Pedro A. *Social Dynamics of Return Migration to Puerto Rico.* Social Sciences Research Center, University of Puerto Rico, 1975.

Figueroa, Sotero. *Ensayo biográfico.* Ponce: Establecimiento Tipográfico "El Vapor," 1888.

Fitzpatrick, Joseph P. *Puerto Rican Americans: The Meaning of Migration to the Mainland.* Englewood Cliffs, N.J.: Prentice-Hall, 1971.

Friedlander, Stanley. *Labor, Migration, and Economic Growth.* Cambridge, Mass.: MIT Press, 1965.

Gayer, Arthur D., Homan, Paul T., and James, Earle K. *The Sugar Economy of Puerto Rico.* New York: Columbia University Press, 1938.

Gil-Bermejo García, Juana. *Panorama histórico de la agricultura en Puerto Rico.* Seville: Instituto de Cultura Puertorriqueña—Escuela de Estudios Hispano-Americanos, 1970.

Glazer, Nathan and Moynihan, Daniel. *Beyond the Melting Pot*. Cambridge, Mass.: MIT Press, 1970.

Goldsen, Rose, Mills, C. Wright, and Senior, Clarence. *Puerto Rican Journey: New York's Newest Migrant*. New York: Harper, 1950.

Gómez Acevedo, Labor. *Organización y reglamentación del trabajo en el Puerto Rico del siglo XIX*. San Juan: Instituto de Cultura Puertorriqueña, 1970.

Goodsell, Charles T. *Administration of a Revolution: The Development of Public Administration in Puerto Rico Under Governor Rexford G. Tugwell, 1941-1946*. Cambridge, Mass.: Harvard University Press, 1965.

Gould, Lyman J. *La Ley Foraker: Raíces de la política colonial de los Estados Unidos*. Río Piedras: Editorial Universidad de Puerto Rico, 1975.

Gutman, Herbert C. *The Black Family in Slavery and Freedom, 1750-1925*. New York: Pantheon, 1976.

Halperin Donghi, Tulio. *Historia contemporánea de América Latina*. Madrid: Alianza Editorial, 1969.

Hansen, Earl Parker. *Puerto Rico: Ally for Progress*. New York: D. Van Nostrand Co., 1962.

Helfgott, Roy B., *et al. Made in New York*. Cambridge, Mass.: Harvard University Press, 1959.

Hernández Alvarez, José. *Return Migration to Puerto Rico*. Berkeley: University of California Press, 1967.

Hostos, Eugenio M. de. *Obras completas*. San Juan: Editorial Coquí, 1969.

Iglesias, César Andreu, ed. *Memorias de Bernardo Vega*. Río Piedras: Editorial Huracán, 1977.

Iglesias, Igualdad. *El obrerismo en Puerto Rico. Epoca de Santiago Iglesias, 1896-1905*. Palencia de Castilla: Editorial Juan Ponce de León, 1973.

Iglesias, Santiago. *Luchas emancipadoras, 1910-1917*. San Juan, 1962.

Jaffe, A. J. and Carreras Carleton, Zaida. *Some Demographic and Economic Characteristics of the Puerto Rican Population Living on the Mainland, USA*. New York: Bureau of Applied Social Research, Columbia University, 1974.

Jaramillo-Yañez, Manuel M. *Factores sociales en el desarrollo económico: El caso de Puerto Rico, 1960-1970*. San Juan: Junta de Planificación, 1974.

Jennings, James. *Puerto Rican Politics in New York City*. Washington, D.C.: University Press of America, 1977.

Labra, Rafael M. de. *La abolición de la esclavitud en las Antillas Españolas*. Madrid: Imprenta a Cargo de J. E. Morete, 1869.

————. *La abolición de la esclavitud en el orden económico*. Madrid: Imprenta de J. Noguera, 1873.

Lewis, Gordon K. *Puerto Rico: Freedom and Power in the Caribbean*. New York: Monthly Review Press, 1963.

López, Alfredo. *The Puerto Rican Papers*. New York: Bobbs Merrill, 1973.

Lowell, Ruth Fabricant. *The Labor Market in New York City: A Study of Jobs and Low-Income Area Workers in 1970*. New York: Department of Social Services, 1975.

Lugo-Silva, Enrique. *The Tugwell Administration in Puerto Rico*. Mexico: Editorial Cultura, 1955.

Maldonado Denis, Manuel. *Puerto Rico y Estados Unidos: Emigración y colonialismo*. Mexico: Siglo XXI, 1976.

Malthus, Thomas Robert. *An Essay on the Principle of Population*. New York: Augustus Kelly, 1971.

Marcus, Joseph. *Labor Conditions in Porto Rico*. Report for the U.S. Department of Labor. Washington, D.C.: U.S. Government Printing Office, 1919.

Marx, Karl. *Capital*. Vol. I. New York: International Publishers, 1967.

————. *Grundrisse*. New York: Vintage, 1973.

————. *Theories of Surplus-Value*. Moscow: Progress Publishers, 1967.

Marx, Karl and Engels, Frederick. *Ireland and the Irish Question*. Moscow: Progress Publishers, 1971.

Mathews, Thomas G. *Puerto Rican Politics and the New Deal*. Gainesville: University of Florida Press, 1960.

Meek, Ronald L., ed. *Marx and Engels on the Population Bomb*. Berkeley: Ramparts Press, 1971.

Memoria descriptiva de la Cuarta Feria y Exposición Pública de la Agricultura, la Industria y Bellas Artes de la Isla de Puerto Rico. Puerto Rico: Imprenta de Acosta, 1865.

Memoria Unión Mercantil e Industrial de Ponce. Ponce: Establecimiento Tipográfico "El Vapor," 1886.

Muñoz Rivera, Luis. *Campañas políticas 1901-1916*. Madrid: Editorial Puerto Rico, 1925.

Nieves Falcón, Luis. *El emigrante puertorriqueño*. Río Piedras: Editorial Edil, 1975.

Pagán, Bolívar. *Historia de los partidos políticos puertorriqueños*. San Juan: Librería Campos, 1959.

Perloff, Harvey S. *Puerto Rico's Economic Future*. Chicago: University of Chicago Press, 1950.

Piven, Frances Fox and Cloward, Richard. *Regulating the Poor*. New York: Vintage Books, 1971.

Poulantzas, Nicos. *Las clases sociales en América Latina*. Mexico: Siglo XXI, 1973.

—————. *Political Power and Social Classes*. London: Sheed and Ward, 1973.

Ramos de Santiago, Carmen. *El desarrollo constituciónal de Puerto Rico: Documentos y casos*. Río Piedras: Editorial Universidad de Puerto Rico, 1973.

Reisman, Michael N. *Puerto Rico and the International Process: New Roles in Association*. Washington, D.C.: American Society of International Law, 1975.

Reynolds, Lloyd D. and Gregory, Peter. *Wages, Productivity, and Industrialization in Puerto Rico*. Homewood, Ill.: Richard D. Irwin, 1965.

Rigual, Néstor. *Incidencias parlamentarias en Puerto Rico*. San Juan: Instituto de Cultura Puertorriqueña, 1972.

Rodríguez, Clara. *The Ethnic Queue in the United States: The Case of Puerto Ricans*. San Francisco: R&E Research Associates, 1973.

Rojas, Manuel F. *Estudios sociales o frutos del sistema*. San Juan: Federación Libre Press, 1918.

Ross, David F. *The Long Uphill Path*. San Juan: Editorial Edil, 1969.

Ruiz Belvis, Segundo, *et al. Proyecto para la abolición de la esclavitud en Puerto Rico, April 10, 1897*. San Juan: Instituto de Cultura Puertorriqueña, 1969.

Schaffer, Alan. *Vito Marcantonio: Radical in Congress*. Syracuse, N.Y.: Syracuse University Press, 1966.

Senior, Clarence. *Puerto Rican Emigration*. Río Piedras: Social Science Research Center, University of Puerto Rico, 1947.

—————. *The Puerto Ricans: Strangers Then Neighbors*. Chicago: Quadrangle Books, 1965.

Singer, Paulo. *Economia política da urbanização*. São Paulo: Editorial Brasiliense, 1973.

Tapia y Rivera, Alejandro. *Mis memorias*. Río Piedras: Editorial Edil, 1971.

Todaro, Michael. *Internal Migration in Developing Countries*. Geneva: International Labour Office, 1976.

Torres Ramírez, Bibiano. *La Isla de Puerto Rico, 1765-1800*. San Juan: Instituto de Cultura Puertorriqueña, 1968.

Tugwell, Rexford G. *Changing the Colonial Climate*. New York: Arno Press, 1970.

————. *The Stricken Land*. Garden City, N.Y.: Doubleday and Co., 1947.

Ulibarri, George S. *Nineteenth-Century Puerto Rican Immigration and Slave Data*. Conference on the National Archives and Statistical Research, May 1968.

United Nations. *Demographic Aspects of Manual Labor*. New York, 1963.

Vernon, Raymond. *Metropolis, 1985*. Cambridge, Mass.: Harvard University Press, 1960.

Vernon, Raymond and Hoover, Edgar M. *Anatomy of a Metropolis*. New York: Doubleday-Anchor, 1962.

Viña, Andrés. *Estudios sobre la Isla de Puerto Rico*. Madrid: Imprenta de Don Antonio Pérez Dubrull, 1856.

————. *Relaciones mercantiles entre España y Puerto Rico*. Madrid: Imprenta de Don Antonio Pérez Dubrull, 1855.

Wagenheim, Kal. *A Survey of Puerto Ricans in the U.S. Mainland in the 1970s*. New York: Praeger Publishers, 1975.

Wantman, Morey J., Israel, Morton, and Kagan, Leonard S. *Population Health Survey*. New York: Center for Social Research, City University of New York, 1972.

Wilhelm, Sidney M. *Who Needs the Negro?* New York: Doubleday-Anchor, 1971.

Will, Robert and Vatter, Harold, eds. *Poverty in Affluence*. New York: Harcourt, Brace & World, 1970.

Articles

Ames, Azel. "Labor Conditions in Porto Rico." *Bulletin of the Bureau of Labor* 34 (May 1901).

Aspira of America. "Social Factors in Educational Attainment among Puerto Ricans in U.S. Metropolitan Areas." New York, 1976.

Augelli, John P. "San Lorenzo: A Case Study of Recent Migrations in Interior Puerto Rico." *American Journal of Economics and Sociology* (1952).

Berríos, Rubén. "Independence for Puerto Rico: The Only Solution." *Foreign Affairs* 55, no. 3 (April 1977).

Bird, Esteban. "The Sugar Industry in Relation to the Social and Economic System of Puerto Rico." Sen. Doc. No. 1. San Juan, 1941.

Campos, Ricardo and Bonilla, Frank. "Industrialization and Migration: Some Effects on the Puerto Rican Working Class," *Latin American Perspectives* 3, no. 3 (1976).

Cardoso, Fernando Henrique. "Comentarios sobre los conceptos de sobrepoblación relativa y marginalidad." *Revista Latinoamericana de Sociología* 1 and 2 (1971).

Carleton, Robert O. "New Aspects of Puerto Rican Migration." *Monthly Labor Review* 83, no. 2 (February 1960).

Cowgill, George L. "On Causes and Consequences of Ancient and Modern Population Change." *American Anthropologist* 77, no. 3 (1975).

Gordon, David M. "Income and Welfare in New York City." *The Public Interest* 16 (1969).

Gray, Lois. "The Jobs Puerto Ricans Hold in New York City." *Monthly Labor Review* 99, no. 10 (October 1976).

Henderson, Julia. "Foreign Labor in the U.S. During the War." *International Labor Review* (December 1945).

Hill, Herbert. "Guardians of the Sweatshop: The Trade Union, Racism, and the Garment Industry." In Adalberto López and James Petras, eds., *Puerto Rico and Puerto Ricans*. New York: Schenkman Publishing, 1974.

Hobsbawm, Eric. "Some Reflections on the Break-Up of Britain." *New Left Review* 105 (1977).

Lenin, V. I. "Capitalism and Workers' Immigration." *Collected Works*. Vol. 19. Moscow: Progress Publishers, 1973.

———. "The Working Class and Neo-Malthusianism." *Collected Works*. Vol. 19. Moscow: Progress Publishers, 1973.

López, Adalberto. "The Puerto Rican Diaspora." In Adalberto López and James Petras, eds., *Puerto Rico and Puerto Ricans*. New York: Schenkman Publishing, 1974.

Maldonado, Rita M. "Why Puerto Ricans Migrated to the United States in 1947-73." *Monthly Labor Review* 99, no. 9 (September 1976).

Mandle, Jay R. "The Plantation Economy and Its Aftermath." *Review of Radical Political Economics* (Spring 1974).

Marazzi, Rosa. "El impacto de la inmigración a Puerto Rico 1800-1830: Análisis estadístico." *Revista de Ciencias Sociales* 18, nos. 1-2 (1974).

Marx, Karl. "The Struggle for the Normal Working-Day. Compulsory Limitation by Law of the Working-Time." In *Capital*, vol. I. New York: International Publishers, 1970.

Mascisco, John J. "Assimilation of the Puerto Ricans on the Mainland: A Sociodemographic Approach." *International Migration Review* 2 (Spring 1968).

Monserrat, Joseph. "Symposium on Puerto Rico in the Year 2000." *Harvard Law Journal* 15, no. 1 (Fall 1968).

Morley, Morris. "Dependence and Development in Puerto Rico." In Adalberto López and James Petras, eds., *Puerto Rico and Puerto Ricans*. New York: Schenkman Publishing, 1974.

NACLA's Latin America and Empire Report 9, no. 5 (July-August 1975).

Nun, José. "Sobrepoblación relativa, ejército industrial de reserva y masa marginal." *Revista Latinoamericana de Sociología* 2 (1969).

Offe, Claus. "The Abolition of Market Control and the Problem of Legitimacy." *Kapitalistate* 1, no. 1 (May 1973).

Oppenheimer, Martin. *Transaction* 12, no. 4 (May-June 1975).

Pantoja, Antonia. "Puerto Rican Migration." *Preliminary Report to the U.S. Commission on the Civil Rights of Puerto Ricans* (1972).

Picó Vidal, Isabel. "La mujer puertorriqueña y la recesión económica." *Avance* 3, no. 145 (May 1975).

"The Puerto Rican Experience on the United States Mainland." *International Migration Review* 2, no. 2 (Spring 1968).

"Puerto Ricans on Contract." *NACLA* 11, no. 8 (1977).

Quintero Rivera, Angel. "Bases sociales de la transformación ideológica del PPD, 1940-1950." *Cuadernos* 6 (1975).

————. "La clase obrera y el proceso político en Puerto Rico." *Revista de Ciencias Sociales* 3, no. 19 (1975).

————. "Conflictos de clase en la política colonial. Puerto Rico bajo España y bajo los Estados Unidos, 1870-1924." *Cuadernos* 2 (1974).

Ramos Mattei, Andrés. "Apuntes sobre la transición hacia el sistema de centrales en la industria azucarera. Contabilidad de la hacienda Mercedita, 1861-1900." *Cuadernos* 4 (1975).

Rodríguez, Clara. "Puerto Ricans and the New York City School System." *Urban Review* (June 1974).

Rodríguez Bou, Ismael. "Significant Factors in the Development of Education in Puerto Rico." In U.S.-Puerto Rico Commission on the Status of Puerto Rico, *Status of Puerto Rico: Selected*

Background Studies. Washington, D.C.: U.S. Government Printing Office, 1965.

Sawyers, Larry. "Urban Form and the Mode of Production." *Review of Radical Political Economics* 8, no. 1 (1975).

Senior, Clarence and Watkins, Donald. "Toward a Balance Sheet of Puerto Rican Migration." In U.S.-Puerto Rico Commission on the Status of Puerto Rico, *Status of Puerto Rico: Selected Background Studies.* Washington, D.C.: U.S. Government Printing Office, 1966.

U.S. Department of Labor. "Unemployment in Porto Rico, 1928-29." *Monthly Labor Review* 31, no. 5 (May 1930).

————. "Unemployment in Porto Rico, 1929." *Monthly Labor Review* 31, no. 3 (September 1930).

————. "Labor Conditions in Porto Rico, 1930." *Monthly Labor Review* 31, no. 35 (December 1930).

Valentine, Charles. "Black Studies and Anthropology: Scholarly and Political Interests in Afro-American Culture." *Addison Wesley Modular Publications*, Module 15 (1972).

Vanderkamp, John. "Migration Flows, Their Determinants and the Effects of Return Migration." *Journal of Political Economy* (September-October 1971).

Vaughan, Mary K. "Tourism in Puerto Rico." In Adalberto López and James Petras, eds., *Puerto Rico and Puerto Ricans*. New York: Schenkman Publishing, 1974.

Weyl, Walter. "Labor Conditions in Puerto Rico." *Bulletin of the Bureau of Labor* 61 (November 1905).

Woytinsky, W. J. "Postwar Economic Perspectives." *Social Security Bulletin* 9, no. 1 (January 1946).

Public Documents: Puerto Rico

Anuarios estadísticos de España, 1854-1860.

Asamblea de Aibonito. *Informes presentados por las comisiones departamentales. Acta de las sesiones—Exposición al Excsmo. Sr. Ministro de Ultramar. Documentos varios.* Mayagüez: Tipografía Comercial, 1886.

Balanza mercantil de la isla de Puerto Rico, 1849-1861.

Bureau of Labor. *Special Report to the Legislature of Porto Rico,* no. 1. San Juan, 1912.

————. *Second Annual Report* (February 1914); *Fourth An-nual Report* (February 1916); *Seventh Annual Report* (April 1920); *Eighth Annual Report* (May 1921); *Ninth Annual Report* (February 1923).

Censos de población de España, 1877 y 1887.

Commonwealth of Puerto Rico, Migration Division. *A Sum-mary in Facts and Figures.* New York, January, 1959.

Corporación de Fomento. *The Industrial Development Pro-gram, 1942-1960.* San Juan, December 1959.

Estadística general del comercio exterior de la provincia de Puerto Rico, 1870-1897.

Governor of Porto Rico. *Annual Report 1900-1901.*

————. *Annual Report 1930.*

————. "Fundamental Social and Political Problems of Porto Rico." Report by Arthur Yager at the Lake Mohonk Confer-ence, October 22, 1915.

Junta de Planificación de Puerto Rico. *Informe económico al gobernador,* 1976, 1977. San Juan, 1977, 1978.

Land Authority of Puerto Rico. *Land Law of Puerto Rico.* San Juan: Insular Procurement Office, 1943.

Memoria estadística referente a la Isla de Puerto Rico, 1860.

Planning Board. *Puerto Rican Migrants: A Socio-Economic Study.* San Juan, 1972.

————. *A Comparative Study of the Labor Market Charac-teristics of Return Migrants and Non-Migrants in Puerto Rico.* San Juan, 1973.

Planning, Urbanizing, and Zoning Board. *A Development Plan for Puerto Rico.* San Juan, 1944.

Public Documents: United States

Bureau of the Census. *Census of Population: 1970, Detailed Characteristics, Puerto Rico.* PCCD, D 53. Washington, D.C.: U.S. Government Printing Office, 1973.

————. *Current Population Survey: Persons of Spanish Origin in the U.S., March 1974.* Washington, D.C.: U.S. Government Printing Office, 1974.

————. *Thirteenth Census of the United States, 1910. Supplement for Porto Rico.* Washington, D.C.: U.S. Gov-ernment Printing Office, 1913.

————. *Fourteenth Census of the United States, 1920.* Washington, D.C.: U.S. Government Printing Office, 1923.

————. *Fifteenth Census of the United States, 1930. Outlying Territories and Possessions.* Washington, D.C.: U.S. Government Printing Office, 1932.

————. *Sixteenth Census of the United States, 1940.* Washington, D.C.: U.S. Government Printing Office, 1942.

————. *Puerto Ricans in the United States, 1960.* Washington, D.C.: U.S. Government Printing Office.

————. *Puerto Ricans in the United States, 1970.* Washington, D.C.: U.S. Government Printing Office.

————. *U.S. Census of Population, 1950.* Washington, D.C.: U.S. Government Printing Office, 1953.

————. *U.S. Census of Population, 1960.* Washington, D.C.: U.S. Government Printing Office, 1960-1964.

————. *U.S. Census of Population: 1970, General Social and Economic Characteristics.* PC(1)-C34. Washington, D.C.: U.S. Government Printing Office, 1973.

Commission on Civil Rights. *Counting the Forgotten.* April 1974.

————. "Demographic, Social, and Economic Characteristics of New York City and the New York Metropolitan Area." *Hearings on the Civil Rights of Puerto Ricans.* Staff report, February 1972.

————. *Puerto Ricans in the Continental United States: An Uncertain Future.* Washington, D.C., 1976.

Department of Commerce and Labor, Bureau of Statistics. *Commercial Porto Rico in 1906.* Washington, D.C.: U.S. Government Printing Office, 1907.

Department of Labor. *Report of the Commissioner of Labor in Hawaii. Bulletin of the Department of Labor* 47 (July 1903).

Department of Labor, Bureau of Labor Statistics. "The New York Puerto Rican: Patterns of Work Experience." *Regional Report No. 19,* Poverty Area Profiles. New York, 1972.

New York City Commission on Human Rights. "The Employment of Minorities, Women and the Handicapped in City Government." New York, 1973.

New York City Council on Economic Education. *Fact Book on the New York Metropolitan Region.* New York: Pace University, 1976.

New York City Department of Social Services. *The Labor Market in New York City: A Study of Jobs and Low Income Area Workers in 1970.*

276   *Bibliography*

New York City Manpower Area Planning Council. *Comprehensive Manpower Plan for New York City, Fiscal Year 1974.* New York: Office of the Mayor.

Puerto Rico Reconstruction Administration. *Census of Puerto Rico, 1935.* Washington, D.C.: U.S. Government Printing Office, 1938.

Regional Plan Association. "Linking Skills, Jobs, and Housing in the New York Urban Region." New York, 1972.

State Charter Revision Commission for New York City. "New York City Today: Demographic and Economic Background Information." Staff report, December 1973.

U.S.-Puerto Rico Commission on the Status of Puerto Rico. *Status of Puerto Rico.* August 1966.

War Department. *Report of the U.S. Insular Commission to the Secretary of War Upon Investigations into the Civil Affairs of the Island of Porto Rico.* Washington, D.C.: U.S. Government Printing Office, 1899.

————. *Report on the Census of Puerto Rico, 1899.* Washington, D.C.: U.S. Government Printing Office, 1900.

Welfare and Health Council of New York City. *Population of Puerto Rican Birth or Parentage, New York City: 1950.* New York, September 1952.

Unpublished Materials

Badillo Veiga, Americo. "Las migraciones internas en Puerto Rico, 1898-1940." New York, 1978.

Beshers, James. "The Measurement of Overpopulation: An Analysis of Puerto Rico." M.A. thesis, University of North Carolina, 1954.

Campos, Ricardo and Bonilla, Frank. "La economía política de la relación colonial: La experiencía puertorriqueña." Mimeo. New York: Centro de Estudios Puertorriqueños, 1977.

Estades, Rosa. "Patterns of Political Participation of Puerto Ricans in New York City." Ph.D. diss., New School for Social Research, 1974.

Fleisher, Belton. "Some Economic Aspects of Puerto Rican Migration to the United States." Ph.D. diss., Stanford University, 1961.

Galvin, Miles Eugene. "Collective Bargaining in the Public Sector in Puerto Rico." Ph.D. diss., University of Wisconsin, 1972.

García, Gervasio. "La economía natural colonial de Puerto Rico en el siglo XIX." Mimeo. Río Piedras: Centro de Estudios de la Realidad Puertorriqueña, 1974.

———. "La primera década de la Federación Libre de Trabajadores de Puerto Rico." Río Piedras: CEREP, 1974.

Gotsch, John W. "Puerto Rican Leadership in New York." M.A. thesis, New York University, 1966.

Gray, Lois. "Economic Incentives to Labor Mobility: The Puerto Rican Case." Ph.D. diss., Columbia University, 1966.

Herrero, José Antonio. "En torno a la mitología del azúcar: Un ensayo en historia económica de Puerto Rico. 1900-1970." Río Piedras: CEREP, 1971.

Moscoso, Francisco. "The Theory of Tribal Consciousness and the Taino." Mimeo. Binghamton: State University of New York, 1975.

Navas Dávila, Gerardo. "The Dialectic of National Development: The Case of Puerto Rico." Ph.D. diss., University of California at Berkeley, 1972.

Piore, Michael J. "The Role of Immigration in Industrial Growth: A Case Study of the Origins and Character of Puerto Rican Migration to Boston." Mimeo. 1973.

Puerto Rican Forum. "The Puerto Rican Community Development Project." 1964.

Quintero Rivera, Angel. "Background to the Emergence of the Capitalist Economy." Mimeo. Río Piedras: CEREP, 1973.

———. "De campesino y agregado a proletario. La economía de plantación." Mimeo. Río Piedras: CEREP, 1974.

Silvestrini Pacheco, Blanca. "Puerto Rican Workers and the Socialist Party, 1932-40." Ph.D. diss., State University of New York at Albany, 1973.

Tabb, William K. "Puerto Ricans in New York City: A Study of Economic and Social Conditions." New York: Bureau of Labor Statistics, 1972.

Valdivieso, Rafael. "Why Puerto Ricans Came to New York." 1971.

Vázquez Calzada, José. "Las causas y efectos de la emigración puertorriqueña." Mimeo. San Juan: Escuela de Medicina, Universidad de Puerto Rico, 1968.

———. "El desbalance entre recursos y población en Puerto Rico." Mimeo. San Juan: Escuela de Medicina, Universidad de Puerto Rico, 1966.

————. "La emigración puertorriqueña: ¿Solución o problema?" Mimeo. San Juan: Escuela de Medicina, Universidad de Puerto Rico, 1963.

————. "La esterilización feminina en Puerto Rico." Mimeo. San Juan: Escuela de Medicina, Universidad de Puerto Rico, 1973.

Index